D1521222

Thick Evaluation

Thick Evaluation

Simon Kirchin

Great Clarendon Street, Oxford, OX2 6DP,
United Kingdom

Oxford University Press is a department of the University of Oxford.
It furthers the University's objective of excellence in research, scholarship,
and education by publishing worldwide. Oxford is a registered trade mark of
Oxford University Press in the UK and in certain other countries

Published in the United States of America by Oxford University Press
198 Madison Avenue, New York, NY 10016, United States of America

British Library Cataloguing in Publication Data
Data available

Library of Congress Control Number: 2017942551

ISBN 978–0–19–880343–0

Printed and bound by
CPI Group (UK) Ltd, Croydon, CR0 4YY

Links to third party websites are provided by Oxford in good faith and
for information only. Oxford disclaims any responsibility for the materials
contained in any third party website referenced in this work.

For my parents

Contents

Acknowledgements

This book has been a long time in the making, almost certainly too long. However, one nice aspect of having spent a good while thinking through a number of issues, and stewing on many problems, is that I am able to thank a large number of people. I hope that this does not come across as an over-long Oscars speech. All of my thanks here are genuine and necessary. I also apologize to anyone I have forgotten.

This book started life as two or three pages in a PhD thesis that I wrote while a student at Sheffield, with the groundwork being laid when I was an undergraduate at Oxford. At the latter I had the good fortune to be taught by three excellent philosophers and tutors: Bill Child, David Wiggins, and Tim Williamson. Those familiar with the material in this book may draw the conclusion that David's work influenced me directly. I suspect that isn't the case because I was probably too unreceptive an undergraduate to appreciate his work fully. I do remember that all three taught me the value of rigorous argument and the importance of close attention to the work of others. While at Sheffield I was supervised by David Bell and Richard Joyce, a supervisory team that, from my point of view, could not have been bettered. David taught me—had to teach me again and again, I'm sorry to say—the importance of being precise with one's words and thoughts, while Richard was a fantastic guide to metaethics. I fondly remember the disagreements I had with both of them. Sheffield in the mid-to-late 1990s was a lovely, supportive place to be a graduate student, and I owe much to the many people, both Faculty and postgraduates, who were there, notably: Gavin Boyce, Peter Carruthers, Keith Frankish, Dave Hemp, Chris Hookway, Maria Kasmirli, Steve Makin, Stefano Mafredi, Ewan McEachran, Betty-Ann Muir, David Owens, Jenny Saul, Bob Stern, Todd Thompson, Leif Wenar, and Steve de Wijze.

Following my time at Sheffield I spent three enjoyable years as a lecturer at Bristol. Now, as then, the period when one has finished a PhD and is looking for a permanent academic home is a difficult and trying affair. This is not just because one is hopeful of the prize of a permanent academic position. One is also spreading one's intellectual wings and growing as a thinker. I am grateful to many people at Bristol for the support they gave me as I developed, particularly Chris Bertram, Jessica Brown, Jimmy Doyle, Keith Graham, James Ladyman, Adam Morton, Andrew Pyle, Mauricio Suarez, and Carolyn Wilde. I was a temporary lecturer at Bristol at the same time that David Bain, Rachel Cooper, Patrick Greenough, and Finn Spicer found themselves in the same boat, and I think myself lucky to have had such wonderful comrades-in-arms.

I have been at the University of Kent since 2003, an intellectual home that has more than suited. My horizons have been expanded and my thoughts supported by many colleagues and friends, both within the philosophy department and outside.

I am especially grateful to Kristoffer Ahlstrom-Vij, David Corfield, Graeme Forbes, Jonathan Friday, Helen Frowe, Edward Harcourt, Edward Kanterian, Hans Maes, Todd Mei, Julien Murzi, Richard Norman, Lubomira Radoilska, Kelli Rudolph, Sean Sayers, Julia Tanney, Robin Taylor, Alan Thomas, and Jon Williamson, all of whom have had to listen to me talk about thick concepts on and off for years. Steve Pethick and Murray Smith have been particularly long-suffering and kind with their time and thoughts. I am the current Dean of the Faculty of Humanities, a Faculty that is home to a large number of colleagues who value education as much as research, and for whom creativity in thought and in practice is paramount. Governments and others all around the world threaten what is good in our universities, even if they try to help, and I feel blessed to lead such a talented and friendly group of people who endeavour to keep the flame alive.

My philosophical thought has been supported and challenged by many people outside the universities I have called home, in private reading, in presentations, and in conversation. (Here I am sure to miss one or two names.) The roll call may be large, but it is heartfelt nonetheless: Olle Blomberg, Anna Bergqvist, Michael Brady, Vittorio Bufacchi, Roger Crisp, Daniel Elstein, Guy Fletcher, Miranda Fricker, Brad Hooker, Tom Hurka, Jeanette Kennett, Brent Kyle, Gerald Lang, Iain Law, Jimmy Lenman, Maggie Little, John McDowell, Brian McElwee, David McNaughton, Alex Miller, Aaron Ridley, Toni Rønnow-Rasmussen, Constantine Sandis, Sam Scheffler, Elisabeth Schellekens Dammann, Neil Sinclair, Philip Stratton-Lake, Bart Streumer, John Skorupski, Folke Tersman, Daniel Whiting, Jon Webber, Ralph Wedgwood, Eric Wiland, Nick Zangwill. I'm particularly grateful to Michel Meliopoulos who invited me to Zurich to present parts of this book when it was in draft at a workshop in September 2014. Simon Keller, in an act of complete supererogation, read and commented on the manuscript when it was close to being finished, thus enabling me to polish and improve it.

Seven people stand out as being of particular support as this study was being written. I have learnt a great deal from the work of Simon Blackburn, Sophie-Grace Chappell, Jonathan Dancy, Adrian Moore, and Michael Smith through the years, but I single them out because of the many fruitful conversations I have had with them and for the support they have given. I know I am not the only one who can say that they have benefited from the time and thought of these famous five, and I record my thanks as others have done before me. I was lucky to be working on the topic of thick concepts at the same time as Debbie Roberts and Pekka Väyrynen. I am grateful for all the times we have shared ideas and discussed the material in this book. Debbie read a draft of Chapter Six when I was close to finishing and helped me to strengthen what I was arguing for, and my overall view would not be what it was if it were not for the number of friendly disagreements I have had with Pekka.

Thoughts are one thing, turning them into a book quite another. As many people have experienced, Peter Momtchiloff at Oxford University Press exercises much wise judgement and patience, and is one of the very best of philosophical midwives.

I am also grateful to Matthias Butler, Clement Raj, Christine Ranft, and Jeremy Langworthy who helped see this book through to publication, and to the anonymous referees who helped saved me from many errors and who encouraged me to sharpen my ideas and arguments.

I also acknowledge thanks for publication of previous work. Chapter Five is a rewritten version of my 'The Shapelessness Hypothesis', *Philosophers' Imprint* (2010), pp. 1–28. The early part of Chapter Six is a rewritten version of part of my 'Thick Concepts and Thick Descriptions', which appeared in my edited volume *Thick Concepts* (Oxford: Oxford University Press, 2013), pp. 60–77.

A book that has taken this long to see the light of day needs more than just philosophical support. Many of my non-academic friends and family have had me lecture them on the relevance of the racy and the significance of slobs. They have done so with unfailing politeness, even if some of their suggestions—'Thick Evaluation? Why not just call it Stupid Thoughts and have done with it?'—I have had to put aside. My parents, to their great surprise, produced and nurtured a philosopher, and they have supported me in more ways than one throughout many years. I dedicate this book to them with much love and respect. Penny, Freddie, and Molly have had to put up with my 'book melancholia' and have done so with hugs and kindness. They have also shown insights into my own thought that I had missed. I would not be the thinker or person I am without them.

Kent

Spring 2017

1

Introduction

Imagine I tell you that Maddy is bad. Perhaps you infer from my intonation, or the context in which we are talking, that I mean morally bad. Additionally, you will probably infer that I am disapproving of Maddy, or saying that I think you should disapprove of her, or similar, given typical linguistic conventions and assuming I am sincere. However, you might not get a more detailed sense of the particular sorts of way in which Maddy is bad, her typical character traits, and the like, since people can be bad in many ways. In contrast, if I say that Maddy is wicked, then you get more of a sense of her typical actions and attitudes to others. The word 'wicked' is more specific than 'bad'. I have still not exactly pinpointed Maddy's character since wickedness takes many forms. But there is more detail nevertheless, perhaps a stronger connotation of the sort of person Maddy is. In addition, and again assuming typical linguistic conventions, you should also get a sense that I am disapproving of Maddy, or saying that you should disapprove of her, or similar, assuming that we are still discussing her moral character.

This imaginary and somewhat stilted scenario introduces the topic of this study. Concepts such as BAD and GOOD are normally referred to as thin evaluative concepts (hereafter just *thin concepts*), whereas WICKED, SELFISH, KIND, BRAVE, DECEITFUL and many more examples in ethics, are said to be thick evaluative concepts (hereafter, *thick concepts*).[1] There are many, many examples of thick concepts beyond the ethical realm. Artworks can be elegant and jejune, teachers can be wise and ignorant, children can be angelic and cheeky, adults can be childlike and childish, gardens can be delicate and cluttered, academics can be modest and pompous, and so on, and so on, and so on.

The supposed difference between thin and thick concepts is a phenomenon that is relatively easy to spot: we are picking out evaluative concepts that are more or less specific. Matters become harder when we try to capture exactly what is going on. Here is a rough and ready distinction to get us started. Often the distinction is put so that whereas thin concepts are primarily or wholly evaluative (in whatever sense is given to 'evaluative'), thick concepts mix evaluation, or evaluative conceptual content, with something that might be called nonevaluative, descriptive conceptual

---

[1] When referring to concepts as concepts, I write them capitalized as here. When referring to and mentioning associated terms and words, I write them thus: 'generous'.

content, or mix with it to a more significant degree than happens with thin concepts. In other words, the application of a thin concept is primarily or wholly concerned with giving a sense of approval or disapproval. In contrast, a thick concept will do that *and* give a sense, or more of a sense, of what the thing is like that is so categorized, a sense beyond the fact that it is to be liked or disliked. Often commentators refer to 'normativity'—either in addition to evaluative content or as a substitute for it—and thus make reference to the fact that both thin and thick concepts can provide guidance and reasons for action, even if only defeasibly. Within this framework, thin concepts' prime or whole function is typically thought to be to provide such guidance and reasons, while thick concepts do this and additionally reflect the world somehow. So, for example, we could say that it would be (prudentially) wrong to walk along the cliff edge, and we could also say that the edge is dangerous. The 'wrong' is simply an expression of a reason not to do something, while the 'dangerous' will indicate such a reason and also indicate something about what the edge is like, such as the fact that it is crumbling, craggy, and high up.

From this rough and ready discussion much philosophical intrigue follows. For example, how is evaluative content and descriptive content supposed to relate in a thick concept? What do we mean by these two labels anyway? Is talk of evaluative and descriptive content the best way of capturing the phenomenon? Perhaps the evaluative element should be seen as functioning in a different way, not as some conceptual content that aims to capture or map onto the world, but as an attitude that we express towards that world, for instance. Is there a difference in kind between thin and thick concepts, or is the difference only one of degree? Do the differences between evaluative concepts from different domains (ethical, aesthetic, prudential, etc.) affect what story we tell about the thin and the thick? Why think there are different evaluative domains anyway?

Some of these questions and others will be raised and answered in this book. My chief concern is the nature of evaluative concepts: can we always separate them into different conceptual contents, and what is the character and function of those supposed different contents in the first place?

In the rest of this Introduction I do five things. First, I lay out what I discuss and argue for in this study. Second, I outline each chapter. Third, I offer a brief history of the distinction between thin and thick concepts that alights on some of the thoughts mentioned. Fourth, I pick out a few contrasts that are at work in my discussion. Lastly, I briefly indicate some interesting and relevant questions that, unfortunately, have to be left aside. In Chapter Two I begin my discussion in earnest.

(a) In this book battle lines are drawn between separationists and nonseparationists. I argue for a version of nonseparationism.

Separationists believe that all putative thick concepts can be divided into different elements. Many separationists divide thick concepts into some very thin evaluative element and some descriptive, nonevaluative element or elements. It is part of their picture that not only should we so separate, but also that evaluation and description are radically different kinds of thing or different kinds of conceptual content. Just now I wrote of some 'descriptive, nonevaluative element'. In this debate this phrasing is strictly a redundancy: descriptive conceptual content *just is* nonevaluative conceptual content.[2] But this point is worth making and drawing our attention to. It is also worth dwelling a little on the English involved. Separationists should typically speak of evaluative and descriptive *elements* or *parts* or *components* because these words imply that what are primary are the separable, independently intelligible factors that make up the thick concept, not the thick concept itself.

Separationists, although united in their core belief, differ on many matters. They disagree about what the evaluative and descriptive elements are and how thin the evaluative element needs to be. They also disagree about how many elements are typically part of a thick concept and about how they are related to each other. Further, they also disagree as to how to treat the evaluative element. To elaborate, the most famous types of separationist are noncognitivists. They typically characterize the evaluative element as an evinced attitude or command. However, cognitivist treatments are also possible. Cognitivist-separationists treat some thin evaluative element, such as GOOD, as a free-standing, independently intelligible concept that is separable from any nonevaluative concept.[3]

As mentioned, I argue for a *nonseparationist* account of thick concepts, and argue further for a particular understanding of this broad view. All nonseparationists believe that thick concepts unite in some way both evaluative and descriptive conceptual content: such content cannot be separated. As such, they may well refer to evaluative and descriptive *aspects* (rather than *elements* or *parts*), as such phrasing implies the primacy of the thick concept not its features. However, I am particularly keen to stress that we should go beyond merely thinking that thick concepts unite evaluative and descriptive content.[4] Why? Expressing matters in this way could be taken to assume that there is some separation between two things or parts, albeit a separation that is then overcome. I emphasize strongly and positively that thick concepts are evaluative concepts, plain and simple; they are as evaluative as thin concepts are, just that they are more specific. This theme gives this book its title, *Thick Evaluation*. The simple—perhaps seemingly simplistic—way in which I introduced matters at the start, by saying that thick concepts are more specific and that thin concepts are more general, turns out to be the key way of thinking about thick concepts and their relation to thin ones. So, to put this another way, I worry whenever I hear other commentators saying that thin concepts are purely evaluative

---

[2] However, innocent and acceptable as this identity is, I do draw attention to it and question it in Chapter Six when I discuss the labels that one applies to the various conceptual categories that are in play.

[3] See Elstein and Hurka (2009), pp. 516–17 for discussion.

[4] I use this phrasing myself from time to time. It is just that I do not think we can leave matters there, and we should not aim only to show that there is this intertwining. That last idea is really the point behind Chapter Five.

whereas in contrast thick concepts mix evaluative and descriptive conceptual content. I think that thick concepts are also 'purely' or 'wholly' evaluative, simply because I have a certain view of what it is for something to be evaluative. This idea will be elaborated and defended throughout my study.[5]

All nonseparationists are cognitivists. They all think that thick and thin concepts can be used to describe the world by picking out parts of it—the parts of it that are good, just, unfair, elegant, and the like—and that in some sense knowledge of the world might be conveyed by their use. Note that we should not confuse the two uses of 'descriptive' I have introduced. I have just used 'describe' to indicate how any word or idea might function: used in a suitable fashion in a language, any word, evaluative or not, can be used to try to pick out some aspect of the world. Earlier, when I wrote of 'descriptive content', I meant something different: a type of conceptual content that does not capture or convey any value judgement. We should be alive to this difference throughout.

Despite being united in their cognitivism, nonseparationists also come in several varieties. To explain how my nonseparationism differs from other types, here are three further points I argue for. First, and carrying on from the main theme of thick concepts being purely evaluative, I argue that while there are clearly some non-evaluative concepts, there is a huge grey area of concepts that cannot be clearly categorized as either evaluative or descriptive by the lights of a more traditional, separationist understanding of 'evaluative'. And, I do stick my neck out: I suggest strongly that there is this grey area, as opposed to there being a sharp distinction between the evaluative and the nonevaluative or descriptive. This follows from the view I develop about thick concepts and the way in which many real-life examples work. I do not regard the lack of a sharp distinction as a flaw, for to so assume is partly to buy into the view of evaluation propagated by separationists. Indeed, the fact that real-life examples threaten such a sharp distinction should indicate the implausibility of separationism.

The second point elaborates the first. I think that there are some concepts that can be counted as evaluative (on a certain understanding of that notion) that some theories and theorists think should not be. Some of the most radical contenders that I suggest are SIMILAR and RELEVANT, but there are far less radical examples such as MACABRE, CONTORTED, and GROTESQUE. Such examples raise this question: do such concepts, whenever legitimately applied, have to have either a positive or negative point to them in order to count as evaluative concepts? My answer to this question is a clear 'no'. I set up a disagreement between two broad views. The *conservative* view of evaluation restricts evaluation to clear positive and negative judgements alone. In

---

[5] This possibility is barely discussed in the literature. There is a flavour of it in Wiggins (2006), pp. 378–9, note 20, and more strongly in Dancy (1995), p. 268. The most detailed discussion is Roberts (2013) which takes the articulation of this view as its main topic. I discuss this last paper in note 29, Chapter Six.

more detail, it is the view that a concept can be counted as an evaluative concept only if in every instance of its use there is a clear and obvious positive or negative stance or view being expressed. The *liberal* view—which is the view I favour—claims that a concept can be evaluative overall and in any particular instance of its use even if in some instances there is no positive or negative stance being expressed when it is employed.[6] Much of this book is an attempt to move us away from thinking of evaluation as simply exhausted by the bare, minimal notions of good and bad, right and wrong, a yes and a no, and, as I frequently put it, the concepts of PRO and CON or of pro and con evaluation. This last pair of options I use as my barest thin concepts. As such, this whole work is a meditation on the notion of evaluation and an argument for a particular conception of what evaluation is.

Third, I argue for 'evaluative flexibility'. A thick concept can be used to indicate some pro stance in one case, and a con stance in another, and yet we can still be talking of the very same concept. (For example, the dangerous nature of a cliff can be a reason not to walk along it, but it can also, in some contexts, be a reason to do so.) My view is opposed to the idea that we have two different yet similar concepts being applied in these two instances, one that is a pro version and one that is a con version. In my view thick concepts hold together a range of pointed evaluations—basically pro, con and neither—of various strengths. I suggest that evaluative flexibility fits very nicely with the nonseparationism I argue for, and nonseparationism in general. Note that it does not cut against the idea expressed in the previous paragraph. Positive and negative stances are essential to a thick concept being a thick concept, that is they are a necessary part of the range. It is just that I do not think they have to be present and apparent in every single use for a concept to be treated as an evaluative concept.

With these three points introduced we can contrast my nonseparationism with other sorts. First, a nonseparationist might say that any and every thick concept only ever has one type of pointed evaluation, be it pro or con. Second, a nonseparationist might say that while thick concepts have both evaluative and descriptive aspects, such concepts are different from, and perhaps clearly and sharply different from, non-evaluative, descriptive concepts. (And, almost certainly, also different from thin concepts.) This second, different sort of nonseparationism shows up clearly the importance and value of the overall position I advocate. Someone may be swept along with the idea I have already mentioned about evaluative and descriptive conceptual content being nonseparably intertwined. However, as I have already said, if we accept this at face value and think that this is the key idea to argue for, then we seem to be implicitly buying the idea that there are always two sorts of conceptual content, albeit two sorts that when they come together cannot then be

---

[6] I leave aside throughout this study the complication of speaker versus hearer meaning so we can focus on the differences between the views themselves. In Chapter Six I sharpen these two views a little more and contrast them with two more views of evaluation.

pulled apart. In my view that gives too much to separationism in the first place, for this view essentially relies on there being two sorts of conceptual content and, indeed, of treating evaluative content as being uniform. The more interesting and better opposition to separationism is the sort of nonseparationism I favour, one that says explicitly that thick concepts are just evaluative concepts that are as evaluative as thin concepts, and that there is a variety of types of evaluation. In addition, I think that my view makes very good sense of everyday thick concepts. In case it needs underlining, I think there are thin concepts and nonevaluative concepts as well. It is just that I believe that thick concepts are not simply products of their combination, nonseparable or otherwise.

I have thought hard about labels. 'Nonseparationism' may suggest the type of position that I have indicated a worry about: two or more parts that cannot be separated instead of a position that casts doubt on thick concepts being made up of parts in any fashion. However, I do not want to proliferate labels and my attention is for the most part focused on arguing against separationism. It is enough for us to be alive to the difference I have drawn between types of nonseparationism and be aware that *all* nonseparationists think of thick concepts as being 'unitary concepts'.[7] It is just that I wish to emphasize something that others do not, that there are dangers in being swept along by the phrase 'nonseparable intertwining of evaluative and descriptive content'.

(b) Before I summarize each chapter, I should say something about the underlying currents at work in my writing. I believe strongly that when arguing for a positive philosophical view it is often vital to understand the whole terrain and begin by getting under the skin of one's (seeming) opponents. So it is with this debate. The whole discussion of thin and thick concepts draws upon a number of ideas and questions—the distinction between evaluation and description, the nature of their relation, what it is to be 'thin'—that are foundational and that can be asked and answered in a variety of ways. Getting a handle on the terrain itself, and framing things correctly, is crucial in shaping a decent final view. Further, I believe strongly in this case that one can see the merits of the nonseparationist view I argue for only by thinking in detail about separationism first: what separationists have argued for, and what they could possibly argue for.

In this spirit, then, the first half of the book is devoted wholly to understanding the terrain. Nonseparationism will emerge as we go through this first half, but the focus is on separationism.

Note also that although I say something about the nature of evaluation at the start of the next chapter so as to start us off—in effect outlining something of the conservative view introduced above—I do not begin with a lengthy meditation on

---

[7] This term is from Altham (1995), p. 162.

the character and conception of the evaluative and then plunge into debates between separationism and nonseparationism. That would be to put the cart before the horse. A mature understanding of evaluation has to come later, once other matters are in place.

This book presents three argumentative strategies by which nonseparationists can defend their view against separationism: (i) a focus on the (supposed) evaluative element, arguing that separationists cannot think of thin concepts being prior to thick concepts; (ii) a focus on the (supposed) descriptive element, arguing that it cannot be identified so as to give us a fully formed concept that, when joined with some thin evaluative element, is enough to mimic a thick concept; and (iii) a focus on the nature of the evaluative in the first place. Strategies (i) and (ii) are not mutually exclusive and, in fact, they are best viewed as working together. I think they are important but that they ultimately do not wholly convince. I think that it is (iii) that is the most important and fertile idea to raise against separationism. Along with detailing the terrain, I regard my development of (iii) as my main contribution in this work. As an argumentative strategy it sits on its own, although one can understand it and how it is supposed to work *only if* one understands the first two and their limitations, which is why I spend time detailing them. The broad negative thought that emerges against separationism is that when one reflects on the nature of the evaluative and thinks through examples, separationism is shown to be a very curious and strange way to understand thick concepts.

That last point is important to understand. This book does not contain *any* knock-down arguments against separationism or for nonseparationism. I do not believe that separationism is incoherent or that it can be revealed as fundamentally inconsistent with something we all take to be basic and important in our everyday lives, for example. Instead, by thinking through various aspects of our everyday evaluative lives I think that the nonseparationist picture I paint makes better sense of these aspects, and the separationist picture less sense, indeed that it is a strange way to view evaluation.

Talk of different pictures may sound pleasant, but it can result in a depressing end point. A clash between two fundamentally different philosophical views can result in argumentative moves being made by both sides that simply beg the question. That can make the heart sink. I think there is no point in denying that there may be something of that in this debate, however I do prefer to emphasize the positive. I believe that a deepening of the account provided by nonseparationism proves to be instructive. Even if no knock-down argument can be given against separationism, I think that neutrals should be persuaded to my side. That is the task I set myself. If I am lucky, some separationists will question their affiliation in addition.

I begin, in **Chapter Two**, by thinking about separationism. Separationists believe that supposed thick concepts can be analysed as containing different elements and aspects, normally some value-free descriptive conceptual content, and some evaluative content, which is normally very thin. This itself brings with it the idea that to evaluate is in some way either simply to approve or to disapprove, and that this is what marks the difference between evaluative content and descriptive content. Despite a broad sweep of agreement, separationists disagree about many things, some of which I have listed earlier. In Chapter Two I discuss two broad types of separationism and present their advantages and disadvantages. I also think about the strengths of the position overall while drawing attention to its likely weaknesses.

In **Chapter Three** I extend our understanding of the terrain by thinking about two important models of conceptual relations, models that attempt to capture the relation between families of general and specific concepts. The two models are the *genus-species* model and the determinable–determinate model. In short I argue that separationists are committed to the former. Indeed, I argue that the *genus-species* model when applied to thin and thick concepts *just is* an expression of separationism. Integral to this model is that each individual *species* concept is created from the combination of the overall *genus* concept and some unique *differentia*.[8] In the case of separationism, some thin evaluative content is the *genus* concept, while the *differentia* is the descriptive content seen as unique to each thick concept.

As well as detailing both conceptual models, I suggest that neither is appropriate for understanding thin and thick concepts. (Although separationism appears to be the *genus-species* model in another guise, that does not mean that nonseparationists should adopt the determinable–determinate model.) Why draw suspicion on both models? The reason is that both sit badly with evaluative flexibility, the idea I introduced above. I detail this idea in Chapter Three, cast it in a positive light, and show why it does not combine well with separationism. Here we have only 'suggestion', not 'conclusive argument'. Evaluative flexibility returns in Chapter Six because other elements of my view will enrich it and be enriched in turn by it. Progress is made in Chapter Three, however, because we are beginning to understand the terrain more and we can see the limitations of the *genus-species* model and separationism. At the end of Chapter Three I briefly diagnose where a different way of understanding thick and thin conceptual relations can enter.

At this point in the book I will have introduced and examined separationism, and detailed the terrain of the debate. I am then in a position, in **Chapter Four**, to introduce and consider the first anti-separationist strategy, that which focuses on the evaluative aspect of thick concepts.

I first argue that there is a difference in kind between the thin and the thick; both our conceptual models depend on that. (I also note, in passing, that the way in which the boundary should be drawn should in turn make us query whether the separationist enterprise is as plausible as it initially appears.[9] I pick this up again in

---

[8] Or, unique to two thick concepts that share the same *differentia* but which have a different thin *genus*.
[9] This discussion brings out the difference between saying that thin concepts are 'wholly' or 'mostly' evaluative. The first may indicate a difference in kind between the thin and the thick, while the second indicates a difference of degree.

Chapter Six.) I use the barest thin concepts, PRO and CON, a lot here. I argue, through consideration of the work of Allan Gibbard, that separationists are better off working with a very thin sort of evaluative element in their analyses of thick concepts.

This builds to the main part of Chapter Four. In order for the *genus–species* model to apply to thin and thick concepts, thin *genus* concepts have to be thought to be conceptually prior to thick *species* concepts, thick concepts being the creation of '*genus* plus some *differentia*'. I consider what 'conceptual priority' might amount to in this debate, and argue that there is no convincing argument for the conceptual priority of the thin. But, in addition, I argue that 'thick prioritarianism' is not a good idea either.[10] If anything emerges with some plausibility, it is a third position I label 'no prioritarianism'. This is the assertion that neither thin nor thick concepts have conceptual priority over the other when considering how these two broad types of concept relate. That said, although I think that this discussion is instructive and that it shows the weaknesses of separationism, I also say that *at most* it stands as a set of weighty considerations with which separationists have to deal. A neutral may not be wholly convinced by the best arguments I lay out against 'thin prioritarianism', let alone a separationist.

This is all to the good in my overall discussion, because this first argumentative strategy, while helping to understand the debate more clearly, also shows that more is required for nonseparationists to challenge separationists successfully.

This takes us to **Chapter Five**. While the first argumentative strategy concentrates on the *genus* part of the model, the second concentrates on the *differentia* that is supposedly unique to each and every thick concept. This brings in the so-called *disentangling argument* and the *shapelessness hypothesis*. The disentangling argument is an argument to the effect that we cannot separate evaluative from descriptive content in the way that separationists envisage for thick concepts. This is because evaluative concepts are shapeless with respect to descriptive concepts: we cannot mimic the extension of evaluative concepts by descriptive conceptual content alone. There is a lot to say about the argument and hypothesis and they have undoubtedly been influential. I claim that the argument is not wholly successful, although that does not mean that separationism walks away unscathed. I suggest a possible different conclusion from the one often reached. However—and again this chimes with my overall narrative—this is weaker than ideal for nonseparationists. In short, they need something more than the first two argumentative strategies discussed in the first half of this book.

One idea that emerges from my treatment of the second argumentative strategy is that it meets separationism on its own terms, something mentioned above. This sets the scene for **Chapter Six**. Separationists believe that evaluative and descriptive conceptual content are not just separate but different. The second strategy, if

---

[10] With apologies for the ugliness of this and other labels.

adopted, is an attempt by nonseparationists to show that evaluative and descriptive content can intertwine in some nonseparable fashion. But, as I have already indicated, taken at face value and alone, this phrasing gives away too much to separationists. It assumes implicitly that one can divide evaluative from descriptive content in the first place. Further, it fails to question explicitly the narrow and conservative view of the evaluative that is being assumed. It is in Chapter Six where I make good on the various positive ideas I hold. Much of this chapter concerns how thick concepts threaten the supposedly clear and obvious distinction between the evaluative and the nonevaluative in part by showing as plausible the liberal view of evaluation. I also conclude my argument for evaluative flexibility.

As should be apparent, a lot of my discussion comes together in Chapter Six. Readers will have to forgive me as every so often I say that I will elaborate or discuss something further in Chapter Six. As also may be apparent as we go through, Chapters Two to Six are the core of the book. The final three chapters are briefer, and designed to be so, but discuss important topics all the same.

In **Chapter Seven** I continue my motivation for and defence of the liberal view of evaluation specifically by focusing on recent arguments from Pekka Väyrynen. He argues that thick terms—for he focuses on these rather than concepts—can convey pro and con evaluations, but it is best to assume that they typically do so only because of context, tone of voice, and other factors. In effect, he denies the claim that they are, in his words, 'inherently evaluative'. What evaluations such terms carry or convey is a matter of pragmatics, not semantics, and are therefore only accidental or nonessential to them. This cuts against my view of thick concepts and my view of evaluation in general, for I do think that pro and con evaluations, and the more general evaluative conceptual content that thick concepts have (that which reaches beyond pointed pro and con points) is part of what they essentially are and marks them as a special part of our everyday thought. Väyrynen lays bare his view of evaluation that is clearly conservative. Having outlined my positive view in the previous chapter, in this chapter I deepen it by showing that Väyrynen's arguments are questionable.

In **Chapter Eight** I discuss two more topics, both of which relate to the social aspect of thick concepts. The first is a potential worry for nonseparationists. One reason people have for believing in the shapelessness hypothesis—and one I accept to some extent—is that one cannot fully appreciate a thick concept (what it is, how it is used), unless one somehow appreciates the evaluative point of the concept. But this raises an interesting question: to what extent does one have to accept and hold sincerely the evaluative point of the concept? If one answers that an anthropologist has to hold sincerely the views of the people she is studying, for example, then it might make many if not all such investigations impossible. I map a way out of this problem for nonseparationism and this leads me to extend my conclusion of Chapter Six, that the real problem faces separationism: it makes anthropological understanding look difficult to achieve because it has a curious way of understanding thick concepts.

This leads me to a second topic. Bernard Williams argues, quite famously, that thick concepts form more of our social world than thin ones, and that they offer a better hope for us maintaining confidence that our evaluative practices are justified. This role for thick concepts is contextualized by us imagining how we might treat our evaluative practices when we confront other groups that think and conceptualize differently from how we do. I argue that Williams is wrong to think that thick concepts offer better hope than thin concepts on this point. Overall Williams presents a fairly pessimistic view of our evaluative practices. I offer something that is more optimistic.

In **Chapter Nine** I draw things to a conclusion. Although this is a study of a topic in the philosophy of value that is quite specific, it has implications for metaethics generally. One issue that requires discussion is how we conceive of thick concepts and terms in relation to (supposed) thick features or properties. That is, how do the ways in which humans think and communicate relate to the stuff that may exist and to which we may be trying to refer? In this final chapter I consider what my previous discussion means for evaluative cognitivism and evaluative realism. My aim here is to set debates about thin and thick concepts in some context and to show what is at stake when it comes to discussions of realism. My aim is not to argue for the brand of cognitivism that I favour. That is a topic for another time.

(c) Although I draw upon a number of writers in this study, this is not a historical treatment of how thick concepts have become a focus of philosophical debate. In this section, however, I situate my debate in the recent history.

As far as I am aware, Williams coined the term 'thick concept', in his *Ethics and the Limits of Philosophy* (abbreviated as *ELP*). Interestingly, in this work the term 'thin concept' never appears. Instead, Williams uses phrases such as 'the most abstract concepts'.[11] It is worth noting, first, that he explicitly defines thin and thick concepts differently from how I have done, and instead uses a frame that suggests 'normativity' and the possibility of concepts encoding reasons. The slogan often used when discussing Williams' view is thus: thin concepts are 'action-guiding' while thick concepts are both 'action-guiding' and 'world-guided'. Despite this difference between us, we can see that Williams' chief concern is to argue against the supposed separation of thick concepts into component parts, no matter how those parts are captured. He also thinks, as I have said, that thick concepts are more important than thin ones when it comes to the possibility of evaluative knowledge and understanding our social world.

Although Williams is famous for exciting interest in thin and thick concepts, to start our story about thick concepts here would be unwise. Many intellectual histories

---

[11] He mentions 'thin concepts' by that label in Williams (1996), p. 25, but does so without any indication that this is a new development. Samuel Scheffler in his 1987 review of *ELP* talks of 'thin concepts'. Scheffler tells me that his memory is of Williams happily using 'thin concept' at the time of his writing *ELP*, so its absence is probably some quirk of no philosophical significance.

are themselves aimed at telling a particular view.[12] Here is my brief, impressionistic version that notes two other sources.

First, during the late 1950s Philippa Foot and Iris Murdoch ran an Oxford seminar in which they began to question recent work in noncognitivism, specifically the prescriptivism of R. M. Hare.[13] They also had in their sights the fact–value distinction more generally. For many prominent thinkers during the twentieth century, the separation of and clear distinction between facts and values was an article of faith. When Maddy says that Paddy is wearing brown trousers or that today is Sunday, she is trying to state facts. When she says that Paddy is good she is ascribing a value to him. Although it looks as if we can pick out values as much as we pick out facts, and that they form part of the stuff of the world, for those that hold to the fact–value distinction the two are very different. Facts are things in the world, while values seem as if they may well not be. Often the fact–value distinction was given a naturalistic edge, with theorists thinking that to be a (proper) fact is to be the sort of thing that is studied, or could be studied, by the natural sciences. Modern natural science has no room for values: it cannot measure them, or test them, and it seems impossible to sense them with any of the normal five human senses. So some other and quite different explanation is needed of our value judgements. As part of this view, doubt was cast on the reality of values. Additionally, questions were raised about the character of our language and psychology when we judge that a particular thing has a certain value. Some of those that relied on the fact–value distinction explicitly conceived of it as a development of Hume's is–ought distinction.[14]

It is easy to see how Hare's prescriptivism and, say, A. J. Ayer's emotivism step in here. We have some supposed nonevaluative, factual, descriptive stuff. We have nonevaluative concepts that we use to pick this stuff out and categorize it as different things. Some of this stuff is further seen as good and some of it as bad. We then have some theory that tells us how it is that such value judgements are conveyed and what their exact function is. Some noncognitivists emphasize the emotive stance that such

---

[12]   See Appiah (2008), chapter 1 for a nice discussion of this idea.

[13]   The best discussions of their ideas are in Foot (1958) and (1958–9), and Murdoch (1956), (1957), and (1962). Williams notes that this seminar was one of the inspirations for his work on thick concepts: Williams (1985), note 7 pp. 217–18. The precise idea he cites is that one cannot understand an idea unless one sees its evaluative point, an idea I discuss in Chapter Eight.

[14]   Putnam (2002), esp. chapter 1, is very good on the history of the development of the fact–value distinction (although Putnam prefers 'dichotomy') and its relation to Hume. One short discussion is worth repeating. He ends that first chapter with thoughts about Carnap and the distinction between observational and theoretical terms. Observational terms are those that refer to properties for which there is a simple test procedure that can determine whether the supposed property in question exists. (Examples include 'blue', 'hot', and 'warmer than'.) Theoretical terms are those that refer to hypothetical physical properties (such as 'charge') that we introduce to explain and predict certain observable phenomena. Putnam (p. 25) imagines a historian describing someone as cruel. This, instead of being a theoretical term in Carnap's sense, is a "term that figures in a certain kind of reflective understanding of the *rationale* of conduct, in understanding both how the agent feels and acts and how others perceive the agent's feelings and actions". Putnam imagines Carnap dismissing cruelty, therefore, as some "metaphysical nonsense".

judgements have, and get us to think about evinced Boos and Hurrahs. Others, such as Hare, get us to think about commands and prescriptions.

Present-day philosophers are used to the fact–value distinction coming under pressure from a number of sources. Foot and Murdoch, through concentration on Hare, can be seen as questioning whether there is such a distinction, and what one might mean by talking of the 'factual' in particular. When we say of Paddy that he is honest, or fair, or wicked, or stylish, are we trying to pick out some fact about him or ascribe a value to him? For Foot and Murdoch it is very likely that we are ascribing values. But it is not so obvious that we are not also picking out something factual and, further, that it would be unwise to separate these two aspects of the one thing. Their reasons—or at least Foot's—for thinking this will be outlined in Chapter Six.

A second point worth noting in our brief history is that although Williams coined 'thick concept', before him Gilbert Ryle used the phrase 'thick description' to describe ideas in the general ballpark.[15] A thick description is simply a more specific sort of description that is required in order to categorize an action or thing. To give a hint of the idea, consider the difference between the more general THINKING and the more specific REFLECTING, MEDITATING, and DAYDREAMING. Ryle mixes this with his idea that among relevantly similar actions and things, described in similar ways, there need not be a separable and identifiable core or base thing that they all have in common. So reflection, meditation, and daydreaming are all types of thinking, but it is not as if there is a specific isolatable thing—thinking—that is common to all of the individual instances and which is attached to three other (separable) things in turn to create those three instances of thinking.

I mention Ryle here, not just because of his use of the word 'thick', but also because he thinks of some descriptions as being abstractions from other, thicker descriptions, echoing Williams' labelling in *ELP*. Williams would have been aware of Ryle's work and a comparison of their ideas is instructive. I discuss Ryle's view of thick descriptions and compare his thoughts with Williams' views of thick concepts, again in Chapter Six.

Alongside these points, it is worth remarking that writers other than Williams—prominently Simon Blackburn, Jonathan Dancy, Allan Gibbard, Susan Hurley, John McDowell, Hilary Putnam, and David Wiggins—were making interesting points about thick concepts during the 1980s and 1990s. Although my study is primarily ahistorical, I will draw on the work of some of these writers in the coming chapters.[16]

---

[15] Ryle (1966–7) and (1968). Although the phrase features prominently in these late papers, the idea of there being higher-levels of description that contrast with bare or minimal descriptions is something that runs through a lot of Ryle's work. I have not been able to ascertain the extent to which Ryle—or Hare—knew of the Foot–Murdoch seminar, let alone whether they attended.

[16] It is also worth mentioning Clifford Geertz who, in Geertz (1973), used Ryle's ideas to great effect in reflecting on what goes on when one attempts to understand other cultures. Although I do not discuss her work, Lovibond (1983) is also relevant.

Key to their discussions was the aforementioned idea of whether evaluative and descriptive conceptual content were separable and, hence, whether thick concepts could be reduced to more basic concepts.

(d) In the previous few pages, and certainly in what is to come, a number of contrasts and ideas appear. Here I highlight three so as to orientate the reader.

(i) *The fact–value distinction.* I have just mentioned this. I do not speculate as to the origins of the distinction, nor as to how scientifically respectable it is.[17] Suffice it to say, in this study I assume a fairly simple-minded characterization: there is stuff in and of the world, and there are values that humans attach to some of that stuff that take either a positive or negative cast. There is assumed to be a distinction between stuff and how we value that stuff, and that distinction is thought to be very deep and unbridgeable. Once the distinction is accepted, another question looms: even if facts and values are radically different types of thing, do values exist and, indeed, are they as ontologically respectable as facts?[18] Some modern theorists may accept the distinction while trying to show that values, or evaluative properties, are still onto-logically respectable. However, many who wielded the distinction originally did so with the explicit or implicit intent of casting doubt on the reality of values. These theorists thought it unwise to think of values as being part of the world of stuff *really* (and their theories may further explain this point), and that such values are in the world merely in some broader sense, namely in the sense that humans create values and humans are themselves part of the world.

There are different ways of charactering the fact–value distinction.[19] Most discus-sions are based on this assumption: we are trying to characterize the world and what is fundamental to our ontology (and some discussions drop the 'fundamental'; they just care about what exists, fundamental or not). Our language and our concepts are essential to that, for reflection on our concepts and how we carve the world reveals to us what our ontological commitments are.

I take it that the broad distinction I am interested in shows up essentially with other terms and phrases: in the 'evaluative' and the 'descriptive', obviously, but also in the 'normative' and the 'positive' used in the social sciences, and in Hume's distinction between is and ought, which in modern-day terms has a narrower focus on normativity and the guidance of action. No matter what labels we use, there is

---

[17] For example, we might think first of all about what facts are, and whether they can be respectable to and in modern science. The fact that the chair is over there is very different from the chair itself, and different again from the atoms that make up a chair. Often 'fact' in the mouths of some thinkers was just a placeholder for 'a thing that exists'.

[18] And further, if they are assumed to be real, should they be thought of naturalistically or nonnatur-alistically? There are many discussions of this in modern metaethics. For a brief flavour see Brink (1989), Enoch (2011), and Shafer-Landau (2003). Kirchin (2012) discusses many positions in metaethics.

[19] As well as Putnam (2002) on this topic see both Blackburn (2013) and Väyrynen (2013), pp. 15–18 for responses.

assumed to be some sharp distinction between how things are, on the one hand, and how we positively or negatively react to those things and how we might like things to be in the future, on the other. Use of Hume's distinction will emphasize this latter idea, where the focus may be on reasoning: 'if this *is* the case, then what *ought* to be done?'[20]

In this book my focus is not on arguing for the reality of evaluative properties. My aim is to question the fact–value distinction in the first place, and to provide *but one* building block in a defence (in fact, a family of different defences) of the reality of values and of a certain view of what happens when we reason and judge. The introduction of thick concepts, or their promise, is designed to cast doubt on the plausibility of the distinction between facts and values. The aim is to make us question what is going on in our language and concepts, our judgement and reasoning that uses them, and what we can conclude about the structure and character of our ontology.

(ii) *Concepts and properties.* This whole study is focused on thinking about conceptual content. I use 'stuff' as a colloquial and general term to indicate things in the world, with concepts being thought of in a simple way: they are the tools by which we characterize and capture that stuff.

Although this book is not a defence of (my version of) evaluative realism, as mentioned I indicate what implications my thoughts have for properties and reality in Chapter Nine, given that I discuss matters wholly in terms of concepts.

(iii) *Concepts and terms.* Again I am assuming something simple here. Terms are the linguistic tools by which we represent the world to ourselves, while concepts are the non-linguistic tools by which we do the same. The philosophical characterization of concepts is a controversial matter, and in this study I want to bracket this dispute because otherwise it will divert us from the main issues between separationists and nonseparationists.[21] Indeed, it is fair to say that this has been the approach that most writers on thick concepts have taken. However, I will say here that I do not think of concepts as literal mental representations, as may be found in cognitive psychology. More positively, I think both that concepts are those non-linguistic entities that help us to present the world in a certain way to ourselves (such that they can be contrasted with the referents of such modes of presentation) and that they can be and are revealed in how people use terms to identify, categorize, communicate, and the like.

---

[20] There is a very interesting and different frame to be used for all of these discussions: perhaps there could be a three-way distinction between facts, value, and reasons (or similar ideas), and perhaps we should be casting doubt on clear distinctions between these three notions. Or perhaps we should simply be interested in exploring the relations more. Why put values and reasons on the same side against facts? Perhaps they are as different from each other as either is from facts. This is really interesting, but in order to make some progress I choose to focus just on the evaluative and the descriptive, although reasons and actions do make appearances every so often. A focus on the relation between and differences between reasons and values is a matter for another time.

[21] See Margolis and Laurence (2014), especially §1 for a flavour. Note that after they list three main views, including the family of 'concepts as mental representations' Margolis and Lawrence indicate that one could try to combine them.

One important distinction between concepts and terms is this. Just as a single word can have more than one meaning and more than one concept—think of 'bank'—so a number of words can have a single concept standing behind them. For example, a number of words such as 'fair', 'fine', 'good', and 'great' can be used not only to indicate the concepts linked explicitly to those terms, but they can all be used, in everyday conversation, to pick out some same, general concept PRO. Note something already mentioned in passing: Pekka Väyrynen, one of my chief interlocutors, casts the debates using 'thick terms', but I take it that our debate is about the same issues.

(e)   One last set of comments. There are topics I would like to have discussed in detail but have decided to leave out for matters of space. Here are three. First, thick concepts are traditionally thought of as one word 'things', reflecting one word terms. But there is no reason to think that matters have to be like this; there could easily be, and probably are, inseparable evaluative concepts that require a number of words to express them, be they in English or any other language. Indeed, further, we might then think that all sorts of linguistic device, such as simile, metaphor, and the like might be useful (or necessary) in indicating some thick evaluations. For simplicity's sake, however, I deal only with one word concepts in this study.[22] Second, because of my language throughout this book I may give the impression that we have distinct evaluative domains, such as *the* ethical, *the* aesthetic, and so on. While some concepts and ideas are solidly within one domain, I do not believe for one moment that there are hard and clear demarcations between various types of evaluation and that every evaluative concept sits squarely in one domain and no others. For example, we can call an artwork grotesque, offensive, heroic, and the like. Such claims can be meant non-metaphorically and may have both aesthetic and ethical connotations. Other such examples abound when considering other borders, such as the ethical–prudential and the aesthetic–epistemic. Further to this, ethical evaluations can be offered without using clear and obvious ethical terminology.[23] These are all interesting ideas, but I do not detail them here. I hope that all I say in this book is both consistent with these ideas and conducive to them.

Lastly, I keep to one side, as much as possible, the idea that if there are concepts then there are very likely to be different conceptions of those concepts and, hence, we need some way to distinguish when a concept is a conception of another concept, and when it is a different concept altogether. Making good on this task is crucial in understanding, for example, whether people are in genuine dispute with one another, and in understanding the very conditions for agreement first of all. I find this whole topic of great interest, but I leave it aside here for another time.

Having indicated ideas that do not get detailed in this book, I now start on those questions I do wish to discuss.

---

[22]   See Zangwill (2013) for more on this idea.
[23]   This is a key theme of Crary (2007). See Kirchin (2008) for commentary.

PART I

Understanding the Debate

2

Separationism

2.1 Introduction

The main aim of this chapter is to detail one of the two main accounts that seek to characterize thick concepts. As mentioned in Chapter One, I label this account 'separationism'. Although I list and explore some of its advantages towards the end of this chapter, I do not advocate it. In later chapters I do argue against separationism, but my present task is to describe and understand it so as to outline its appeal.

There are some ghosts at our feast. The first is mentioned in passing a few times and it made an appearance in Chapter One. The disentangling argument, which employs the shapelessness hypothesis, is often raised against separationism. Some of the points made by separationists will make sense only once we have considered this argument and hypothesis in Chapter Five. But we must start somewhere; we would find it hard to understand the disentangling argument without understanding what it was an argument against. I trust that what I say below makes enough sense for now without articulating what the argument and hypothesis are.

Two other ghosts are evaluative conceptual content (or 'evaluation' generally) and descriptive conceptual content. As mentioned in Chapter One, I do not begin by examining these labels in detail, but will merely employ them after a little discussion. For a start, I think the difference is something that can be said only once we have discussed the various battles between separationists and nonseparationists. Thick concepts are interesting because they call into question the claim that there is a hard and fast boundary between evaluation and descriptive conceptual content. So it would get matters the wrong way round to think that we have to articulate fully what evaluation is before we began to discuss thick concepts. In addition, it seems a fool's task to aim to give detailed necessary and sufficient conditions, say, to mark the difference between evaluative and descriptive content; or so I will suggest in this study.[1] It therefore seems good enough for our purposes to rely on rules of thumb and intuitions about familiar examples to tell the difference between thin and thick concepts. It seems better to let a view of the evaluative and the descriptive emerge

---

[1] Aristotle's advice from *Nicomachean Ethics* 1094b–1095a about the precision of explanation being appropriate for the subject matter seems apt here; Aristotle (2000). Furthermore, in what language would such necessary and sufficient conditions be spelt out? Descriptive language? This would obviously be viciously circular.

through examples and attempts at characterization, and then try to make that view more concrete.

In that spirit let me begin by saying that evaluative content *seems* to be the sort of content which expresses, or *is*, our approval and disapproval of certain things.[2] Its most basic and bare form can be expressed by two concepts that I mentioned in Chapter One, PRO and CON. I assume throughout that these are the most basic and minimal positive and negative stances we can take towards things. Philosophers may often talk of simple approval and disapproval in this regard, or like and dislike, and both distinctions seem good enough. Alternatively, we might be inclined to refer to PRO, say, as a 'positive preference', but that may pack too much into the idea. As we will see later in this book, a positive view may not imply that we want the thing, or want to do something with the thing, or that we prefer the thing to something else, and 'preference' carries these connotations. (Or, it does in my view, anyway.) We may not wish to *do* anything with something we think of positively; we may simply think and feel positively about it. Whatever our view about what a preference is, or if similar worries plague approval and likings, all I mean by PRO and CON is, again, the most minimal positive and negative views we can imagine.

I emphasize a point made in passing in Chapter One. Although we may not use the words 'pro' and 'con' very much, I think that we use the concepts, explicitly or implicitly, all the time. We might use various words to express PRO, for example, words such as 'good', 'fair', 'fine', 'cool', 'wicked', the many various slang words that come and go, and various linguistic expressions and tics such as 'uh-huh', 'alright', and 'yeah'. These words and expressions can obviously be used of other concepts, but in some contexts they are used to indicate only PRO.[3] I will have more to say about PRO and CON throughout this book.

Although we may use PRO and CON every day, evaluation is not confined simply to such bare evaluation. We can express our attractions and repulsions, our joys and annoyances, and so on. Our thick concepts in particular seem to be indicating content that is pro-in-a-way and con-in-a-way. For example, to label something as generous is to praise it for being a certain way, and the way in which it exists is what gives—or *is*—the reason for the praise. This praise and the 'certain way' in which something exists are united in or by a thick concept. The debate between separationists and nonseparationists centres on how to understand that uniting. Such content can alter in strength, of course; if something is excellent it is typically better than if it is just nice, okay, or acceptable.

---

[2] Here I loosely articulate the conservative view of evaluation, mentioned in Chapter One. I tighten this up and compare it with the liberal view in Chapter Six.

[3] For a different view about such thin concepts—that they are merely a philosopher's construct—see Chappell (2013). I think that Chappell is correct that very often philosophers are not alive to the encrustation that supposed thin concepts have, and that this may render such concepts less thin than is usually thought. However, I also think this paper misses something else that is of the everyday and ordinary, namely the sort of positive and negative judgement that I indicate in the main text.

Although I argue in this book for an understanding of evaluation which is not exhausted by pro and con stances, this starting idea is not a bad one. This idea of evaluation provides a nice, clear contrast with descriptive content, which seems to be the sort of content that describes features of things in a value-free way. This starting characterization might not be that helpful since I have defined descriptive content in relation to evaluative content, rather than giving it a characterization that stands free. But this interdefining, or rough-characterization-of-one-broad-family-of-concept-only-after-the-other-is-introduced, might well be inevitable. At least some clear-cut examples of descriptive content are easy to give. After all, there does not seem to be any evaluation involved in saying that some piece of Paddy's clothing is brown or that the table is 'over there'. However and as advertised, once we think harder about matters, we should see that the domain of evaluative is larger than we may at first think. That idea will occupy us in Chapter Six. For now, we should think about separationism, and in doing so assume that we have a good initial grasp of the distinction between evaluative and descriptive conceptual content.

One final word of warning. Chapter One started us off quite gently, and Chapters Three and Four should also be relatively easy to follow even if both contain a few detailed topics. This present chapter, however, is more technical and abstract. If one is uninterested in the niceties of different sorts of separationism, then the main message to take from this chapter is that separationism is not a single, narrow position. It contains within itself scope for splintering into different accounts.

2.2 Introducing Separationism

In Chapter One I described briefly the very essence of a thick concept, namely a concept that in some way has both an evaluative aspect and a descriptive aspect or, as separationists may prefer to say, evaluative and descriptive elements or parts. A key question for all theorists is how the evaluative and descriptive combine. What unites all separationist theories is the thought that any story about evaluative and descriptive conceptual content must assume that these are two distinct and separable sorts of content.

Alongside this first idea, further points need stating. Separationists do not claim, first, that thick concepts feel phenomenologically disjointed or feel as if they are a mixture. Nor do they claim, second, that it is easy for everyday users of thick concepts to note exactly where the descriptive starts and the evaluative begins. What they claim is that any thick concept contains parts that can be separated in the abstract, in theory, upon reflection. Nor, third, are they claiming that the relation between the evaluative and descriptive parts of all thick concepts is exactly the same. Separationists can and do state that while some thick concepts have to carry the same sort of evaluation, even to the same strength, in most or all contexts, others do not. An example of the former might be JUST (or JUSTICE). Can we ever imagine something being just and being bad for that reason? The positive evaluation seems quite tightly wedded to the overall concept. An example of the latter might be ELEGANT (or ELEGANCE). The elegance of one poem might add positively to its value, whereas the elegance of another might be neither here nor there, or might be its greatest failing. Some poems' ideas and moods are better expressed through a rough style and messy structure so as to convey urgency or rawness.[4]

Fourth, separationists do not routinely claim that thick concepts are bogus or useless. They might claim that it is erroneous to characterize thick concepts in the way that nonseparationists do, but that is a different point. We can legitimately describe institutions as just and poems as elegant, just as we describe them as old or long. It is just that we should understand what lies behind the use of such terms and concepts. So, returning to the general point, separationists' key claim is simply that thick concepts are not unitary concepts, and are instead the product of separable conceptual contents or other elements, which in turn might themselves be full-blown concepts.

Fifth, it is open to separationists to cast evaluation in different ways. I have switched in my introductory comments from 'evaluative conceptual content' to 'evaluation' and 'evaluative element'. The first idea is something that cognitivist-separationists will happily embrace, but is something that their noncognitivist cousins will reject. (We met this distinction in Chapter One.) Although a lot of the discussion in this chapter is run in terms of attitudes that are evinced, I am not so concerned at all with how the evaluation is treated; I am more concerned with other ways in which separationists differ.

That is the general position. Why should we adopt it? I detail various reasons for doing so at the end of this chapter, reasons that can be expressed better after my discussion of the positions. But in essence all of these reasons stem from an idea I have already voiced, namely the difference between evaluation and descriptive conceptual content, between facts and values. These seem to be two radically different ways of responding to or capturing the world. It makes sense, goes the thought, to be suspicious of the claim that any conceptual content that has aspects of both evaluation and descriptive content is a unitary concept, a concept that cannot be analysed into separable parts. The positive, separationist views that stem from this suspicion try to make sense of how we can go about analysing thick concepts into component parts.

In what follows I detail various sorts of separationism, using two broad headings. I consider their rival merits, both in comparison to one another and in comparison to a general form of nonseparationism. Towards the end I sow seeds of doubt regarding separationism as a whole.

---

[4] I use JUST and ELEGANT only to illustrate the general contention. Things can be said against the claims made about both examples. For instance, maintaining a strict form of justice can at times be detrimental to friendship and familial love. However, this point should not detain us.

One last point. My set-up has a fictional quality. It is easy to indicate views that constitute our two broad headings and associate them with particular philosophers. However, there is a grey area where it is not so clear what sort of separationism we have, and my talk of two headings may mislead. This greyness is partly because of the philosophical issues involved, and partly because people have fine-tuned their views over time. I have Simon Blackburn particularly in mind regarding this last point. I sort this issue out towards the end, but we first need to understand the broad views.

2.3 Simple Separationism

The first sort of separationism I label 'simple separationism'. I take work by Blackburn during the 1980s and 1990s as my main example.[5] 'Simple' here indicates that this position is less complicated than its rival. It is not being used pejoratively; indeed, the position has virtues.

The idea is this. Imagine we have a wholly nonevaluative, purely descriptive concept, such as CHAIR.[6] A certain extension of the concept will be fixed: *these* things will be chairs and *those* things will not be. Imagine now that we begin to find some chairs completely lovely for whatever reason. We could write this as 'chair↑', which indicates the descriptive *term* 'chair' said sincerely with a positive tone of voice. We then introduce this term and tone into our vocabulary. Indeed, imagine that it becomes so entrenched in what we and our peer group think and do that a new concept develops, CHAIR-PRO. (We might not literally say 'chair-pro', but this is the concept standing behind 'chair↑'.) CHAIR-PRO could be used of all chairs, although it will probably be used of only a subset. We can imagine a related term and concept, 'chair↓' and CHAIR-CON that cover some of the other chairs, as well as our original CHAIR.[7] We can imagine further examples that indicate toleration, infatuation (with two arrows) and the like. This proposal identifies the evaluative content in the concept as some thin concept throughout, typically PRO or CON depending on whether the evaluation is positive or negative. Note that what has happened in this scenario is that we have started with a certain tone of voice or evinced attitude and, because of

---

[5] See Blackburn (1984), pp. 148–51; (1992), pp. 285–99; and (1998), pp. 92–104. Across these pieces there is a fine-tuning of Blackburn's view, which culminates in something he says in Blackburn (1998) and something he says in Blackburn (2013). I discuss this in §2.4. Thinking about his central and earlier work on the topic will be instructive, however, as many ideas still hold. Other examples of simple separationism include Stevenson (1944), chapter 3, and Hare (1952), p. 121; and (1963), pp. 21–9. Daniel Elstein and Thomas Hurka seem to cast Blackburn as a simple separationist in Elstein and Hurka (2009), notes 10 and 11, and do not comment on the fine-tuning of his view that I pick out. Another notable separationist paper is Smith (2013), which draws on Hare's work.

[6] I believe that CHAIR is a pretty good bet for being a nonevaluative, descriptive concept, and that stands despite my arguments in Chapter Six that are designed to make us question what the difference is between the evaluative and the descriptive.

[7] A new concept, CHAIR-NEUTRAL, may come about, which serves to indicate no evaluation where one could be expected to be given. That would be a different concept from that which involved just 'no evaluation', that is just CHAIR.

some cultural entrenching, we have begun to think that we have some evaluative conceptual content. This content has become connected to or, better, has become intertwined with some descriptive content.

Concepts such as CHAIR-PRO are interesting because they unite what are two separate sorts of conceptual content and they do so obviously. Such examples are odd, however, since they are mere philosophical constructs. Of course, we may on an odd occasion say 'chair↑'. Imagine, for example, a situation where you are relieved that finally someone has brought in the chair you have been requesting for ages, rather than the unwanted tables with which you have been left. An exclamation of 'chair↑!' might be perfectly natural. But despite such rare examples, we do not have a fully fledged concept of CHAIR-PRO. We simply do not need such a thing. We manage perfectly well with CHAIR and when the occasion arises indicate a positive or negative attitude with tone of voice or through other things. The evaluation connected to 'chair' and CHAIR is only accidental. So CHAIR-PRO is most definitely a strange philosophical construct.

This matters because surely the aim of such examples is to make vivid what is going on with familiar, everyday thick concepts. We do not really care about silly concepts made up by philosophers. What have they to teach us?

Luckily, Blackburn constructs a quite famous case that has exactly the same structure as 'chair↑', but which is far closer to familiar concerns.[8] His example is 'fat↓'. He imagines a culture in which it is perfectly fine to be fat, perhaps it is even admirable. Then, some people—"slim, active, lithe teenagers, perhaps"—begin to be disgusted by fat people, and describe them as 'fat↓'.[9] It is clear from this example that 'fat↓' should be separated into two distinct parts, 'description+tone' as Blackburn puts it.[10] We can imagine the story extending and the group carrying on speaking in this way, perhaps influencing others, so that over time or because of significant incidents a new concept is born, FAT-CON.[11] It is clear from what Blackburn says about 'fat↓', and his comments about the work of chief nonseparationist John McDowell, that he is committed to thinking that we should separate concepts such as FAT-CON into their evaluative and descriptive elements, and that we should further see the evaluation as something that should be given a noncognitivist treatment of some sort. Perhaps other concepts might be forthcoming in an extended scenario. Perhaps some

---

[8] The example is first introduced in Blackburn (1992), p. 290, but is given more detail in (1998), specifically pp. 94–7 and with other points made across pp. 97–104.

[9] Blackburn (1998), p. 95.   [10] This is used primarily in Blackburn (1992).

[11] Blackburn sticks throughout his writings to 'fat↓' and emphasizes tone of voice and the like. Nowhere does he refer to a possible *concept*, with some attached evaluation, which is entirely in keeping with his noncognitivism. To keep things strict, and because it helps with points I make later, I introduce FAT-CON. I use this concept a lot in this chapter because 'fat↓' is a well-used example in Blackburn's writings and it is easy to manipulate so as to make points. We could worry that FAT is itself an evaluative concept, but I leave that nicety aside and employ it as Blackburn intends it, as a nonevaluative concept. (Thanks to Graeme A. Forbes for this final point.)

rejoice in being fat and the concept FAT-PRO is born. There might be a range of reactions attached to the same descriptive content of fat. And, as always, all of these attitudes can be indicated through tone of voice, body language, and the like.[12]

We can characterize other concepts similarly. For example, Blackburn, following R. M. Hare, has drawn attention to the fact that while some people's industry is a good thing, we often bemoan others' industry. Perhaps in the latter case what is being worked towards is disagreeable or, more pertinently, the industry itself is holding the person back. Perhaps a graduate student is working too hard and cannot see the wood for the trees. She needs to relax and lighten up.[13] Blackburn says similar things about tidiness. An insistence that my university office is kept impeccably tidy aids my work, but keeping to this ideal at home can drive my family mad.[14]

The point of such examples should be obvious. Blackburn, Hare, and others are trying to show that familiar everyday thick concepts such as KIND and WICKED work in the same way. We have some descriptive content to which some evaluative element is conjoined. This evaluative element can be signalled through tone of voice and other things. In some cases the evaluative element we might expect is cancelled or reversed, for example when someone speaks sarcastically. In other cases, we might expect an evaluation of some sort, but it is not clear what the 'typical' attitude would be. (And so on.) Furthermore, the history of certain thick concepts might be quite different from that of 'fat↓' and FAT-CON. We no longer have to signal with tone of voice that we approve of just things. Given typical conventions, judging something to be just in a normal speaking voice is enough to imply that we approve of the thing. But this difference, be it genetic or otherwise, should not put us off the main scent. Everyday, familiar thick concepts should be characterized as involving two distinct and separable sorts of element, the descriptive and the evaluative, where the latter is taken to be something thin.

Hence, the conclusion that Blackburn reaches is that there are, strictly, no thick concepts because there is no thick conceptual content. All familiar, everyday thick concepts can be broken into non-thick component elements. It just so happens that these elements are sometimes conjoined together. So we can talk of FAT-PRO as *a* concept, but really it is the concept FAT conjoined with something else. Some theorists will choose to give a noncognitive analysis of that evaluation, as Blackburn and Hare famously choose to. But, as I have mentioned in Chapter One, we could give the

---

[12] Blackburn discusses this point at length in Blackburn (1992).

[13] Blackburn (1992), p. 286 and Hare (1952), p. 121. Blackburn's example of 'industry of which we disapprove' is some people's attitude towards Margaret Thatcher when she was Prime Minister of the UK. Yet that negative attitude might be focused on her aims, indeed this is how Blackburn portrays it, and any disapproval of the industry may well ride on that rather than being directed at the industry itself. This is not quite what Blackburn needs to support his claim about the flexibility of the evaluative element, hence my example of the student in which the industry itself is viewed negatively.

[14] Which it does.

evaluation element a cognitive analysis while still maintaining the separation of the two parts.[15]

This is all very well, yet I want to expose immediately a slide to avoid. Clearly some people disapprove of people who are fat while others revel in largeness. We have a range of terms in this area—some affectionate, some distasteful—from which we may draw concepts: 'fat', 'obese', 'chunky', 'cuddly', 'gross', 'whale'. Some words can be used nonevaluatively, as in medical charts. Some are typically used positively, while others are typically used negatively. ('Obese' is a medical term, but it can be used by people to chastise and bully.) No one should deny this. Nor should we deny that there is a difference between 'chair↑' and 'fat↓': one example taps into familiar concerns and language use, while the other does not. Similarly, we can readily see that INDUSTRY and TIDY *may* work in the way Blackburn suggests. We seem to have some fairly clear descriptive conceptual content in both cases; indeed such contents form familiar stand-alone concepts.[16] But just because a concept such as FAT-CON taps into familiar concerns, we should not therefore conclude straightaway that all familiar thick concepts work in this way. That would be to slide from one sort of example to another while unthinkingly accepting that they have the same structure, when so far we have not really thought hard about the case that interests us. TIDY and INDUSTRY might be different from KIND and CRUEL.

That said, if we dig a little we can see that this model appeals. We have already uncovered some nice aspects of this proposal. We have a determinate descriptive concept that, in principle, is accessible to everyone. We then have evaluations that are attached to it in some fashion. Such evaluations are allowed to alter in direction (positive, negative, perhaps none at all) and strength, depending on the context. This seems to reflect the reality of our use of some thick concepts. Where there is a fixed attitude, perhaps with things that are deemed just, this is either a phenomenon to be merely noted, or something to be explained simply because we humans are built so as to like the (descriptive) features that form the justice of just things. The strength of this proposal is that we have a simple picture which allows for flexibility of evaluative attitude, and this seems a key feature of our thick concepts.

There are other virtues as well, which we will come to. Before I end this section, however, it is worth exposing the ways in which simple separationism might further divide. We have some distinct and separable descriptive and evaluative elements. But these two elements can combine differently. Here are two models.[17] We could *conjoin* the two elements: we say that something is a descriptive way, then attach an attitude. This is what is going on with Blackburn's example of 'fat↓' as so far

---

[15] See again Elstein and Hurka (2009), pp. 516–17.

[16] Again, reflecting on and questioning this will be done in Chapter Six.

[17] The labels are from Allan Gibbard in Gibbard (1992). See also Blackburn (1984), pp. 148–9 for a full discussion of conjunction and (something very much like) licensing. Blackburn suggests the point about indeterminacy in my next paragraph. Gibbard briefly defines a third model, *presuppositional*. I ignore it here for simplicity's sake but it will appear in Chapter Seven.

presented. A different view is where we say that someone is *licensed* (by rules of language, by conventions) to use a thick term, and say that an item is a certain descriptive way, *only if* she attaches a particular evaluation to that descriptive content. Perhaps this is what is going on with JUST, at least as presented so far. By convention, we simply cannot pick out the features of the item in *that* sort of descriptive way and use the concept unless we are prepared to evaluate the group of such features positively.

Simple separationists are not forced to choose between these models as an explanation for all (supposed) thick concepts. They can say that some concepts work one way while others work another. (And they can introduce more models.) Furthermore, simple separationists might say that talk of two models suggests a sharp contrast, but that need not be the case. Actual use of many concepts might be indeterminate between these two models. The extent to which the descriptive part of a concept can be put forward without a particular evaluation or evaluations being present might be something unclear to concept users. Or, it might be clear, but be dependent on context thus leading to different models being appropriate at different times to explain what is happening. Perhaps in many contexts, where the conjunction model applies, people who disagree about someone being fat-con can at least agree that the person is fat and agree precisely on the descriptive nature of the case; they just have different evaluations. Perhaps in some other contexts it is the licensing model that is appropriate.

On that last point, consider this example. Two people—Betty and Frank—are in the audience of a beauty pageant and it is the convention in their community that in such situations disapproval has to follow if one of the contestants is thought to be fat; it is FAT-CON or nothing. So because one of them, Betty, wishes to refrain from disapproving, she takes issue with whether the descriptive content is instantiated or exemplified. She simply refrains from calling a contestant fat because she does not have a negative evaluation. Frank is different. He takes a negative view of the contestant and so the descriptive content is licensed.[18] In this case, of course, words such as 'cuddly' and 'gross' develop. Frank can legitimately say of a contestant that he is gross, while Betty can legitimately say that he is not gross 'but cuddly instead'. (Realistically, Betty may not be able to deny the relative largeness of the contestant, but she does not conceptualize him straightforwardly as fat.) Frank and Betty differ not just in attitude but in the descriptive content of the concept they employ. The descriptive content of gross is licensed only if users disapprove of things seen to embody it; if they approve of them, they are not allowed to employ that particular descriptive content.[19] Perhaps in other communities and different

[18] In reality, things might be complex in both cases. I say 'negative view', but Frank might be laughing helplessly at the large contestant and enjoying the experience. But here his positive view is a function of the presence of a fat person in a beauty contest; he thinks the fatness itself is definitely not to be admired.
[19] It is harder to develop examples with 'fat' where the licensing model is appropriate. If you find yourself thinking that this example is too far-fetched, then that is no opposition to the validity of the licensing model. It might indicate that this model fits concepts such as KIND better.

contexts the conjunction model is better. Perhaps Terry and June are straightforwardly arguing about some contestant, and agree wholly in the descriptive content.
The difference between them is one of difference in attitude alone. Or, in other
words, Terry's use of 'cuddly' and June's use of 'gross' are used as synonyms for
'fat-pro' and 'fat-con', where the 'fat' part is exactly the same. This is not the case
with Betty and Frank.

These end comments set up a few things for later. Before we contrast all of this
with complex separationism, I should repeat that we have so far not seen any change
in Blackburn's thinking, although we will do later. For now we can add, after the
discussion thus far, that Blackburn thinks of standard thick concepts as typically
better explained by using the licensing model, rather than thinking that both models
are probably equally applicable.

It is now time to consider two rival views.

2.4 Two Kinds of Complex Separationism

There are a number of ways in which we could oppose simple separationism. As a
way of running certain thoughts I am going to use a discussion by Daniel Elstein
and Thomas Hurka as representative. Recall that simple separationism holds that
the best way of characterizing all thick concepts with which we are familiar is to
assume that we have a fully determinate descriptive concept that in some way is
connected to an evaluation. Elstein and Hurka outline two separationist accounts
that are alternatives to this. I refer to Elstein and Hurka's position overall as
'complex separationism'.

(a) Their first account can be introduced in their own words.

We have discussed two types of concept: at one extreme is a thin concept like 'good', which
says nothing about the good-making properties of items falling under it, at the other extreme is
a descriptively determinate concept like 'Kraut', which specifies those properties completely,
and therefore fully determines the concept's extension. Surely there is room between these
extremes for a category of thick (or 'thick-ish') concepts whose descriptive component specifies
good- or right-making properties to some degree but not completely, saying only that they
must be of some specified general type but not selecting specific properties within that type—
that is left to evaluation. Or, to put the point slightly differently, there can be concepts whose
descriptive component defines an area in conceptual space within which admissible good- or
right-making properties must be found, so any use of the concept associating it with
properties outside that area is a misuse, but does not identify any specific point within the
area as uniquely correct, as a concept like 'Kraut' does. The concept therefore has descriptive
content, but this content is not completely determinate. The pattern of this analysis is
something like 'x is good, and there are properties X, Y, and Z (not specified) of general
type A (specified), such that x has X, Y, and Z make anything that has them good'. This
pattern is reductive, because it uses only the thin concept 'good' and the descriptive concept
'A'. But it accommodates the key disentangling argument, because determining *which*

properties of type A are the good-making ones, which we must do to determine the concept's extension, is a matter for evaluative judgement.[20]

Elstein and Hurka view simple separationism as treating all thick concepts as akin to KRAUT. We have some descriptively determinate concept, in this case 'is a German', which is allied to some negative attitude.[21] But why think that all thick concepts should be analysed in this way? Among many examples, Elstein and Hurka consider JUST or, more specifically, DISTRIBUTIVE JUSTICE. Should we characterize this concept as having a clearly and fully determinate descriptive content to which some (typically positive) evaluation is then added? Or, alternatively, should it be characterized as being a positive evaluation which licenses a certain fully determinate descriptive content? We could choose either. But if we did we would not be able to analyse disagreements between different theorists of distributive justice in the correct way, something that is clearly desirable.

Why not? Some people think that just distributions are those that are equal distributions in some sense of the term 'equal', and good for being so, while some others think that just distributions are those that are proportionally distributed according to merit, and good for being so. If we characterized these two conceptions as being two distinct descriptive contents, to which positive evaluations were applied, we would not be able to say that an egalitarian and a desert theorist could meaningfully argue with each other about whether a proposed distribution was just. On this analysis JUST or DISTRIBUTIVE justice would mean different things to different theorists and they would be talking past each other, as the philosophical cliché has it. Although political theorists differ, there is some locus of agreement about what counts as a just distribution, and this should be captured by our philosophical characterization. So even if their conceptions of DISTRIBUTIVE JUSTICE differ, political theorists agree about what the general concept is concerned with.[22]

---

[20] Elstein and Hurka (2009), p. 521. Elstein and Hurka's starting motivation is to show that separationism can accommodate the disentangling argument. They worry that simple separationism cannot, and this is a flaw both in terms of strategy, since it is the main argument against separationism, and a flaw generally, since they think that there is something correct that lies behind the argument. I believe that they do not fully understand the argument and that their position is also vulnerable to it, as I show in Chapter Five. I also believe that what they think of as being the argument can be accommodated to some extent by simple separationism, as I show later in this chapter.
[21] KRAUT is discussed in Blackburn (1984), pp. 148–51, although the context is slightly different. For what it is worth, I dislike Elstein and Hurka's bracketed suggestion in the quotation that what they might be developing is a characterization of 'thick-ish' concepts that lie in the middle, as if KRAUT were 'fully thick'. As far as I am concerned, even if the descriptive aspect or part of a thick concept is less specific than related concepts, I still take it to be 'fully' thick, since this is just a matter of there being some sort of union of descriptive content and evaluation. For example, COMPASSIONATE is more specific than KIND, yet both are standardly assumed to be fully fledged thick concepts, as are the concepts characterized by Elstein and Hurka that have less than completely specified descriptive content. I return to this point in Chapter Four.
[22] Both the example and the distinction between concepts and conceptions calls to mind John Rawls' discussion in Rawls (1971), p. 5.

Elstein and Hurka suggest the following as a first stab: 'x is distributively just' will mean something such as 'x is good, and there are properties X, Y, Z (not specified) that distributions have as distributions, or in virtue of their distributive shape, such that x has X, Y, and Z, and X, Y, and Z make any distribution that has them good'.[23] There are some restrictions on our concept: it cannot be used of generous actions, say, or at least it cannot be used of them in so far as they are generous. But such restrictions do not completely determine the extension of the concept. The descriptive part of the concept only partly determines the extension of the concept since we have to plug descriptive ideas into the X, Y, and Z. We get those once we approve of certain elements being part of our concept and exclude others. Importantly, our approval is not just an approval of an element being part of a concept that allows us to fine-tune it. In approving of a feature we are saying that any distribution that has this sort of feature will be a distribution that is good, and be so for that reason.

This final point sets this separationist position apart from simple separationism. We might have to think hard about where the boundary lies between the fat and the thin. This is not just a matter of thinking about one thing: we might have to think about the balance between (obvious) bodily shape, and something more scientific, such as height–weight ratios. However, when we make such decisions—decisions about what is to be included in the descriptive content of the concept—according to simple separationism the evaluation is separate. This is obviously so according to the conjunction model. We have some fully determinate descriptive content to which an evaluation is added. Even in the licensing model, what is licensed by a certain sort of evaluation is a fully formed determinate descriptive content. In contrast, complex separationism says that many thick concepts should be characterized such that when we pick out certain descriptive features as being part of the concept, this picking out is an evaluation. Why? Such features directly feed into explaining why the item that falls under the concept is seen as good or bad (or, more minimally, pro or con). In the case of DISTRIBUTIVE JUSTICE, it is not only that the egalitarian picks out a feature—equal treatment in respect of X—which helps to locate the purely descriptive contours of the concept and *then further* says that an item that falls under this concept is just, as if she could choose to withhold such an assessment. The distribution is seen as just, and hence good, precisely because it has the feature picked out, and the picking out of this feature is a matter of approving of it in the first place.

In all of this we supposedly still have a separationist account, as Elstein and Hurka state. At every stage, and across the whole concept, we are dealing with (supposed) descriptive content—equal treatment, things given according to merit, distributions— and concepts such as GOODNESS (or, I think better, PRO) are applied to and mixed with such descriptive ideas.[24]

---

[23] Elstein and Hurka (2009), p. 522.

[24] Elstein and Hurka's first account is also found in Gibbard (1992). His account incorporates an element concerned with whether a reaction—typically a more specific reaction than pro or con—is

(b) Elstein and Hurka's second account is more complicated than the first. They are unsure whether their first account fits thick virtue concepts adequately, and they see a further account as necessary. As they say:

This second pattern involves a three-part analysis, because it supplements the global thin evaluation that governs the whole concept (the 'x is good...' or 'x is right...' of the first pattern) with a further thin evaluation that is embedded within the descriptive content. Its presence means we cannot determine the extension of the thick concept without determining the extensions of the embedded thin one, that is, without making evaluations.[25]

They illustrate this using a number of concepts. Here I pick their example of INTEGRITY. Integrity involves sticking to one's goals, but not just any goals count, at least on certain conceptions of integrity. These goals themselves have to be seen as important ones, first of all. Elstein and Hurka's example of a non-starter is someone who persistently adds to her beer-mat collection which draws her energies away from preventing the rise of Nazism. Furthermore, even among the significant goals we then have to consider which ones are good, and this will generate many disputes. Think of people who stand up for what they believe is morally right, even in the face of strong disagreement or danger. People will disagree about whether, for example, it is worth sticking up for the rights of abortion doctors to live peaceful lives, or whether certain words and images should be banned from television. On this particular characterization of integrity, then, we have to make an evaluation about which goals are the good ones.

Elstein and Hurka's stab at INTEGRITY is: 'x is an act of integrity' means that 'x is good, and x involves sticking to a significantly good goal despite distractions and temptations, where this property makes any act that has it good'.[26] So anything that falls under the description is seen as good, but within the description we have made another evaluation, an evaluation of the goal. This clearly sets it apart from simple separationism, since with that account there is no mention of an embedded evaluation within the description that needs to be satisfied and which can be a point of dispute. It is also different from Elstein and Hurka's first account since in that account, like that of simple separationism, there is only one evaluation that governs the whole concept. Or, to put it another way, it is true that according to their first account, Elstein and Hurka think that we evaluate when we are picking out certain descriptive features to be part of the content. However, there is still only one, clear, explicit evaluation that governs the concept. In this second account we allow for another evaluation that explicitly checks or moulds the concept's boundary. In the case of INTEGRITY the suggestion is that the goal aimed at has to be good.

---

warranted. (Gibbard's main example is LEWD, and the relevant feeling is labelled L-censoriousness.) But it is essentially the same account.

[25] Elstein and Hurka (2009), p. 526.   [26] Elstein and Hurka (2009), p. 526.

However, Elstein and Hurka note that we could combine the first and second accounts. The key point about their first account is that the descriptive is not fully determinate, whereas the second embeds an evaluation that does not govern the whole concept. It seems obvious that some thick concepts might require a characterization that embodies *both* ideas. As Elstein and Hurka suggest, perhaps there is a dispute about exactly what integrity involves: is it based on the goal of being good, or is it based on a person's belief that the goal is good (assuming the belief to be non-culpable), or both? We might require a conception of INTEGRITY that has a descriptive element that leaves this open, not least because different contexts might require us to prioritize different specific ideas. Similarly, we might say for some conceptions of DISTRIBUTIVE justice that not every distribution in which things are equalized is a just distribution, for we might need to approve those things as being appropriate for such a characterization. It might—*might*—be seen as just to equalize the number of hairs on people's forearms, but most people would not consider such an equal distribution just, since JUST should be reserved for more important things.[27]

Elstein and Hurka's two accounts, and their combination, show that thick concepts might need more nuanced treatment than simple separationism provides: a separationist treatment might need to do more than wholly divide the descriptive from the evaluative, even if one thinks of the two sorts of content as distinct and separable. The way in which we mix those elements is very important. This takes us to a critical comparison of the accounts.

2.5 A Grey Area

I have mentioned that assuming that we have two clear and distinct sorts of separationism is a fiction. There is some grey area. Why would one think this? After all, it seems as if we have a clear dividing line: one sort of separationism assumes some descriptive content that is fully determined aside from any evaluations, while another allows evaluations to help mould the (still separable) descriptive content.

Consider the following from Blackburn, published recently, where he distinguishes a strong and a weak sense of the disentanglement of thick terms into an evaluative element and some descriptive conceptual content.

One sense would require that the extension of the term is one thing, given by a purely descriptive concept, while the other dimension (usually an evaluative one) simply attaches to what is thereby described. This is roughly the case with, for instance, terms of racial or national abuse: the members of the race or nation are identifiable in empirical terms, and the abuse added. The extension can be identified independently of the 'evaluation' (or abuse). As far as I am aware, nobody now thinks that this model applies to interesting candidates for thickness, such as 'cruel' or 'courageous'.

---

[27] Elstein and Hurka (2009), p. 531.

However there is a much more interesting, but weaker sense of disentangling, in which it is still an open question whether such terms can be disentangled. In this sense, the claim is that there are two vectors or dimensions in question, but that they interact. Most obviously, the evaluative element can help to determine what is put into the extension. So, for instance, you do not call someone 'pig-headed' unless you wish to imply a criticism of them, and this fact goes some way into determining who is so-called. The descriptive dimension is that of being resolute or firm, disinclined to change your mind under discursive pressure from others; the other dimension is that of being so *unduly* or inappropriately. The term signals both things, but there is no identifying its extension without employing the evaluative side. There is still disentangling, since there are so clearly two different vectors, and there is predictably going to be disagreement over when 'unduly' kicks in. One man's admirable resolution is another man's pig-headedness. So the descriptions and the valuations interact, and only when they harmonise, in one mind or another, will the term get used. Clearly the common argument that there is no determining the extension of any particular term without deploying an evaluation (or piggy-backing on an evaluation that one does not share) is of no force whatsoever against this view, since it simply seizes on exactly what the view describes.[28]

This is a version of the licensing model. A certain attitude helps to determine the descriptive content of the concept one is using. The difference between what Blackburn says here and what we imagined happening before is that in this passage he now notes that there may be some general description that fits the specific descriptive contents that are licensed by the various attitudes and which together form the various concepts in play. In the case of the beauty contest, perhaps that general description is BIG or BIG FOR A PERSON. Betty's positive view means that she is licensed to fill in the descriptive content by picking out certain things and ignoring others, perhaps, and uses words such as 'cuddly'. Frank's negative view licenses him in assuming different specific descriptive content, and this results in him using derogatory words.

This comes close to saying what Elstein and Hurka say in their first model. We have some evaluative attitude which does not just license a description, but influences what that precise descriptive content is. However, there is a difference. Elstein and Hurka explicitly assume that we have some general description that can be held by all disputants, and then the differences between them are a function of clearly isolatable and different Xs, Ys, and Zs. Blackburn does not go down this route. Instead, we have a general description: in the case imagined 'being resolute or firm'. Once that is in place we have people being placed on some descriptive dimension according to their attitudes towards any candidate example, and the strength of such attitudes.

This difference may just be a matter of presentation.[29] But given some of their examples, such as DISTRIBUTIVE JUSTICE, it is clear that Elstein and Hurka think their

[28] Blackburn (2013), p. 122.

[29] Indeed, in personal communication Blackburn said that he quite liked Elstein and Hurka's first proposal, although he also said that he did not want to backtrack on what he said in Blackburn (1984). I hope that my discussion pitches his view neatly between these two thoughts.

analysis as presented is needed. Even if we have a general description common to all disputants, that does not mean we have a single dimension or scale along which such disputants then plant themselves. The content of the specific descriptions that are covered by the general description may be quite different, even radically so, and this may be best captured by talking of quite different Xs, Ys, and Zs, isolatable in this analysis because they are so different.[30] In contrast, even though Blackburn is indicating some general content, which then gets specified differently because of the evaluation, it seems fair to describe him as thinking that this general content is determinate, and that the evaluation just helps to locate what sort of exact content one gets. Or, in other words, one can specify the descriptive content of a concept, and this itself will give a good indication of the descriptive content of the concept even if that content needs to be specified. The general description given in Elstein and Hurka's first model needs some specific ideas to move us beyond any general ballpark idea: a general ballpark descriptive content on its own is not enough to fill out the concept. This is enough to justify initial discussion of two broad models, and to retain our idea of two models when looking at the details of various theories.[31]

---

[30] The different specifics of the rival theories of Rawls and Nozick come readily to mind again here. One could not capture the differences between Rawls and Nozick in disputing whether something was just or unjust by thinking in terms of a single and general descriptive dimension along which Rawls and Nozick planted themselves because of their attitudes towards certain instances.

[31] If more justification is needed, consider this. At no point in his writings does Blackburn *clearly* state something along the lines of Elstein and Hurka's first form of complex separationism. We might imagine that 'fat↓' gives him ample opportunity to do so. Perhaps some think of FAT as having something to do with bodily shape, while others prefer to prioritize clear medical measures. Or just with regards to the former, some might think that someone qualifies as fat if his stomach is large and bulging, while others look in addition to the thickness of the limbs and the neck. These differences, particularly the first, would require different dimensions, I think.

At one point in Blackburn (1992) he compares his account with Gibbard's. (In note 24 I mentioned that Gibbard's account can be seen as a version of the first sort of complex separationism.) It seems as if he will come close to agreeing with Gibbard, but in doing so only confirms their differences. He says, "So far, it might seem that examples of description+tone must be distinct from those of 'gopa' and 'lewd' [Gibbard's main examples] in that the descriptive side is fixed, and the sneer or other tone optional.... But that is not quite right. For we can easily imagine just the same kinds of dispute over terms of description+tone. Amanda and Beryl may have been card-carrying fattists until Amanda met Clive. 'Clive is so fat↓' challenges Beryl. 'No, not fat↓—stocky, well-built' dreams Amanda. The dispute need not be one about vagueness, as we can see if we play it through with Pavarotti instead of Clive. Pavarotti is unquestionably fat, but many fattists would recoil from calling him fat↓.... 'fat↓' shares with other derog. terms the property that where you do not want to express or endorse the attitude, you will refuse application of the term" (p. 290). Or, in other words, Blackburn's explanation of the dispute between Amanda and Clive relies on the licensing model. Amanda will not call Clive 'fat↓', simply because she does not have the negative attitude towards him that licenses the associated descriptive content. By implication, Blackburn thinks that this, or the conjunction model, or some combination, can explain all such disagreements.

As well as the quotation in the main text, see also Blackburn (1998), p. 103. Here Blackburn comes close to advocating the first model of complex separationism, but again, when thinking about the general description of something being lewd, he claims that the evaluative and descriptive elements can be "moulded in different ways", claiming, I think, that we have two sorts of range here that collide and which result in different but related concepts being applied by different people.

However, two points are pertinent here. First, I leave it open as to whether (if one is a separationist) just one of these models should be thought to fit all concepts or, as I suspect, some models are better suited to some concepts and some contexts, and other models are better suited to others. After all, it is this reasoning which leads Elstein and Hurka to develop two models, and as Blackburn says, in some contexts use might be indeterminate between the conjunction and licensing models.

Second, although it is still helpful to think in terms of there being two models, it is pretty obvious now that there is some grey area. How the evaluation is used to pick out the descriptive content is a complicated issue, and it may not produce stark contrasts. Similarly, how the specific descriptive content is to be analysed may not be something that can be packaged as isolatable Xs and Ys, and it may be unclear what the descriptive scale is like along which judges find themselves. What is meant by 'general' here and what is meant by 'specific' is unclear. All of this suggests untidy mess rather than clear-cut difference. We should be alive to the fact that the two sorts of separationism introduced may be closer than may appear at first, both to outsiders and even separationists themselves.

So we have some mess. However, we can think about the criticisms separationists give of each other, at least to indicate an interesting trade-off that has implications for the whole terrain and debate about thick concepts.

2.6 Some Critical Points

I pursue two points of critical comparison: Elstein and Hurka's first account is designed to explain disagreements, while simple separationism allows for flexibility of evaluative attitude. After this I introduce a worry with separationism more generally, to sow some seeds of doubt. I end by listing reasons why one might wish to be a separationist.

(a) I first consider how simple separationism fares against Elstein and Hurka's idea that disagreements cannot be analysed properly.

Note immediately the difference between the conjunction and licensing models. The licensing model has it that by convention some evaluation has to be in place *before* a descriptive content is licensed. We imagined both models applying to people's disagreements concerning fat people. In the licensing scenario we noted that because an evaluation has to be in place for a certain descriptive content to be licensed, then this model applies only if we were happy to say that the two concepts employed—CUDDLY and GROSS—also had slightly different descriptive content. If not, the conjunction model would capture things better. So on the licensing model, we can still talk of there being flexibility of attitude, but only if we also admit that the specific descriptive content is flexible.

This means, further, that on this characterization we have to be careful when speaking of there being disagreement. When Frank says that a beauty contestant is gross, while Betty says that he is cuddly, and where both concepts are interpreted as 'licensed' concepts, then we can say that the concepts are opposed in a sense. But it is not as if Frank and Betty agree that the person is fat yet differ only in attitude. (That was why I introduced Terry and June.) Rather, Frank and Betty are partly disagreeing about what exactly it is to be fat and what the term 'fat' means in the first place, and that will probably be influenced by what sort of attitude they take towards fat people in certain contexts. Frank is conceptualizing, encoding, and communicating specific descriptive content different from the content Betty is working with. If we are unhappy with this characterization of any particular debate and use of a concept (or concepts)—if we want to say that there is complete agreement in descriptive content—we need to choose the conjunction model to provide explanation.

With that said, let us see how each model fares when compared with Elstein and Hurka's worry. (Note that Elstein and Hurka do not explicitly consider each model in turn.) First, consider the conjunction model with its assumed sameness of specific descriptive content in disputes. That model is all very well in explaining disagreements where the disputants agree (exactly) about descriptive content but disagree in attitude. Yet, there are other sorts of disagreement—surely a large number—where the two disputants agree in attitude about the general concept that they wish to employ *and* agree with the general contours of the concept, but still disagree about whether the concept applies in a particular case. That is the point lying behind Elstein and Hurka's first account and examples such as DISTRIBUTIVE JUSTICE. It seems obvious that the conjunction model fails to capture many disagreements for many uses of concepts.

What of the licensing model, as understood by Blackburn in the more recent piece I quoted? Its prospects are a lot better. When Betty and Frank are exchanging terms and concepts when they are at the beauty pageant (and where we interpret their use of CUDDLY and GROSS along the lines of the licensing model), there is some general dimension which they have in common that influences their terms, and this seems enough to ward off the challenge. Elstein and Hurka analyse what happens as there being a general and common descriptive element that is made more specific with the introduction of isolatable elements, indicated by X, Y, and Z. The fact that Blackburn chooses to have some general descriptive dimension and eschews talk of further isolatable elements in his analysis does not mean at all that he cannot meet their challenge about disagreements.

A further worry may crop up, which should be raised if only to be dealt with. Elstein and Hurka's analysis gives equal weight and importance to the descriptive and evaluative elements, or at least the overall pattern of analysis is flexible enough to allow different weightings for different concepts in different contexts. It seems right that there be this flexibility and likely equal weighting. A theorist thinks of *this* distribution as just because of how she sees it descriptively and her overall positive impression. But, in contrast, the licensing model seems to see the evaluation as prime, at least symbolically. This is suggested by the label: the evaluation licenses—allows, admits of, gives access to—the descriptive content. The evaluation is in place and this licenses the description. It can certainly seem that things are this way when compared to the conjunction model. However, again I think we have a worry that can be cleared up. After all, it is not as if Frank and Betty have some evaluation and then fill in the descriptive details when they are arguing. (Well, phenomenologically speaking this might happen, but this seems wrong as a theoretical characterization of their concept use.) Sure, they adopt a certain descriptive content only because they have a certain evaluation. But one reason that they adopt the evaluation is because they are inclined to pick out and conceptualize the descriptive features of a contestant in a certain way. To my mind, the licensing model can admit that the descriptive part of the concept, and any particular conception of it, is as important as the evaluation that licenses it.

So I am not so sure that simple separationism for those cases where the licensing model applies fully (or somewhat) lacks the resources to be adapted to answer Elstein and Hurka's worry. Of course, the extent to which the licensing model is applicable to our concepts, even if separationism is correct overall, is moot.

(b) How do Elstein and Hurka fare against the strength already mentioned of simple separationism, namely the flexibility of attitude?[32]

Let us begin with their first analysis. In the definitions cited from them we had only one thin concept mentioned, namely GOOD, and this is the case with other analyses. Is it possible for them to develop analyses of concepts where the flexibility of attitude is explicitly encoded? For a start, one might challenge whether we should be interested in the flexibility of attitude. A familiar general position in ethics has it that our everyday virtue (and vice) concepts have only one attitude attached: it is conceptually impossible for something to be just and bad for that reason. But this is a controversial position for such concepts, and there seem plenty of thick concepts that are not virtue or vice concepts, so I think the challenge to Elstein and Hurka needs to be followed.

So how might their analysis, suitably developed, work for a concept such as ELEGANT?[33] We might say that 'x is elegant' means something such as 'x is either good or bad or neutral, and there are properties X, Y, Z (not specified) that things (in a wide sense) have in virtue of appearing to the eye as refined and efficient, such that x has X, Y, and Z, and X, Y, and Z make any object that has them good or bad or neutral'. (The 'appearing to the eye as refined and efficient' part is obviously my initial stab at getting us into the right ballpark. It is imperfect, but our focus should rest on other matters.) In some respect this analysis is not itself bad. We just have some additional stuff—more evaluations and how they link to the Xs and Ys—to take

---

[32] As with the conjunction and licensing models, Elstein and Hurka do not consider this issue explicitly. Note that they are neutral between cognitivist- and noncognitivist-separationist analyses, but I retain 'attitude' here for continuity with Blackburn's criticism.
[33] I am taking this as a *prima facie* good example of a concept where we want to have flexibility of attitude.

into account when trying to analyse a concept. And it might be something that, before we consider nonseparationism, seems to capture the phenomena perfectly well. But, despite this, there is a general worry, which is only a hunch for now. With this analysis there is now more stuff to account for and fill in or, in other words, we have far less anchoring and far more flexibility then we had previously. There may be no way in advance of predicting how the different evaluations and different Xs, Ys, and Zs interact. It is certainly going to be more complex then was envisaged previously. How can we be confident that we understand the concept and its application without understanding how the descriptive and the evaluative can connect in the first place, particularly when the contours of the concept as given are so loose? As we will see, this inchoate suspicion will develop into the disentangling argument.

At this stage we can raise a similar worry for Blackburn. He has fine-tuned his licensing model to include a general descriptive dimension linking two related concepts and their uses. This hides a problem and is in tune with that just raised against Elstein and Hurka. How can we be certain that Betty and Frank are using concepts that are related such that when Betty says that someone is cuddly and Frank says he is gross we can say that they are in a real dispute? What is this descriptive dimension along which they both lie? It seems as if the interplay between the (separable) evaluations and this general but common descriptive content may be complex. Again, I will make good on this inchoate worry later in the book.

Does this worry about evaluative flexibility apply to Elstein and Hurka's second analysis? Probably not, since they introduce it explicitly for cases where there is a thin concept embedded in the descriptive part that, roughly speaking, helps us to make sense of it. Think of the account of INTEGRITY: an action is one of integrity only if we approve of it. It would be odd, following Elstein and Hurka, to have something such as 'x is an act of integrity' meaning 'x is good or bad and x involves sticking to a significantly good or bad goal despite distractions and temptations, where this property makes any act that has it good or bad or neutral'. This does not fit what they are trying to do with integrity (and similar concepts), because including two 'bad's would make an action one of foolhardiness, or zealotry, or something worse. This changes the concept being analysed, rather than accounting for one concept accommodating the flexibility of attitude or evaluation.

Of course, a defence of Elstein and Hurka on this score works only in so far as there are concepts that we think need to be analysed in the way they do with their second account. We could imagine someone saying that integrity and other concepts should be analysed differently, perhaps in terms of the licensing model. But, as a neutral between these two sorts of separationism, I have to say I side with Elstein and Hurka here, at least given how people use a concept such as INTEGRITY. If I were given to separationist analyses, I would concur that the descriptive content has to embed an evaluation: people do not have in mind just any goal when thinking about integrity.

So, thus far, a score draw: Elstein and Hurka's best point works very well against one model that can be favoured by simple separationists, but not at all well against another. Similarly, only one of their two analyses fails when it comes to the point about flexibility of attitude. We can see this as indicative of a trade-off when it comes to separationism: the more we play up the idea that some separable evaluation can be flexible, the harder it is to develop an understanding of how disputes work, while the more we try to harness and nail elements in our characterization of concepts, the harder it is to accommodate the supposed phenomenon of evaluative flexibility.

The main point here—and the main point to emerge from this whole chapter as we move from looking at the details of the position to look at its overall nature and point—is to realize that ideally an account of thick concepts would aim to satisfy both demands: we want an account that allows us to talk meaningfully about disagreement and also one that accommodates evaluative flexibility (if one indeed thinks it is a desideratum). These twin demands will come back later in the book.

(c) Here is one further point. I discuss it briefly so as to set up a worry that links to my discussion of shapelessness in Chapter Five.

In note 20 I mentioned that Elstein and Hurka believe that their separationist analysis can accommodate the best point ranged against simple separationist accounts from nonseparationists. This connects with the aforementioned point about disentangling and shapelessness. We will concentrate on this later in Chapter Five. For now, we need merely discuss that Elstein and Hurka believe the key part of the nonseparationist challenge is that separationism cannot accommodate the idea that evaluative content determines concepts' extensions.[34] (It is obvious that both of their analyses do take this into account.) Now, I do not believe this idea, as stated this simply, is the main nonseparationist point. We can see quite easily that in some sense even simple separationists can accommodate this idea of extension, and so Elstein and Hurka's criticism of their rivals fails.

Simple separationists think quite plainly that we will have to have knowledge of the evaluative point or points of a concept in order to predict its extension. After all, it is very likely, even determined, that CHAIR-PRO and FAT-CON have more limited extension than CHAIR and FAT. Knowledge of the evaluative content in our first pair of concepts is *crucial* to knowing the boundaries of the whole concept since it provides limits. Only a certain number of chairs will have CHAIR-PRO applied to them, and which ones are so categorized will be determined by the evaluation. So, strictly, what Elstein and Hurka say is false.

That said, they are attempting to cope with the *spirit* of the nonseparationist charge much more. The spirit of the charge, in their eyes, is that evaluative content is more involved than a simple conjunction or licensing account will allow. This is particularly apparent in their second model, where some evaluative element is

---

[34] Elstein and Hurka (2009), pp. 519–20.

embedded in the descriptive content. But this leads to another worry. If Elstein and Hurka think that nonseparationists will be dissatisfied with the response by simple separationists—because what they are requesting is some acknowledgement that concept users have to appreciate the evaluative point of the concept as a whole— then nonseparationists will also be left dissatisfied with what Elstein and Hurka say. This is because, in brief, one cannot really understand what descriptions are relevant to the concept as a whole unless one 'imbues' the whole of the concept with evaluation; inserting a separable pro or con evaluation to govern some of the separable description does not cut it. This is a more refined echo of the 'inchoate suspicion' raised in the middle of (b). I elaborate on and deepen this idea in Chapter Five.

(d) Why should we adopt separationism in the first place? As mentioned in Chapter One, the general adoption of the fact–value distinction has much to do with it. This leads to four points. First, adoption of the fact–value distinction is seen by some as uncontroversial since it seems to encapsulate much of modern thinking, especially that encapsulated by the rise of modern science. Any philosophical analysis worth its salt cannot afford to ignore the demands and intellectual currents of modern science. If we agree that the evaluative and the descriptive should be held apart, then it seems that any analysis of evaluative concepts—especially thick ones— has to place this idea at the very centre. The second point in favour of separationism links nicely to the first: not only is the separation of evaluation and description supposedly reflected in much of modern thinking, it is simple and clear. *These* things are values, *those* things are (nonevaluative) facts, and never the twain shall meet.

The third point in favour of separationism is easiest to understand when focused on simple separationism. Making the descriptive part fully determinate allows for a relative ease of understanding on the part of people only slightly familiar or very unfamiliar with the concept. Let me explain. Sometimes it is easy to understand what a concept is and how it is applied by others. But sometimes it can be very hard and can take much time and energy. For example, an anthropologist might take months or years when investigating some alien tribe and how they conceive of the world. The concepts that the members of the tribe employ might be quite different from the anthropologist's; they might not simply apply TABOO to different things, but they might have a new and strange concept, such as SCHMABOO, the contours of which may be difficult to discern. We typically think that understanding is possible, even in hard cases. Simple separationism supposedly gives a nice account of how such under- standing is possible. There are two things we need to do. First, we have only to work out what the descriptive content of the concept is, perhaps by considering a number of cases and having some dialogue with a user, in order to understand the whole concept. Second, we have to work out, or simply be given the knowledge of, which evaluation accompanies the descriptive content or, more complicatedly, which evaluations are appropriate in which context. If we parcel things up in this way, it seems that understanding others' concepts will be a fairly easy matter. The part of the concept that is nonevaluative seems to be the driving force and senior partner in many cases; just think back to our CHAIR and FAT examples where some thin evaluation is simply tacked on.[35] By definition, apparently, nonevaluative, descriptive content is something that is accessible and understandable to everyone. We can have any value system we like and still be able to understand which thing is a chair and which thing is a table. So although some work will have to be done, and some anthropologists may have to find some friendly insiders to help them navigate their way through which thin evaluations are given at which times, understanding others is, in principle, no great mystery.

In contrast, if nonseparationists really think that the evaluative is intertwined in some nonseparable fashion with the descriptive and, hence, further, that we need to appreciate and even share the evaluation of those that sincerely employ the value concepts we are trying to understand, then the seemingly routine task of understanding others does become a great mystery. Do anthropologists really have to share and sincerely apply SCHMABOO in order to understand this concept? Surely not. So why not assume that the key part of the concept is something accessible and understandable to all?

Although I have run this third point in terms of simple separationism, the moral holds for complex versions. Complexity is introduced because we have to have more knowledge of which nonevaluative elements are being seen in a positive or negative light. But those evaluations are still thin and the building blocks are still simple, as in the first version of separationism. The concepts we investigate as 'outsiders' should still be fairly easy to grasp, especially if we have an insider friend to help guide us through the concepts.

This links to a fourth reason in favour of separationism. Blackburn argues that a point in favour of his account—which applies to all separationist accounts—is that it allows for normative criticism.[36] We can all agree that this descriptive element is 'the' or 'a' part of a concept or, alternatively, that some nonevaluative stuff can be grouped in a certain way using a concept. And then, as a separate process, some people will wish to approve of the part included in the concept or approve of the stuff that is being categorized. Some will disapprove of it. According to Blackburn this is the basis for normative criticism. Here is what he says about CUTE as applied to women:

Now it is *morally* vital that we proceed by splitting the input from the output in [the case of CUTE]. By refusing to split we fail to open an essentially specifically *normative* dimension of criticism. If the last word is that these people perceive cuteness and react to it with the appropriate cuteness reaction, whereas other people do not, we have lost the analytic tools with which to recognize what is wrong with them. What is wrong with them is along these lines: they react to an infantile, unthreatening appearance or self-presentation in women, or

---

[35] Hare in Hare (1952), pp. 121ff thinks that the descriptive meaning of TIDY and INDUSTRIOUS, for example, as being more important than the evaluative meaning.

[36] Blackburn (1998), pp. 101–5. He repeats this idea early on in Blackburn (2013).

overt indications of willingness to be subservient to men, with admiration or desire (the men) or envy and emulation (the women). Cute things are those to which we can show affection without threat, or patronizingly, or even with contempt. Children and pets are quintessentially cute. Applied to women, I say, this is a bad thing. Once we can separate input from output enough to see that this is what is going on, the talk of whirls of organism, or single 'thick' rules, or a special perception available only to those who have been acculturated, simply sounds hollow: disguises for a conservative and ultimately self-serving complacency.[37]

His worry is that nonseparationist accounts of the thick just accept concepts and their applications as they are. But that cannot be the end of the matter, for some concepts are bad and are applied in a bad way. It is important that we are able to note what the concept is about, and this appreciation be available to people outside of those that use the concept in a certain social milieu. (Think back to the third point.) From that we can then see whether a certain sort of categorization applied with approval to a certain sort of thing is itself good or bad. This is all supposedly made a lot easier if we can separate evaluation from descriptive content.

The introduction of complex separationism—and Blackburn's recent points about simple separationism—may seem to muddy the waters, things are in fact still clear. To repeat a word introduced by Blackburn earlier, we have two separate vectors. And it is perfectly to the point regarding normative criticism to think whether the attachment of *that* evaluation to *that* specific sort of description (along *that* general descriptive vector) when applied to *that* person or thing or action is itself good.

I think all four of these challenges can be met. The first challenge is the largest and broadest. It will be addressed in Chapter Six, as will the second. In response to both points, I can say now that I do not think the reality of our use of concepts is as simple and clear as separationists think. The third and fourth points are discussed in Chapter Eight.

2.7 Conclusion

In this chapter we have begun to understand how one might capture thick concepts. We now have some handle on separationism. We can see how it might splinter into different views and we can appreciate that there is some grey area between those views. I have also introduced some advantages of the overall position. Lastly, we are getting a sense of the terrain and at the end of §2.6(b) I introduced a trade-off which itself introduces two desiderata: we may wish to accommodate evaluative flexibility, and we need also to ensure that we can account for how disputes work. Those two desiderata will return: the first in Chapter Three and the second in Chapter Eight.

I now turn my attention to what unites separationists in Chapter Three, in order to prepare the ground for how one can argue against their position. How exactly do they understand and model the relationship between thin and thick concepts?

---

[37] Blackburn (1998), pp. 101–2.

3
Conceptual Relations

3.1 Introduction

We now have an idea of what separationism amounts to, the form of some of its varieties, and its appeal. The aim of this chapter is to dig deeper and put us in a position—in Chapters Four and Five—to introduce and understand arguments that have been raised against it.

In this chapter I introduce two models of conceptual relations: '*genus–species*' and '*determinable–determinate*'. Both models tell us how exactly the relations are to be conceived between families of general and specific concepts. Given that thin concepts are thought to be general concepts and thick concepts are thought to be specific concepts, and given also that both thin and thick concepts are evaluative and, thus, related, then it stands to reason that these models are worth investigation.

My overall claim is that neither model applies to thin and thick concepts. I believe that neither model can satisfactorily accommodate evaluative flexibility, and I believe that doing so is highly desirable. In addition, I believe that the *genus–species* model is separationism in disguise. That additional belief is important, for the introduction of the *genus–species* model will enable us both to understand separationism better and to put pressure on it in Chapters Four and Five.

The structure and aims of this chapter are as follows. In §3.2 I outline the *genus–species* model. In §3.3 I outline the determinable–determinate model. In §3.4 I briefly show why we should think the two models are distinct. (Although keeping them distinct is not crucial to my overall argument because I disregard both, keeping them apart makes my argumentative narrative cleaner.) In §3.5 I explain evaluative flexibility and motivate it. My case for evaluative flexibility concludes when we reach Chapter Six where I show how it relates to other parts of my view. So I aim only to show evaluative flexibility in a positive light in this chapter, not conclusively show it as correct. Even with that modest aim, this present chapter still makes progress. First, I show that separationists who wish to adopt evaluative flexibility need to pause, as this idea seems to be in tension with the *genus–species* model. The tension can be resolved only by changing the idea of evaluative flexibility into something different from the idea I argue for. Second, I also show why nonseparationists should be wary of the determinable–determinate model, because it also is in tension with evaluative flexibility and this is something they should think of adopting. In §3.6 I discuss evaluative flexibility and the *genus–species* model, and in §3.7 I discuss it in relation to the determinable–determinate model.[1] Having shown problems with both models, I briefly suggest what sort of model of conceptual relations nonseparationists should find agreeable.

One final note. The idea of there being relations involves the idea that there are *relata*—in this case thin and thick concepts—and it is natural and essential to assume that the *relata* differ in kind in such relations. I will not argue in this chapter that thin and thick concepts differ in kind, but it will be the first claim argued for in the next chapter. I discuss it later rather than now because what I say in connection with it immediately opens up a criticism of separationism. So, for now, when entertaining the idea of conceptual relations I assume that thin and thick concepts differ in kind.

3.2 The *Genus–Species* Model

The *genus–species* model has it that we begin with some general concept, which is assumed to be our *genus* concept, and then, in order to derive a specific concept assumed to be the *species* concept, we have to be able to isolate some unique *differentia* that picks out that *species* concept from the other *species* concepts that belong to the same *genus*.[2] For example, we might begin with the *genus* concept ANIMAL or ANIMALHOOD. How might we capture what it is to be *homo sapiens*? One way in which to distinguish *homo sapiens* from other animals is to introduce the idea of rationality. That is, *homo sapiens* are, uniquely, the rational animals.

Two features of this model mark it as the model it is. First, we *begin* with the *genus* concept and then we *derive* the *species* concept. The idea is that the *genus* concept is thought to be conceptually or logically prior to the *species* concept. The one is defined in terms of the other. In everyday thought we clearly have knowledge both of what it is to be an animal and of various animals. But in order for the model to apply to this case, we must in theory have to have understanding of what it is to be an animal, understanding that makes no reference to any particular animals and their traits, such that it then makes sense to think of the relationship between the general and specific concepts in terms of conceptual priority and derivation. Second, not only has

---

[1] Some writers have suggested that we should apply the determinable–determinate model to thin and thick concepts. Graham Oddie in Oddie (2005), pp. 160–2 introduces the application of the model, albeit in a brief fashion with no discussion of the *genus–species* model. Christine Tappolet in Tappolet (2004) argues for its application primarily because she argues against applying its rival. Edward Harcourt and Alan Thomas in Harcourt and Thomas (2013) think that thin and thick concepts fulfil the minimal requirements for the determinable–determinate relation, and in doing so explicitly cite Tappolet as an inspiration, although they also criticize her.

[2] It could be that two or more concepts can have the same *differentia*, but their *genus* would be different. This may be the case for thick concepts. So on this view—although I do not believe this at all—BRAVE and FOOLHARDY look like they have the same *differentia*, but one belongs to the *genus* GOOD or PRO, and the other belongs to BAD or CON. Although I sometimes talk of a unique *differentia* in the main text for simplicity's sake, I always have this clause in mind.

the *differentia* to be unique to the *species*, but it also has to be something that can be understood separately from, and prior to, the *species* concept, otherwise talk of derivation is misplaced. In other words, we have two independent ingredients that are prior to our outcome and which come together to form it.

There are problems with this model. First, we might worry how widely applicable it is. For a start, we need to make sure that the *genus* concept really is understood in a way that is decent enough to enable the derivation. Perhaps in the case of *homo sapiens* we can avoid this worry by concentrating on matters of reproduction, respiration, and the like when trying to characterize what it is to be an animal. But, besides this, we need to think about the *differentia*. Talking simply of rationality in the case of humans seems inadequate since, arguably, other animals are rational in some fashion. Recall that the *differentia* has to be characterized prior to the *species* concept, so we cannot say that the rationality in which we are interested is the rationality typical of *homo sapiens*. Finding some way of picking out the *differentia* can be harder than it seems in some cases.[3] These points do not threaten the distinctive nature of the model, but they do threaten the extent of its applicability.

Second, and aside from this general issue of applicability, we might worry whether this model applies to thin and thick concepts. As mentioned, it is natural enough that our thin concepts will be the *genus* concepts and our thick ones will be the *species* concepts. KIND, COMPASSIONATE, WISE, and BEAUTIFUL all seem to be *species* of GOOD. If we think that the model applies then it seems, briefly, that we assume that we have some decent understanding of what it is for something to be good *apart from* any understanding of what it is for anything to be kind, wise, and so on. Also, it seems that we will have to think that there will be some particular *differentia* that will uniquely pick out the kind, and some particular differentia that will uniquely pick out the wise, and so on. Adoption of this model should strongly incline us towards viewing thick concepts as constructed from separable elements. In fact, on further reflection we can see that adoption of this model entails this view of the thick or even—my view in this study—that this model when applied to the thick *simply is* separationism by another name. We have our evaluative thin *genus* concept, we add to it a *differentia*—characterized in wholly nonevaluative, descriptive terms, presumably—and, hence, a thick concept is constructed and captured. On this understanding thick concepts are concepts that can be decomposed into separable, smaller elements.[4]

This idea holds whether we adopt simple separationism or a more complex version. The basic idea behind any type of separationism is that we have distinct elements that are added together to create thick concepts, and which are intelligible independently of our understanding of the thick. It is this run of ideas that I take to be key in providing the link between separationism and the *genus–species* model.

---

[3] Sanford (2006), §3 points this out, citing among others Aristotle (1994), pp. 176–84.
[4] Tappolet (2004), pp. 213–17 discusses this point. See also Hurley (1989), chapter 2.

Of course, there are different ways of construing the elements that constitute thick concepts. Many separationists, as we know, are noncognitivists. As I pointed out in the previous chapter, it is not quite right to talk of them thinking there is some thin *conceptual content* that is the *genus*. Rather, there is some thin attitude, characterized as something evinced by judges, that plays the role as our *genus*. But the general point remains. In order to analyse what thick concepts are, we have two (or more) types of element that are thought to be conceptually or logically prior to the thick, and which are moulded together to create it.

Another way in which separationists disagree among themselves is how thin they characterize the *genus* thin concept or element. Some construe it in a very thin way. Although they may use GOOD or BAD in their analyses and discussion, they pretty obviously really mean PRO or CON. Alternatively, we could identify it with some noncognitive feeling that is more specific than a bare approval. As mentioned in note 24 in Chapter Two, Gibbard, in his analysis of LEWD, imagines a feeling that he labels 'L-censoriousness'.[5] I discuss this in Chapter Four, but it is worth noting the issue now. The key point, again, is that thick concepts are created and constructed from ingredients that are independently intelligible and conceptually prior to thick concepts, so they cannot be understood, characterized, isolated, or identified by using thick concepts.

Because the *genus–species* model is so clearly in tune with separationism, non-separationists need to think about other models of conceptual relations.

3.3 The Determinable–Determinate Model

The modern characterization and labelling of the determinable–determinate model is due to W. E. Johnson, primarily in Johnson (1921), chapter XI, supplemented by discussions spread around Johnson (1922) and (1924).[6] This model links general and specific concepts, but we do not have to understand the general concept prior to the specific one, and there is no separable, prior *differentiae* that uniquely pick out individual specific concepts. For illustration, consider the canonical example of COLOUR (or COLOURED or BEING A COLOUR) and various colour concepts such as RED (or REDNESS or BEING RED).[7] Do these concepts fit the *genus–species* model? One worry is whether we have enough understanding of what it is to be coloured aside from understanding what it is to be any of the specific colours. Even if that can be solved, the possibility of supplying *differentia* is considered highly problematic. If the *genus–species* model is applicable, we should be able to claim that RED is the 'X sort of colour', or 'the colour with X-ness', say, where the uniquely identifying X is

---

[5] Gibbard (1992).
[6] For commentary see Prior (1949), and Searle (1959) and (1967), as well as the aforementioned Sanford (2006).
[7] For ease of writing I stick to COLOUR and RED, but clearly we may wish to adjust our English.

something independently intelligible from and conceptually prior to RED. But there seems to be nothing to fill this role. Saying 'RED is the colour with *this* sort of wavelength' will not do, it is commonly supposed, because talk of wavelengths is simply a different presentation of RED itself, not something independent of and conceptually prior to it. Hence, we need a different model to accommodate such an example.

According to the determinable–determinate model we simply state that there is some link, but that the general concept (the determinable) is not conceptually prior to any specific concept (some determinate), nor is there any *differentia*. As well as the case of colours, other examples that fit this model are lengths, ages, and sizes. For example, A LENGTH OF 5 METRES and A LENGTH OF 6 METRES are both determinates of the determinable A LENGTH BETWEEN 4 METRES AND 7 METRES. It is clear also that the application of this model to thin and thick concepts will be amenable to those who think that thick concepts are, in some fashion, concepts that admit of no separation into component parts.

There are two further points that it is useful to make in readiness for later discussion. First, a concept can be both a determinable and a determinate. RED is a determinate of COLOUR, but it is a determinable towards other colour determinates, such as SCARLET and CHERRY. Second, we might ask what links various concepts together in a family. With the *genus–species* model the answer is obvious: various *species* concepts are linked by being derived from the same *genus* concept. What of this model? Why are RED and BLUE, but not SQUARE, deemed to be determinates of a common determinable concept?

Here is the commonly given explanation. We cannot pursue any strategy that explains why RED and BLUE are part of the same family in terms of a commonality or commonalities between them, and further say they are distinguished from each other by something unique to them individually, for this is simply a restatement of the *genus–species* model. Instead, Johnson and subsequent writers pursued a different strategy, by focusing not on commonality but on exclusivity or, in David Armstrong's words, by considering 'mutual detestation societies'.[8] What makes it the case that RED and BLUE are determinates of a common determinable is that both concepts cannot apply, or be instantiated if one prefers, at the same time in the same place (or, at the same time by the same object). Similarly, in the case of lengths, nothing can instantiate the same concepts (ONLY) A LENGTH OF 5 METRES and (ONLY) A LENGTH OF 6 METRES at the same time, at least along the same side. However, it is clear that something can be both red and square at the same time. We can link this to our first point. Some colour patch cannot be both red and blue at the same time, and this reflects our intuitive thought that RED and BLUE are at the same 'conceptual level'. But clearly something can be both red and scarlet at the same time. This simply reflects

[8] Armstrong (1978), p. 112.

another common intuition, namely that RED and SCARLET are at different conceptual levels. One is more specific than the other, just as COLOUR and RED are. I return to the phenomenon of exclusion below.

3.4 Are the Models Distinct?

In this section I raise and briefly answer this question: are the two models distinct?[9] I have followed many commentators in assuming they are. But this assumption is arguable. In a moment I consider and briefly reject two reasons for thinking that the distinction can be questioned. As I have mentioned, whether or not we keep to a sharp dividing line between the models does not affect my overall argumentative narrative, since in the end I reject both models for thin and thick concepts. My main target is the *genus–species* model since it seems so obviously in tune with separationism. If the determinable–determinate model is closer to it than appears, then it may also be affected by my general arguments in later chapters. That is something I do not mind. It is just cleaner for my narrative to keep them apart.

Here are two reasons for not thinking them distinct, both found in Sanford (2006), especially §1.3 and §3.[10] First, it is not as if the two models have *nothing* in common: they both deal with general and specific concepts and, importantly, they both have exclusion as part of what they say. So perhaps they are a lot closer than we may think. But we should also note, *contra* Sanford's simple challenge, that the explanation of exclusion provided by the two models is very different. On the *genus–species* model *homo sapiens* and cats exclude each other in the sense that no animal can be both, and this is just because the *differentia* for each is unique. Exclusion works differently in the case of the determinable–determinate model. While it is true that no object can instantiate both red and blue at the same time for example, this is just what exclusion means. In the case of this model, the phenomenon of exclusion does not depend on there being a specific element being different in the case of the two (supposedly) exclusionary concepts which are, in turn, linked by having an element in common.

Second, Sanford thinks that we can construct various conjunctive and disjunctive definitions of some supposedly clear-cut determinable–determinate examples. These definitions show how easy it is to transform these examples into *genus–species* examples, and thus our confidence in the sharpness of the division between the two models should be undermined. For example, he characterizes, that is defines, RED as: 'x is red = (df.) (x is colored) & (x is red or x is not colored)'. We have a unique *differentia*, which is a (gerrymandered) concept (or predicate) that is not RED. One quick and fatal counter to this, however, is that this concept still includes RED and so presupposes some understanding of it. This clearly cuts against applying the

---

[9] This short section adds nothing to my overall argumentative narrative, so readers who are uninterested in this question can skip ahead to §3.5.

[10] Sanford notes that Johnson himself provides only equivocal support for the distinction.

genus–species model. It is still very unclear whether we will be able to construct *differentiae* for staple determinable–determinate examples, and hence cast doubt on the division between the two models.

There is more to say on this complicated matter, but I am confident that we can proceed in thinking the two models are distinct. As I say, given I reject both of them for thin and thick concepts, then their division is of little importance to me. It just keeps my narrative cleaner if we treat them separately.

3.5 Evaluative Flexibility

I return to the two models in a while. For now we need to establish that it is attractive to think that thick concepts exhibit evaluative flexibility, for this has a bearing on both models. Remember that the point of this section is *not* to argue conclusively for this phenomenon. As I have indicated, I argue for evaluative flexibility by seeing how well it fits with other aspects of my position, something we will appreciate only in later chapters. For now, it is enough merely to show evaluative flexibility in a positive light. In the following sections I indicate why the two models cannot accommodate evaluative flexibility, at least as I define it.

We have met this phenomenon earlier, in Chapter Two, when I talked of simple separationists thinking about the flexibility of the evaluative or attitudinative part of thick concepts. Recall an example from Chapter Two, mentioned briefly. We may often praise a poem for its elegance, and its elegance can be manifested in a number of ways: the words chosen, the mood created to capture the topic, the lay-out on the page, or the rhythms of the spoken word. But we often damn a poem and do so because it is elegant. We have a certain sort of topic that really cries out for raw and earthy words, or a disjointed, jerky presentation, or something else. The poem's elegance is completely out of place and spoils what could be something good. To employ some technical words, we might say that in some contexts elegance is bad- or wrong-making: it contributes negatively in some way to the overall thing of which it is a part.

When we start to think like this, examples abound. Cherubic children can often be a bore. Cheekiness and even naughtiness in children have their rightful place: such children show spirit, independence, and invention. We are often sick of crotchety people. But crotchetiness can be a virtue in some cases, in refusing to suffer or compromise with foolishness, and the exhibited temper may be just the right thing to shock those with whom one is arguing into a better course of action. We have previously met, in Chapter Two, Blackburn's and Hare's examples of people being industrious and tidy. It appears that we can create such examples at will. It appears that many, if not all, thick evaluative concepts can vary in the evaluations that they carry or embody.

This appears fine. But can our case for evaluative flexibility lie here? No. For evaluative flexibility to be correct then the *very same* concept has to alter in evaluation depending on context. What if, instead, we have a range of evaluations (broadly positive, negative, and neutral) across a range of concepts, albeit concepts that are related and where in some instances the concepts in the range are covered by the same word?

Consider the following train of thought. We can call a poem 'too elegant' implying that it would be okay if it was elegant to some extent, but in this instance we have too much of it. We have the same concept in play, but we acknowledge that we can have too much of what is normally a good thing which results in a bad thing. (Similarly, we can have too little of a good thing, which results in something bad.) For some concepts, these excesses and deficiencies might themselves have neat, different English words. When it comes to ELEGANT we might hear people talk of something being 'over-styled' or 'affected'. So even though we have the same concept, we should not forget that concepts can be used in this way.

This might lead us to wonder whether we have, in fact, the same concept. Perhaps what we really have are two concepts, ELEGANT-PRO and ELEGANT-CON. (We may have more than that. There may be some concept which is 'extremely-pro', for example, but I will keep things simple.) My talk of excesses and deficiencies just now was deliberate, for this way of thinking recalls Aristotle in *Nicomachean Ethics*. In some contexts, too much of something (or the wrong amount of something in the wrong context) means that what could have been brave is in fact rash or reckless; giving us not just new words, but also new concepts, even if they are clearly related to BRAVE.[11]

This takes us back to Blackburn and the idea of the licensing model. We earlier had CUDDLY and GROSS, but we discussed them to death so I shall switch examples. When someone is short-tempered and is so unreasonably—perhaps it is not so obvious that other people are being foolish and annoying—we might call them crotchety, or awkward, or petulant, or gruff, or many other such things. When we admire some-one's stance and their refusal to be sweet and polite to those they should be quick to be angry with, we might prefer to describe such behaviour with softer words, such as 'indignant', or 'riled', or employ the more neutral 'angry', and even use 'heroic' if their aims and the situation demand it. So, goes the thought, it seems that if some behaviour or object is deemed good, one sort of concept will apply, while if it is deemed bad then another sort will apply. Why bother with talk of the flexibility of a *single* concept? Crotchety behaviour is *always* bad. That is a central reason it gets to be crotchety. Indeed, our debate about whether or not an action is crotchety is a way of debating whether or not it is good. In conclusion—and this is the important thought—this analysis generalizes for most or all thick concepts.

This train of thought raises a few issues and gives us a few ways of capturing the various phenomena. I will deal with a nonseparationist option I do not like first of all,

---

[11] I prefer something along the lines in the parentheses to explain what Aristotle is getting at in his doctrine of the mean, but I do not push it as this is not a book of Aristotelian scholarship.

and then separationism afterwards. That will allow me to say something about my positive view.

First of all, here is the nonseparationist option that I introduce only to cover the logical terrain. It is possible to agree with the previous train of thought and be a nonseparationist about thick concepts. That is, we will multiply and allow various ELEGANCE concepts—ELEGANT-PRO and ELEGANT-CON, for example—but for each one say it is impossible to separate the evaluative from the descriptive. Note that the English presentation of these more specific concepts would be judged misleading by advocates of this view, for the hyphen clearly separates what might be thought descriptive content from an evaluation. Crucial to this nonseparationist view, however, is that we can say that there is something that these two concepts share—they are both types of ELEGANT after all—but we should not think of there being some isolatable descriptive content that is the shared element.

I do not like this view at all. True, the qualifiers at the end distinguish it in logical space from separationist views. But how is one to argue for the idea that our two concepts are both nonseparable and yet they have shared, common content that can seemingly be seen as distinct from the two different evaluative points? Arguing for this seems very difficult. Further to that, who is to say that we have just two concepts, ELEGANT-PRO and ELEGANT-CON? What are we also to make of ELEGANT-VERY-PRO? Is it a different (nonseparable) concept, or just a stronger version of the first example? Similarly, what are we to make of how our elegance concepts are linked to STYLISH-PRO and STYLISH-CON? And what are we to make of poems being HARMONIOUS-PRO and HARMONIOUS-CON, CONSTRAINED-PRO and CONSTRAINED-CON, JERKY-PRO and JERKY-CON, and so on?

To my mind, if you think that an evaluative concept is nonseparable, then it is far easier to imagine that the evaluative aspect of the concept can itself alter—in terms of specific positive or negative view that is conveyed—depending on context and this not require you to multiply the number of concepts you have. There is no reason to pursue the nonseparationist view that we are allowed only one distinct sort of evaluative content per each concept because the alternative is too messy to contemplate. On the contrary, I think this alternative is beautifully simple.

Now consider separationism. Separationists will argue that it is routine to analyse thick concepts into more specific varieties to reflect the separation of evaluation from description. We will get some differences between separationists beyond this. The difference for Elstein and Hurka between ELEGANT and contrary concepts such as AFFECTED and CONSTRAINED when applied to our poem might be analysed in terms of isolatable conceptual elements, that is in terms of some Xs and Ys. For Blackburn, there may be some *general* descriptive dimension along which judges and their evaluations plant themselves, but then we get different specifications of this general vector because of the different attitudes to which they are conjoined. In both cases we may have many words that are used, as in our ELEGANT example. These may well indicate different concepts. In other words, and to summarize, behind the everyday

English words that may be used, what unites all of these separationist positions is the idea that putting matters in terms of ELEGANT-PRO and ELEGANT-CON is not a misleading presentation in the least.

Both separationism and the nonseparationist alternative I have considered just before include the idea that once we have a different evaluation—strictly, a different bare thin concept or elements—then this justifies us in speaking of two (or more) concepts. It may even entail it. My suggested view is different.

When we call two poems elegant, yet praise one for being elegant and damn the other in the same way, we can still note and pick out the elegance. We are using the same word in the same sort of way, at least, and despite the *theoretical* possibility of there being different concepts (ELEGANCE-PRO and ELEGANCE-CON) standing behind this word, the ease with which we can in many everyday contexts see the similarity and compare in that light is surely telling. This is a first suggested point in my view's favour, designed to show that what I am entertaining is not so strange. Second, we should note that the two opposing views I have canvassed seem based only on the overly quick thought that if we have different, specific evaluations being employed— in terms of PRO and CON—that automatically means we must have at least two concepts in play. Where is the argument for that? We surely need some extensive argument, for this is a fundamental point. Further and third, I worry that adopting the position I oppose will lead to an over-multiplication of concepts, all separate and all performing their very specific role. My worry here mirrors my first point. The idea standing behind both, perhaps, is this. Those that oppose my view seem to think that if one has a variation in function or specific evaluative stance that is expressed, then one must have different concepts. I do not see that at all. Indeed, in Chapter Six I illustrate, through discussion of Williams and Ryle, that a concept—especially an evaluative concept—can have a number of functions across a range of instances, and yet it be natural to assume that it is the same concept. As I express it there, an evaluative concept can be such that it holds together a range of specific evaluative stances of varying strengths, and this be part of the evaluative aspect of the concept; indeed and further, such evaluative stances are of and express the entire concept. (I add this rider to underline the point that the entire concept is evaluative, not just some aspect of it.)

These few thoughts are not enough to argue against separationism as yet. But they, and the previous examples, should make us pause to let evaluative flexibility in as a live possibility at least. It is also important to see that evaluative flexibility as I have characterized it slots very nicely into a nonseparationist view that I favour (and not the one from logical terrain canvassed earlier). We have a single, evaluative concept, even if we initially capture this idea by saying that it has aspects of evaluation and description. Further, a key argument raised by nonseparationists against separationists—one which has cropped up every so often—is that one can under- stand the descriptive aspect of a thick concept (that is, why it applies to items with certain sorts of feature) only by understanding its evaluation or evaluative point, in part because such concepts are so complex. We shall see this develop into the thought that the best way of understanding what nonseparationists have been saying is that this is true because we have a range of specific evaluations, and appreciation of this range is required to understand which concepts apply and why.

We have enough motivation to think how our two conceptual models fare when we see if they can accommodate it. Evaluative flexibility has some attraction, and it seems to sit nicely with nonseparationism.

One final note before I return to those two models. I talked of Blackburn advocating evaluative flexibility, but what he supports is different from what I advocate. He thinks of there being a separable descriptive content, to which different attitudes can be conjoined; recall his 'description+tone' from Chapter Two. So even though we may sloppily say that ELEGANT can change its evaluation on his view, what we really mean is that there is some general descriptive dimension along which certain different attitudes are placed, resulting in different words ('elegant', 'constrained', 'prim', 'stifled').[12] They have something general in common, but the 'description+tone's that result are different. This may also result in us saying, for convenience's sake, that we have 'evaluative flexibility', even if, strictly, what we have is the same general descriptive concept with different attitudes attached, thus resulting in *different things* with different attitudes, not the *same thing* embracing different evaluative points.[13]

3.6 The *Genus–Species* Model and Separationism

If evaluative flexibility turns out to be a real phenomenon, where it is understood as I have characterized it as referring to the flexible evaluative nature of a single concept, then we cannot adopt either of the two conceptual models discussed earlier. The same reasoning applies to both models, although it is easier to show in the case of the *genus–species* model.

Recall that in order to get a thick concept we supposedly have a thin *genus* concept to which some *differentia* is added. If we adopt evaluative flexibility (for a single

---

[12] What that general descriptive dimension might be I do not know. If one thinks of it purely descriptively, one might well call it 'elegant'.

[13] This whole discussion of evaluative flexibility calls to mind the debate between particularists and generalists. The two best books on the subject are Dancy (2004) and McKeever and Ridge (2006). Particularists come in varieties, and discussion of what the dispute between the two camps amounts to is thorny. However, for simplicity's sake we can note that some particularists, including Dancy, argue that features (or reasons) can vary in their valency in a way that is influenced by context: sometimes a feature can be right-making and sometimes it can be wrong-making. This short claim can then be given a modal edge, and particularists can choose to say that it is not necessary for moral reasoning having a rational structure that it be based on codified principles in which features are deemed to be either always right-making or always wrong-making. This is not a book on the intricacies of the debate about particularism. Suffice it to say that one can be a particularist about thick concepts or thick features. My discussion in the main text is an expression of my acceptance of this sort of particularism. I have defended this view in more detail in Kirchin (2003b), which is a response to Crisp (2000) and McNaughton and Rawling (2000).

concept), then we are imagining that we can have at times a PRO *genus* and at times a CON *genus* to which some *differentia* is added, which then results in something which is the same concept in both additions. That plainly makes no sense. This is why putting things explicitly in terms of ELEGANT-PRO and ELEGANT-CON is so right for this model. ELEGANT-PRO and BRAVE-PRO, say, have the same *genus*, but are distinguished by their descriptive *differentiae*, and our two elegance concepts are distinguished by belonging to different *genera*.[14]

This is not to say that separationism and the *genus–species* model come apart. We should remind ourselves what is meant by evaluative flexibility in the mouths of separationists and, chiefly, Blackburn. The point was just made, but I make it again in case it was lost.

There is no tension here for Blackburn simply because he does not in the end think of evaluative flexibility as being something to do with the same concept. What we have is a general descriptive concept to which different attitudes, often conveyed through tone of voice, are then added. He might then not even want to say that we have different concepts that are constructed, strictly, although he might allow that we can talk loosely as if there are. The attitudes are placed along a descriptive dimension and we have different words that pick out those different and distinct placings. There is no notion here of the very same concept changing its evaluative aspect. By changing the evaluative part, as separationists conceive of it, you change the concept, or whatever it is that we call it.

The moral, from this simple review of Blackburn's position, is that this goes for all separationist positions: by changing one of the ingredients, you thereby change the product, rather than alter the very same product from one instance to another.

For completeness, here is what happens with complex separationism. Complex separationists are committed to there being independent ingredients that result in a product, but the descriptive ingredient is not 'fully' determinate. I made play in Chapter Two with the thought that Elstein and Hurka's analysis for ELEGANT would get more complicated if we had both a GOOD and a BAD, or both a PRO and a CON. Here we can see that it would be unwise to think that we would end up with the same concept. Part of the worry with the analysis I presented was that it was so vague and so general as to cover very many different expressions of 'elegant'. True it helps us to see that there will be some connection between ELEGANT-PRO and ELEGANT-CON— namely the 'ELEGANT' part—but then we would be better off with two distinct sorts of concept. (Or, if our language and thought typically expressed a need for a separation between ELEGANT-PRO and ELEGANT-VERY-PRO, say, then more than two distinct sorts of concept.)

---

[14] We can carve things differently by having the descriptive 'ELEGANT' part as the *genus*, and the evaluation as the *differentia*, but in our imagined scenario that will not result in many concepts. Given the prevalence of the number of pro- and con-concepts, and given that *genus* is supposed to be a general idea, then it is better to conceive things as I have done in the main text.

Thus, to summarize, there seems to be tension between the adoption of the *genus–species* model and evaluative flexibility *of some sort*, but this is only a passing worry. As a separationist one can adopt the *genus–species* model, and one can sign up to some general idea of evaluative flexibility, but the key rider is that this second idea cannot be the evaluative flexibility of a single concept. The view has instead to be that there is some descriptive core, which itself may be tagged with the typical thick term such as 'elegant' or 'brave', and then we end up with different resulting products, distinguished because of different evaluations, indicated by different tones of voice and the like.

This little discussion may seem unimportant. But it will help set things up for the next section, and it helps to build up a picture of separationism and the *genus–species* model. With that in mind, I summarize what has gone on in the rest of this chapter.

The *genus–species* model as applied to thin and thick concepts is simply separationism with a different name. Four aspects seem pertinent: (i) There are two or more elements that go to make any concept deemed to be a *species* concept. (ii) All elements that are assumed to be ingredients of the *species* concept have to be intelligible independently of our understanding of any *species* concept. (iii) All elements have to be conceptually prior to the *species* concept. (iv) The *differentia* has to be unique to the *species* concept. Given that the *genus* concept is likely to be shared, it is the *differentia* that will typically mark the *species* concept out as being different from other concepts.[15]

It would be easy to slide between (ii) and (iii). Undoubtedly they are linked and go nicely together. But aspect (ii) concerns the content of the two concepts, as it were, whereas aspect (iii) concerns which element, if any, comes first and which should be seen as being constructed from the other. I discuss 'conceptual priority' in Chapter Four. Furthermore, although I will often have simple separationism in mind when criticizing separationism generally, my comments will apply equally to various forms of complex separationism. Putting things in terms of the *genus–species* model sets the scene for two main sorts of criticism that I have already advertised. In Chapter Four I concentrate on the thin, *genus* element: what is it for something to be thin and what is involved in assuming that thin concepts or elements are conceptually prior to thick concepts? In Chapter Five I concentrate on the *differentia*.

3.7 Nonseparationism and the Determinable–Determinate Model

Before that, one last question. I shall soon begin, in Chapter Four, to argue directly that separationism and the *genus–species* model should not be used to understand the relationship between thin and thick concepts. (I have, thus far, cast suspicion only,

---

[15] The 'typically' is designed to cope with analyses such as Gibbard's, which I discuss in Chapter Four.

since evaluative flexibility of a single concept cannot be accommodated within separationism.) So, therefore, does that mean that nonseparationists should adopt the determinable–determinate model? I think the answer is 'no'.[16]

On the face of it there is a very strong reason for nonseparationists to adopt the determinable–determinate model. It seems that the two models exhaust the choices that face us when choosing between models of conceptual relations where we are assuming a link between general and specific concepts. Given that separationism just is the *genus–species* model applied to thin and thick concepts, then it seems nonseparationists must choose the determinable–determinate model. However, why should we think that the two models exhaust the options?

It goes back to the phenomenon of exclusion. Recall that our aim is to explain how general and specific concepts that are assumed to be families are linked. The *genus–species* model encapsulates one very natural answer to that question, namely commonality. That commonality is of a particular kind: namely a defined and isolatable common element that can be identified as appearing in each and every one of the concepts that are, therefore, treated as *species* of the *genus*, or *species* of the common element or root. (That will be important in a moment.) Against this, the determinable–determinate model bases relations on exclusion. So it appears as if we have only two choices: relations can be based either on commonality or exclusion.

Some nonseparationists may be happy to leave things there. But I am not because evaluative flexibility cannot be handled by the determinable–determinate model. Why not? As with the *genus–species* model, the determinable–determinate model is a model between concepts considered as whole things. Thus, for example, when we say that RED is a determinate of the determinable COLOUR, what we mean to say is that every red thing is also a coloured thing or, if one prefers, every time the concept RED is instantiated, then COLOUR is instantiated. So if we want to say that, for example, HONEST is a determinate of the determinable GOOD, then we have to be committed to saying that every honest thing is also a good thing, not merely that some honest things are good things and some other honest things are not. Thus, the commitment to HONEST, for example, being a determinate of GOOD, does not respect evaluative flexibility. And, to repeat, it is not just a matter of these specific examples: we have a general commitment about determinates always being linked to some determinable.

Just for completeness, let us consider very briefly one possible defence. There is nothing in the model that says that a concept cannot be a determinate of more than one determinable. SCARLET is a determinate of both RED and COLOUR. It even works for determinables that are at the same conceptual level. A LENGTH OF 6 METRES is always a determinate of many different determinables of the form BETWEEN X METRES AND Y METRES. So, if we favour evaluative flexibility, it seems as if we could say that HONEST is a determinate of both GOOD and BAD. However, the case of value is different from

---

[16] I used to think that they should. I am grateful to Debbie Roberts for convincing me that I was wrong.

the case of lengths. It is plausible to assume—and perhaps necessary to our use of these concepts to assume—that paired thin concepts such as GOOD and BAD, and RIGHT and WRONG, are opposed. Although it may not appear to be at first glance, saying that a concept can be both always good-making and always bad-making (or even be always good-making and occasionally bad-making) is as contradictory as saying that red things can be both always coloured and occasionally not-coloured. So this avenue is closed. And, in short, the determinable–determinate model is inconsistent with evaluative flexibility of a single concept.

Having said all of this, there is a gaping hole in my story. If I sign up to evaluative flexibility, and assume that this cannot be accommodated by either model of conceptual relations, then what model of conceptual relations between the general and the specific *do* I favour? This point presses a great deal given that I have set things up so that the two models that have preoccupied us apparently exhaust the options.

I here offer a broad response. We should revisit what it means to say that some general concept, for example GOOD, is a concept that is 'held in common by', or 'which is part of', or 'which is exhibited by', or 'which is shown in' more specific evaluative concepts. The *genus–species* model has it that this can be understood only if the conceptual content is something that itself is an independent ingredient that retains this character even when brought into contact with some *differentia*, thereby producing a new concept. But it need not be like that at all. Thoughts familiar from the later Wittgenstein on family resemblance teach us that there may be many concepts—or 'things', understood very broadly—that go together and which, sometimes, can be seen as specific versions of some general thing by exhibiting it or by some other relation. Even if we can say, confidently, that all of these examples are examples of X, in doing so we need not be committed to saying that the way in which X is in each example is exactly the same way such that we can isolate and identify the X part, thus justifying us in separating it. Perhaps instead we can abstract from the various examples and get a sense of what X or the X is like, even if that sense is not to be found in each example in exactly the same way. Wittgenstein's idea can be exemplified literally: this is how things often work when it comes to the noses and cheekbones of certain family members. The same is true of certain concepts, I think.

This general sort of stance can unite specific concepts with general concepts. We can say that *this* group of specific concepts exhibit or are linked to a general concept, although *those other* specific concepts do not. We can also say that these specific concepts can exhibit more than one general concept; some specific evaluative concepts can even exhibit both GOOD and BAD, although they need not do it at the very same time with regards to the very same thing being categorized. We can say this sort of thing because there is no tie or recipe independent of and different from our exercise of evaluative judgement between concepts considered as general types. We have, instead, thoughts about judgement that allows for more flexibility in the nature of concepts and the relations they can form with other concepts. The justification for a specific concept being a member of a family of general concepts need not rely on an individual, isolatable, separable part that is held in common by both parent and child and which, in the extreme case, is wholly the parent concept itself.

This is a broadbrush treatment of judgement. Although I will return to this sort of stance (in Chapters Six and Eight), it will remain broadbrush throughout. For even when we return to it, much of my commentary will be negative, pointing out—as I have done in this chapter—the difficulties we get into when we divert from this general stance for evaluative concepts. Indeed, although this is clearly influenced by thoughts from the later Wittgenstein, I will not offer any Wittgensteinian exegesis in this book. One point I will return to in the next chapter is worth flagging. One might wonder whether the more general—that is, thin—sorts of evaluative concepts are only ever *mere* abstractions of the thicker ones, as was suggested just now. Some theorists have thought this but, despite what I have just written, I do not believe this to be the case; we can think of the thin differently while retaining the idea of a model of conceptual relations different from the two models that have preoccupied us in this chapter.

3.8 Conclusion

Understanding the *genus–species* and determinable–determinate models was import-ant for understanding separationism, and giving us the start of some insight into nonseparationism. As part of this I have also got us thinking about evaluative flexibility.

As I mentioned, thinking in terms of the *genus–species* model will help us to understand how we can criticize separationism and the ways in which it is vulnerable. We now need to turn to think about the type of concept typically thought by separationists to be the *genus* concept, namely the thin.

4

The Thin

4.1 Introduction

One key attack on separationism is to argue that separationists' notion of the thin is wrong. More specifically it can be argued that it does not show enough appreciation of what it is for something to be a thin concept. Furthermore, separationists are committed to the idea that thin concepts enjoy some form of conceptual priority over thick ones: the latter are explicitly assumed to be constructed from the former plus some *differentia*. But what are the reasons for this view and how might one question it?

This chapter has two main topics. First, I investigate the notion of the thin and think about what notion of the thin is best employed by separationists. In order to do this I think about whether there is a dividing line between two broad types of evaluative concept. (I suggest there is.) This itself does not result in an argument, but it does resonate with the line of argument I pursue in Chapter Six: in brief, some so-called thin concepts may be thicker than others. Furthermore, through looking at the work of Allan Gibbard I argue that separationists are better off thinking of the thin as very thin. Having established that, I move to my second main topic: what does it mean to say, as separationists have to say, that the thin is conceptually prior to the thick? Not only do I think about what that means, I also ask whether such a conceptual priority is true. In my view the arguments for it are weak indeed, although crucially I think that much of what I say is inconclusive. My main conclusion is that nonseparationists need to find different ground on which to fight.

In §4.2 and §4.3 I argue for the idea that we can talk with confidence of there being two types of concept, although my end point is designed only to be strongly suggestive not conclusive. In §4.4 I reflect on the argumentative narrative that leads from the first two sections. In §4.5 I argue that separationists should assume that the evaluative element in their analyses has to be construed as very thin, and as mentioned I think about Gibbard's work here. I then consider conceptual priority in §4.6 and §4.7. Even if we assume—as I do—that there are thin concepts, why assume that they are conceptually prior to thick ones, as the *genus–species* model requires? In §4.8 I conclude.

4.2 Two Types of Concept?

It is routine to assume in discussions of thin and thick concepts that we have two broad types of concept: the thin and the thick. However, it is worth challenging that assumption since we can learn a lot. I believe we can understand the thick only if we understand the thin. Indeed, in this and the next section I start to sow seeds that will unsettle the separationist view in later chapters. Despite my challenging the 'binary' assumption of thin and thick concepts, the reader should note that at the end of my discussion I suggest that we *should* keep to the view that there are two broad types of concept. My aim is to show what we can learn from thinking about the thin.

Writers normally introduce thin concepts and talk of GOOD and BAD, RIGHT and WRONG, and then move quickly onto the whole run of thick concepts. I did the same in my Introduction. It also often happens that these thin concepts are described as being evaluative only, and the thick ones are thought to be both evaluative and descriptive. But all of this is simply too quick. Compare two of our thin concepts, GOOD and RIGHT. That these concepts are different concepts is surely unarguable. For a start, philosophical and other writers normally namecheck both of them rather than use one to stand for the other. And, second, they do so because the vast majority of writers and ordinary people think there *is* a difference, even if, in the end, some theorists might argue that the two come together in an interesting way. The whole of modern normative ethics—and much of our everyday thought that it is supposed to reflect—makes no sense unless we assume, at least at the start, that there is a difference between GOOD and RIGHT.

What is that difference? The following may not be exactly correct, but it is decent enough for our purposes. If something is good then it indicates that we both approve of the thing and that we are open to the possibility of other relevantly similar things being things that we can approve of, be that approval stronger, weaker, or the same.[1] If something is right, then we approve of the thing and we think that it is the only thing among all relevantly similar things that we can approve of or want to approve of. In short, we ordinarily think that in a given context or situation there can be many good things but only one right one.[2]

Two points flow from this. First, GOOD and RIGHT are both positive concepts, yet they differ. In what respect do they differ? If we have bought into the idea that evaluative and descriptive content are completely separate, and if we think that evaluative content is exhausted by mere likes and dislikes, then we will have to say that GOOD and RIGHT differ in terms of descriptive content. In which case, we straightaway threaten the thought that these traditionally cast thin concepts are evaluative only and 'purely', at least on our introductory understanding of thin and thick concepts. That idea is reinforced by a second point. We have another evaluative

---

[1] We could frame all of this in terms of 'should be approved of', or similar. That does not make any difference to what I say.

[2] As I said, this is rough. I am sensitive to the idea that 'right' might be used in everyday speech as a synonym for 'good', where people are picking out something that they approve of and want to indicate that they approve of it strongly, not that it is the only approvable thing. However, I reckon that such use is either non-standard or easy to interpret as indicating GOOD. On reflection, my distinction, or something like it, holds.

concept in the mix now, namely PRO. GOOD and RIGHT differ from PRO. They are concepts which we employ to approve of things, but when we approve we do more than simply say 'pro'. We approve of things in a certain way, with extra information.[3] The way in which we approve of good things is different from the way in which we approve of right things.

That, again, should make us worry about how we classify thin concepts. Are they all 'simply' and 'merely' and 'purely' evaluative, with thick concepts being something else? Perhaps the evaluative way in which thin concepts are evaluative can differ. Or, in other words, perhaps thin concepts come in a range of 'thicknesses'? After all, some seem slightly more specific than others; indeed, perhaps we should just drop the inverted commas around 'thicknesses'.

I think that we *can* class thin concepts as being 'simply' and 'purely' evaluative but that is because I have a certain view of the evaluative that allows me to say that thick concepts are also 'simply' and 'purely' evaluative. We could really pursue this current line of thought in a way that becomes a full frontal attack on separationism, by questioning what separationists mean by and include in their notion of 'the evaluative' and from that argue that thick concepts can also be fundamentally and simply evaluative. I do that in Chapter Six and park the argument just mentioned for the present. Right now I stress a *different* idea. We are concerned only with whether we should assume such a clear division between the thin and the thick.

I should point out that the discussion just now can be run for concepts other than just GOOD and RIGHT. Consider a range of concepts that pick out pro-concepts in any language and indicate strength of approval. In English we might have a run of concepts from OUTSTANDING to OKAY and ADEQUATE, that takes in EXCELLENT, FINE, DECENT, and ACCEPTABLE along the way, among other examples.[4] Again, the key idea is that these are all pro-concepts, yet they do more than just indicate approval of something. If that is all they did, we would have the same concept, but we do not. Something else must be going on.

There is another point often missing from the literature. We would surely say that there is a difference between the concepts ETHICALLY GOOD, AESTHETICALLY GOOD, PRUDENTIALLY GOOD, and the like.[5] Yet clearly all of them differ from PRO and CON, and it would take a brave person to argue that they were not more specific versions of GOOD. Are we then committed to the idea that they are all thick concepts? Perhaps. But doing so is unnerving. It seems also possible and justifiable

---

[3] As mentioned in Chapter One, we can use all sorts of word in everyday language to indicate PRO and CON. I am thinking here of the many cases where we are doing something different from merely indicating bare approval or disapproval.

[4] I am well aware that these concepts might themselves be thicker and that some of them may be imperfect for this present point. The thought is simply that some words and concepts in everyday speech are used to indicate a pro-attitude, and some to indicate a con-attitude, where such concepts differ only in terms of strength.

[5] Some might not think there are clear differences in kind here. But surely most will think it plausible that there are at least differences of degree here that are philosophically significant.

to think that we have now added to our range of concepts that can be labelled thin, and that this group is growing as we continue to reflect.

Having thought a little about the thin and exposed the possibility of there being differences, let us do the same with the thick. Compare this family of concepts: KIND, CARING, COMPASSIONATE, EMPATHETIC, SYMPATHETIC, THOUGHTFUL, and CONSIDERATE. It is impossible to be precise here, but to my mind it seems obvious that KIND is thinner and more general than, say, EMPATHETIC and SYMPATHETIC. THOUGHTFUL, at least as meant as part of this family, seems to lie in the middle, it being a certain way in which one can exercise kindness, although I am prepared to be argued out of this claim. The main idea is that there is a host of different thicknesses among all those concepts classed as thick concepts.

In a review of Williams' *ELP*, Samuel Scheffler makes essentially the same point. He notes that Williams assumes that there are just two sorts of concept: the thick and the more abstract. *Contra* Williams, Scheffler gives a list of concepts that seem to fall under neither heading, grouped in families.[6] For example, JUSTICE, FAIRNESS, and IMPARTIALITY form one little family; PRIVACY, SELF-RESPECT, and ENVY form another; and NEEDS, WELL-BEING, AND INTERESTS form a third. Scheffler notes that Williams' bifurcation of thick concepts as being both world-guided and action-guiding, and thin concepts as being action-guiding alone, appears unjustified. In fact, he calls this divide 'incoherent'. Williams, Scheffler claims, ties world-guidedness to agreement in application, but it appears that Williams is not so strict as to see widespread agreement as either necessary or sufficient for a concept being world-guided. Indeed, given that strengths and types of agreement can vary depending on concept (and context), it seems as if we are in territory where it is unwise to think of strict conditions and of clear dividing lines between one type of thing and another. Scheffler explicitly talks of various relevant considerations here being 'matters of degree'.

These preceding comments can now be put together to define the challenge of this section. So far I have done two things. I have indicated that it may be less than obvious that all traditional thin concepts should be lumped together and assumed to be the same. In particular we saw that concepts that are traditionally labelled as thin might differ from PRO (or CON) and do so because some other conceptual content (or something) is added to PRO (or CON), and/or the strength of approval or disapproval changes. A concept traditionally classed as thin may well not be a simple or bare approval or disapproval. This first point can itself be used as a starting point to try to unseat the separationist view of the thin, but here I am using it simply to pursue the idea that the thin comes in a range of thicknesses. I have also, second,

---

[6] Scheffler (1987), pp. 417ff. One of Scheffler's other main worries is that Williams charges modern professional moral philosophy with being interested only in thin concepts such as GOOD and RIGHT, whereas in fact many modern moral philosophers are interested in a whole host of concepts. A note from Chapter One bears repetition: Scheffler, unlike Williams in *ELP*, uses the label 'thin concept'.

indicated that thick concepts can come in a variety of thicknesses. It is very tempting at this stage to put these two ideas together and argue that the distinction between the thin and the thick is only a convenient starting point, an idea that we should look beyond.

This comes into view when we work away at the possible boundary of the thin and the thick. Consider OUGHT, DUTY, DECENT, ACCEPTABLE, and JUST. Are these thin? The first two are often classified in this way, the third and fourth appeared briefly in my discussion of the thin (but I noted that they could be thought to be thick), and the last was included in my brief discussion of thick concepts. The point is that it is not clear that there is any difference between them in terms of their thicknesses. Or, if there is it will take a lot of argumentation, and there may still remain disagreements at the end. Why not, then, just eschew the distinction between the thin and the thick, as Scheffler suggests? Instead of a difference in kind between two types, why not just embrace a difference of degree among our evaluative concepts? Why not just assume some sort of continuum in this matter? It seems likely that our evaluative concepts range from the barely thin at one end to the very thick at the other, taking in all manner of concepts along the way.

The conclusion is just that we have evaluative concepts and that some are more specific than others. (Or if you prefer, for emphasis, some are more general than others.) That is all that can be said. Placing a dividing line to indicate some difference in kind is simply unjustified and a result of sloppy, lazy thinking.

4.3 Back to the Distinction

But is this a product of sloppy, lazy thinking? There seems *something* to the idea that we have general and specific evaluative concepts and there is something important about the difference between them, so much so that we can talk of a dividing line.

Think again about GOOD and RIGHT. When we apply these concepts we approve in both cases. The difference between them comes only in what attitude we take towards those other things that are classed as being relevantly similar to our target things. We do not say anything more about the target things themselves aside from indicating our approval of them. A similar point can be made about our range of concepts that indicate strengths of approval and disapproval, at least on one conception of such matters. One attractive view is that all such judgements are essentially comparative. We can understand the approval of *this* thing only in the light of our consideration of *that other* thing. In a case—an 'odd universe' sort of case—where we approve of only one thing, we cannot really say how strongly we approve of the thing, since we can reach such a view only in the light of approvals towards other things.[7]

---

[7] One alternative is to say that comparisons between different sorts of approval, such as those indicated by OUTSTANDING and OKAY, can be understood fully without the need for comparison. This relies on us being able to understand 'strong approval' on its own, without any reference to, or experience of, say, 'weak

In contrast, think of standard thick concepts. When we say that someone is generous or obnoxious we are not only approving or disapproving of her, if that is what we are doing. We are also approving or disapproving of her in a certain way, where 'that certain way' is focused on her, the target thing. Crucially, unlike the story I have just told for GOOD and RIGHT, our application and understanding of standard thick concepts to one thing does not depend essentially on our view of other things. Note, that we might say, in general, that people can fully understand GENEROUS, say, only by applying it to many things. But that is a different point. The point I am making here is that, even if there has to be a background of many uses of a thick concept in order for understanding to be decent or mature, once that background is in place, any single use of a thick concept need involve reference only to the particular thing that is being characterized. In contrast, any single application of GOOD will involve essential reference to a person's view of other things (or reference to how she might view other things, given the context, task, or question facing her). The way in which we view those other things will be crucial in distinguishing GOOD from RIGHT according to my starting definitions. In other words, with thick concepts we are indicating something more specific than approval and disapproval of the thing in question in a way that is clearly different from how we do so when applying concepts such as GOOD and RIGHT.

Let me summarize this in a different way, as this may be quite abstract. The distinction between the thin and the thick may be thus. Thick concepts pick out certain sorts of liking towards certain things and they carry or can be specific sorts of those likings where such likings are not dependent on us drawing comparisons with other things and their characterizations, or on other matters. On the other hand, when thin concepts pick out or are likings towards certain things, they may give us more information about the thing than a bare approval will, but if so this is achieved only through some comparison with other things and their characterizations or some other matter not to do with the target things themselves. Or, in other words, thick concepts can be used to voice approvals and disapprovals towards things and can do so specifically with a focus, sometimes, only on the things themselves. Thin concepts are not like that. If they do go beyond PRO and CON, the extra information is conveyed through something else, such as a comparison with other objects.

As advertised, I do not believe that this distinction in kind is *definitively* correct. But I cannot help thinking that just as I imagined an opponent to the distinction between thick and thin saying that it is a product of lazy and sloppy thinking, we might also judge that it is too quick to move from the idea that there is a 'range of thicknesses' in our evaluative concepts to the idea that there can be no difference in kind between them. The idea of thin and thick, of being general and specific, has

approval'. I am sceptical about this, but even if I am wrong, then my example of GOOD and RIGHT still works. Thinking in this way about thin concepts is, to my mind, all to the good and shows my worry that more thought about the thin is required.

some roots. We would do well to pause and think about the ways in which concepts work to see if we can uncover some general trends that help mark interesting differences. The one I have marked out above may be imperfect and is certainly not fully worked out. But it is a decent start that should stop us from blithely assuming only differences of degree between our evaluative concepts, even if we assume a range of thicknesses across them.

If my distinction is onto something, we should revisit other examples. ETHICALLY GOOD, AESTHETICALLY GOOD and the others may not be as thin as I first suggested they could be. When we pick out something as ethically good we *are* giving some information about the thing beyond the fact that we think it is good and which is not itself wholly comparative. I find it intuitive that we can pick out the ethical character of an ethical liking without comparison with other things, which may or may not be ethical. And the same is true of things deemed aesthetically good.

What of concepts such as JUST and DECENT? If we are to follow my distinction in some form, then it appears that these concepts turn out to be thick, albeit thinner than some others. Things get trickier when we talk of OUGHT and DUTY, APPROPRIATE and ADEQUATE. OUGHT seems really rather thin and could be as thin as RIGHT or at least close to it. Yet, if we follow most philosophers we can note that 'ought implies can'. We have, then, an additional element not standardly included in RIGHT. Some action ought to be pursued if it is positively endorsed, so long as it is the only thing that can be positively endorsed from a range of relevantly similar options *and* it can be pursued. We have thickened up RIGHT ever so slightly. Perhaps the invocation of what can be pursued is sufficient to push it into the camp of thick concepts as I have just drawn them, but perhaps it should stay on the thin side of things because we have an essential comparative judgement, albeit with an additional clause, which shows the connection of OUGHT to RIGHT. Similar comments could be made of the other concepts mentioned at the start of this paragraph.

The philosophical moral hereabouts is simply that if we wish to maintain some distinction in kind among evaluative concepts, and label the two camps 'thin' and 'thick', we need to think hard about a number of examples and decide where to place them. In doing so, we will bring into focus exactly what the basis is of the distinction between the thick and the thin. We will also see, I strongly think, that within both of the two broad camps there is a range of thicknesses. (Scheffler was absolutely correct to emphasize this range.) Assuming that what we define as being thin is not exhausted by the minimally thin concepts PRO and CON, this point applies to thin concepts and not just the thick.

4.4 A Pause

The argument of the previous chapter assumed that there was going to be a difference in kind between the thin and the thick. I hope that my previous section has at least provided enough inspiration to think that the distinction retains plausibility. It matters somewhat for my discussion. I think that separationism is wrong, but not because separationists erroneously believe that there is a distinction in kind between the thin and the thick. They are wrong for other reasons.

However, if you do not think that the distinction is plausible, that should not stop the interest in this book. True, the structure of my discussion with its talk of the *genus–species* model and how I use that to introduce the arguments will seem beside the point. Yet, the topics that I discuss in what follows will not be. We still need to understand the thin*ner* concepts and how they relate to more specific ones, and we need to understand how, if at all, one can disentangle the thinner sorts of approval from the information and connotations that thick*er* concepts convey and carry. Even those that believe in a difference only of degree believe in a difference, and so they should think hard about how the more and less specific evaluative concepts relate.

One thing we have learned from the previous discussion is that evaluative content is more varied than might at first appear; it may be more than just PRO and CON. As the reader is already aware, this is a key claim of this book. Even by focusing only on thin concepts—which are so often introduced and then quickly ignored in discussions of the thick—we can see that there is more to be said about evaluative content. The difference between GOOD and RIGHT, and the question of where DUTY, OUGHT, and AESTHETICALLY GOOD fit in to the thin/thick divide are questions that require serious thought.

Before we turn our attention to separationism explicitly, I engage with one of the most interesting moral philosophers of recent times. This is partly to position him in relation to the ideas of the previous chapter, but it is mainly to introduce a point of his analysis that is pertinent to how I am treating separationist uses of the thin.

4.5 Gibbard and L-censoriousness

Allan Gibbard, in a 1992 debate with Blackburn, introduces his analysis of thick concepts, which itself is an expansion of his brief discussion in Gibbard (1990). He rejects what he calls 'two component' analyses of thick concepts of the sort we investigated in Chapter Two when looking at conjunction and licensing. Among other reasons for rejection, he mentions that if such analyses were applied, then disputants could end up (incorrectly) characterized as talking past one another.[8] In the end he draws up something like Elstein and Hurka's proposal, in so far as his analysis also has some looseness to the descriptive component. However, as we saw in Chapter Two Blackburn's favoured analysis now accommodates some looseness, so even though some difference between the two writers remains as we shall shortly see, there may not be as much of a difference between Gibbard in 1992 and Blackburn's more recent view as there was in the 1992 debate.

---

[8] Gibbard (1992), p. 277.

I do not pursue all of the details of Gibbard's analysis here. Instead, I focus on one aspect of it. Here, for illustration, is Gibbard's analysis of his target example, LEWD.

So, 'Act X is lewd' means this: L-censoriousness toward the agent is warranted, for passing beyond those limits on sexual display such that (i) in general, passing beyond those limits warrants feelings of L-censoriousness toward the person doing so, and (ii) this holds either on no further grounds or on grounds that apply specially to sexual displays as sexual displays.[9]

What I focus on is Gibbard's 'feeling of L-censoriousness'.

Clearly what we have here is something explicitly different from the PRO and GOOD elements with which I have so far been working. I am not so bothered about the fact that Gibbard's analysis explicitly introduces the idea of a feeling; that is to be expected from someone who is working within the noncognitivist tradition. What *is* interesting is the fact that the noncognitive feeling cited is not as thin as we have been used to. Perhaps this fact exposes something wrong in my discussion thus far.

My discussion has saddled separationists with a view of the thin that is under-developed, both in the sense of there being not much thought about it, but also in the sense that there is an explicit assumption that there is not much to it. I began to poke and prod that idea in §4.2 by showing that there may be a range of thin concepts (or thin elements) that we might wish to work with. That is supposed to introduce us gently to the idea that evaluative content can come in a range of thicknesses, and that be a perfectly natural idea. But with Gibbard we see a separationist who has a very specific sort of noncognitive element explicitly encoded into his analysis. So perhaps I should not keep on working with something really thin when criticizing separation-ism. Perhaps I am attacking a straw man.

I applaud Gibbard's analysis in that it does not work with PRO or some other very thin element. Although he makes hardly anything of this move, it is important to realize that separationists need not be committed, at least *prima facie*, to a very thin element in their analysis. As separationists, all that they are committed to is this familiar run of ideas: thick concepts are created from separable elements that themselves are not thick, typically some thin (or thinner) element (often conceptual content, often noncognitive feeling), plus some descriptive, nonevaluative conceptual content. Gibbard's analysis plumps for an element that is more specific than what we are used to, but—before criticism—that is itself not enough to stop his analysis from being separationist.

However, now I come to that criticism. I raise two general points, and then tie them to what Gibbard says. I assume for the moment that separationists will be noncogni-tivists of some sort, but what I say in relation to this will then allow for a criticism of cognitivist-separationists, one that ties to the first two sections of this chapter.

---

[9] Gibbard (1992), pp. 280–1. The looseness, for example, comes with the "passing beyond those limits", but it leaves it open as to what the limits are and the extent to which passing beyond them gives us something like a lewd action rather than something different and/or even worse.

First, a point about how concepts are supposed to work according to separationists. Recall that separationists are trying to provide an analysis of what is involved in a thick concept, and recall also that any ingredients that go to make the thick concept are, by definition, conceptually prior to their product. In which case, although we can talk, perhaps in an offhand manner, of the thin element in terms of the thick one, we need to be absolutely clear that in the final analysis this thin element cannot be identified and isolated by a theorist simply by their using the target thick concept or term. This is because the target thick concept is what we are trying to characterize in the first place.

This is strictly a point about the thin element and a particular, individual thick concept product. It could be that we identify a thin element using a *different* thick concept or term that has already been analysed. But, of course, the same stricture would apply when characterizing *that* concept. Unless we want to embrace a vicious regress, at some point there has to be some analysis of some thick concept where no thick concept or term is used, even if that thick concept is then used to help define further thick concepts.

My worry with regards to Gibbard is that his invocation of L-censoriousness falls obviously foul of this first point. We are picking out a feeling by explicitly using the thick concept, LEWD, that we are trying to analyse. This seems illegitimate. However, there may be a way out of this thought, for both Gibbard and other noncognitivist-separationists who wish to include in their analysis a 'thicker-than-bare-thin' evaluative element. This brings me to my second point.

The second point concerns psychology. The rescuing move for Gibbard and separationists like him is to say that we can pick out and have knowledge of a specific sort of element without first identifying it through use of any thick concept or term. Sure, we might label it by using some thick term, but that is only for convenience's sake and happens only after we have got used to isolating the feeling. Indeed, the thick concept gets formed because we are so used to the feeling. The key point is that certain sorts of feeling are psychologically real and are clearly felt things that we can isolate and identify in the right way. We can easily see them as prior to any thick concept.

This defence of this sort of separationism stands and falls on the plausibility of the claim about psychology. There is no doubt at all that humans, even just 'typical humans', have a wide range of experiences and feelings and that these could be used as the building blocks in the way envisaged by Gibbard. But—and this is a big 'but'—are we confident that we have a large variety of experiences sufficient to help build all of the thick concepts we wish to build?

Gibbard's own analysis is of an extreme form. It suggests that there is a one-to-one mapping from specific feeling to specific concept. There is no way that L-censoriousness will be involved in any other sort of thick concept. It is true that there is some descriptive content involved in Gibbard's analysis and that will help to define the thick concept. But, even then, if we changed the descriptive content it is hard to imagine a different sort of thick concept emerging once we have plugged in L-censoriousness.[10]

In which case, it seems that we will need as many specific feelings that we can isolate as there are specific concepts to be analysed. This is the first worry we can raise against Gibbard's view. Is there a specific feeling associated with JUST, with ELEGANT, with ILLUMINATING, and with many, many more examples? I doubt this very strongly. Moreover and second, we will have to be confident that there is some fine degree of agreement in feeling across all people such that we can speak of there being common concepts of LEWD and all the rest. In advance of a huge psychological-cum-sociological research programme that investigates this philosophical issue, we should refrain from drawing any definitive conclusion. But I am highly doubtful that we have this range of feelings sufficient to justify this sort of analysis.

A third, connected worry is raised by Blackburn against Gibbard.[11] Blackburn thinks that there is a large variety of feelings (or 'attitudes') that attend to most sorts of thick concept; in short he accuses Gibbard of failing to take account of evaluative flexibility.[12] This familiar point indeed strikes home. We might rejoice in something being lewd, and it "comes from the same neck of the woods as provocative, fruity, naughty, salacious, racy...".[13] Blackburn questions why lewdness should be portrayed in negative terms with talk of 'censoriousness'. As part of that, his examples support my first criticism: are we confident that we can tightly isolate different sorts of fine-grained feeling such that we have the feeling associated only with lewdness, the feeling associated only with raciness, the feeling associated only with naughtiness (and the right sort of naughtiness at that), and so on? Again, I emphasize the point: Gibbard's analysis may work for some thick concept families; the family of KIND, SYMPATHETIC, EMPATHETIC comes to mind. There *are* families and individual concepts that are obviously based on certain sorts of common feeling and emotion. But I do not think it will work for other examples.

So there is a large question mark hanging over the thought that separationists can and should employ highly fine-grained feelings in their analyses of thick concepts.

---

[10] Perhaps a rewording while retaining L-censoriousness might give us some concept that maps onto the idea of sexual activity and display that *is* acceptable. 'The feeling of L-censoriousness would be warranted if...but this is not one of those occasions and the feeling is not warranted and the sexual display is acceptable.' I am not sure what concept this would be, exactly, in English, and the wording is not quite correct anyway, since I think that separationists should be wary of assuming that terms such as 'warranted' and 'acceptable' are nonevaluative. Putting these matters aside, if some feelings do lend themselves to being used by us to analyse two or even a few thick concepts, the spirit of the point in the main text still holds: there will have to be a very large number of individual feelings in order for us to analyse concepts in this way.

[11] Blackburn (1992), pp. 291ff.

[12] Or, given what I said in Chapter Three, 'a range of specific, positive and negative evaluations linked to highly similar concepts'.

[13] Blackburn (1992), p. 295.

Yet, recall that I have characterized Gibbard's analysis as extreme. What if we had worked with feelings that were more coarse-grained than L-censoriousness, yet more fine-grained than some bare pro or con attitude? These feelings are envisaged as helping to isolate the thick concept we require, but are not themselves doing the whole job or even just most of it. In effect, such feelings do less than Gibbard envisages. We then allow the descriptive content to 'fill in' and, in effect, be the thing that helps to individuate every thick concept. This seems a more promising strategy, at least in so far as it is not obviously subject to the criticism I have been making of Gibbard's analysis.

However, this relies on that descriptive conceptual content being sufficient to cover or mimic the thick concept. In Chapter Five we will examine a powerful argument that suggests that it cannot do this job. To finish off this section, I switch to consider what we can say about cognitivist-separationists and this matter, and also reflect more generally.

What drives a lot of the criticism of this section is the idea that we do not have all of the fine-grained feelings sufficient to do the job required. But cognitivist-separationists are not interested in feelings. They prefer to say that we can employ some evaluative ideas, understood cognitivistically, in our analyses of thick concepts. However, they also have a tricky path to tread. They clearly do not wish such ideas of concepts to be themselves thick and components in some analysis, for that would make these components themselves nonseparable and basic. What if they assume that we can employ in our analyses some thin concepts (so-called) which are less than minimally or barely thin? That is, they eschew PRO and CON and work with OUGHT, DUTY, ACCEPTABLE, and other such ideas.

Certainly doing so avoids a worry that we may not have sufficient feelings to map onto the concepts we wish; no doubt we have a range of such thin*ner* concepts. But a different worry arrives, one that lingered in the background of earlier comments. Why would we feel the need to provide an analysis of (so-called) thick concepts and regard them as non-primitive, while also thinking that these thicker-than-bare-thin thin concepts *are* primitive and in no need of analysis? I may have argued across §4.2 and §4.3 that it would be unwise to jettison the idea of a difference in kind between the thin and the thick, but clearly my whole discussion raised the possibility of there being a lot in common between concepts traditionally classed using these two headings. Indeed, I showed that we could provide ways of distinguishing some of the thinner concepts from one another. They fall short of 'analyses', because detail was lacking, but we might very well suspect that analyses of the sort favoured by separationists could be forthcoming. At the very least, cognitivist-separationists who wish to employ in their analyses thin concepts that are thicker than PRO and CON owe us a great deal of discussion and defence as to why they use such concepts and why they are primitive.

It is time to draw some morals and a conclusion in this section. Separationists are committed to there being at least two elements that are to be included in their analyses of thick concepts. These elements cannot be isolated and captured by using thick terms and concepts, at least before any analysis has been carried out. We can assume that any thin evaluative element that is employed can, without problem, be barely thin: noncognitivist analyses can assume that we have some form of pro or con attitude, while cognitivist analyses can assume a simple PRO or CON concept. This, however, means that when we analyse and individuate thick concepts, all of the work is done by the descriptive conceptual content that is included as part of the analysis. (We will look at this in Chapter Five.)

If separationists do not take this route, then they are subject to worries. Non-cognitivists make the feeling or attitude associated with a concept more fine-grained than a simple pro- or con-attitude. The more fine-grained they make it then the more they run the risk of us querying whether we have a range of such feelings that can help to individuate our whole range of concepts. And they need to make sure they stop short of saying something as obviously viciously circular as 'the feeling that helps to isolate thick concept X is the X sort of feeling'. As part of this we may worry, with Blackburn, that there is not a single specific sort of feeling associated with any particular concept. There may be many such feelings, some of which may be positive and some of which may be negative.

Cognitivist-separationists who wish to 'thicken up' the thin element in their analysis are similarly in trouble. We may ask, quite simply, why the thicker-than-bare-thin thin concepts are treated by them as unanalysable and primitive, while thick concepts require analysis of a separationist kind. Such separationists owe us a detailed discussion which, with good reason, shows why it is that GOOD, RIGHT, and OUGHT, say, are primitive, but DUTY, AESTHETICALLY GOOD, WISE, and GROTESQUE are not.

The overall conclusion, then, is that separationists are on far safer ground if they assume that the thin element in their analysis of thick concepts is barely thin, just as Blackburn, and Elstein and Hurka do. As I have mentioned, this puts stress on the descriptive part of any analysis, and I discuss that in Chapter Five. Furthermore, our earlier thoughts in this chapter about the various thicknesses of (supposed) thin concepts might cause a little disquiet: according to the train of thought thus far, separationists are better off working with very thin notions of evaluation, but this may mean that they have to give separationist analyses of so-called thin concepts into some positive or negative part plus some descriptive part. There is nothing inconsistent with this as it stands, but it is an interesting development that I pick up in Chapter Six.

But we cannot jump to these matters now. It is one thing to assume or claim that there are barely thin concepts; I have assumed that, after all, with my invocation of PRO and CON. It is quite another to assume and argue for the idea that such concepts are conceptually prior to thick concepts. Before we tackle the descriptive, we need to tackle this idea. After all, this is the reason why I introduced the *genus–species* model in the first place.

4.6 Susan Hurley and Centralism

As well as asking what reason there is to think that thin concepts are conceptually prior to thick concepts, we also need to ask what is meant by the phrase 'conceptual priority' first of all, at least as it pertains to the debate in which we are interested.[14]

My understanding of 'conceptual priority' is fairly simple and plain: if we say that one concept is prior to another (and assume there to be some link between them) it means that the former has been involved in the creation of the latter, with the latter cast as some type of product. This clearly reflects my discussion in Chapter Three. There may, of course, be reasons why we wish to say that one concept is prior to another. Invoking these may give us only a sense of a particular *type* or *example* of conceptual priority and not give us a better sense of what the whole idea of conceptual priority means. Remember that when separationists think of thin concepts being prior to thick ones, they appear to be making a *general* claim. Even if they favour a particular, specific understanding of conceptual priority, advanced through examples, perhaps, they need a further argument that establishes that that is the best way of understanding the *general* idea. In my discussion below I consider three different examples of conceptual priority: 'social priority', 'learning priority', and 'justificatory priority'. These three illustrative examples do not get separationists close to justifying the priority of the thin over the thick in general, let alone give them conclusive victories.

Before we get to those examples, it is worth starting to think through these issues via someone who has already been here. Susan Hurley is to be credited with giving us some insights in this regard. In her *Natural Reasons* she identifies a position she calls 'centralism', which is the assertion that thin concepts are the central evaluative concepts, with thick concepts being derivative.[15] She opposes this position with 'non-centralism'. I prefer to say that separationists are committed to 'thin prioritarianism'. It is an uglier term, certainly, but speaking in this way allows us to introduce explicitly two opposing positions in a way that Hurley's terminology does not. She recognizes the two opposing options, but her terminology blurs this point. 'Non-centralism' covers two ideas. One could be a 'thick prioritarian' and claim that thick concepts are conceptually prior to thin ones. Or one could hold to a 'no priority' position and argue that across the whole class of evaluative concepts it is wrong to say that either type of concept is prior to the other.[16] There may be small family

---

[14] So I can talk of 'conceptual priority' for simplicity's sake, I talk of thin concepts being prior in the rest of this chapter, while acknowledging that noncognitivists may prefer the more neutral 'thin element'.

[15] Hurley (1989), pp. 13ff. See also Tappolet (2004). Tappolet also assumes that centralism about evaluative concepts fails.

[16] This position of 'no priority' is different from that labelled in the same way in McDowell (1987), p. 160 (cf. Wiggins (1998), pp. 195–6), although McDowell's (and Wiggins') idea is indicated in a different part of this study. The idea behind this other 'no priority' view is that one could see evaluative concepts as prior to feelings that one is identifying, or one could see the feelings as prior. This links with the ideas regarding Gibbard's analysis earlier in this chapter. Another, very closely related idea often labelled as a 'no

groupings that, for whatever reason, exhibit this sort of priority relation. Yet, it is wrong to generalize across all evaluative concepts. So with my terminology we have a clear three-way fight.[17] Below I discuss possible ways of arguing for thin prioritarianism. In doing so I argue against both this and thick prioritarianism, as I favour the no priority view.

Before that, a few comments on Hurley's discussion of the matter. Simply through her labelling she achieved a lot as she was able to identify a key and pervasive idea. However, she provides no knock-down argument against centralism, that is thin prioritarianism. Arguably, much of *Natural Reasons* is designed to show the attractions of the alternative view and the paucity of her opponents'. Despite the absence of a knock-down argument, she does have a promising argumentative strategy. Early on in her book she considers how centralism can and is applied in areas other than (explicit) the area of value and reason, and she tries to show the implausibility of centralism in the value and reason case; those other areas are the use of colour, mathematical, and legal concepts. Some of what she says amounts to the idea that 'we do not think as centralism says we should think in those other cases, so it is likely that we do not think in this way in the evaluative case either'. Put baldly like that, this point is unlikely to convince a neutral, let alone a thin prioritarian. This is partly because centralists may argue that we do think as they say we think, and also because many centralists try to abstract from practice and argue that we are trying to get some analysis of what is involved in the concepts themselves. We can talk of a concept being conceptually prior, in a philosophical analysis, while accepting that in practice ordinary users rely on both thin and thick concepts all the time. Hurley would probably have challenged this methodological guiding idea since her opposition to centralism is heavily informed by work from the later Wittgenstein who, as is well known, privileged the practice of concept use when understanding matters philosophically. That sort of tension in methodology will crop up in the next section. For now, as an illustration, let me talk through Hurley's strategy against colour centralism and how it can be continued.

To my mind she begins by attributing a mistaken view to centralists by assuming that centralism analyses RED in terms of COLOUR plus something that picks out red things, for example wavelength of a certain sort.[18] As mentioned, this is standardly not thought to be a serious option in discussions of the *genus–species* and determinable–determinate models. However, Hurley then usefully comments that we do not apply and understand COLOUR without applying and understanding RED,

---

priority' view is that idea that *properties* and value judgements are fitted to one another, and that neither one is prior to the other: properties do not come before judgements (as a mind-independent realist might think), nor do judgement come before pseudo-properties, as certain noncognitivists are characterized as thinking. See Wiggins (1998), pp. 196ff.

[17]   Hurley, when opposing centralism, seems to favour a 'no priority' approach, but this is not absolutely clear.

[18]   Hurley (1989), p. 15.

BLUE, and the like. However, she does not consider how centralists might respond, and I think in doing so we can extend the discussion in an illuminating manner. I do this now and drop talk of 'centralism'.

It is key to bear in mind that we are interested in the concepts themselves. Clearly anyone familiar with what it is to be coloured, and the colours themselves, will realize that if an object is coloured it is coloured in a certain way, and vice versa. Similarly, if an action is good it is good in a certain way, and we might also say that if an action has some thick concept applicable to it, it entails that there will be some applicable thin concept. But, *contra* Hurley, thin prioritarians about colour might say that this is a slightly different point from having decent understanding of the concepts themselves. They might argue that when we focus just on the concept COLOUR (or COLOUREDNESS), we have some related ideas of 'objects being filled in visually'. We have enough understanding of what being coloured is apart from any understanding we have of the various colour concepts. Well, perhaps. But my example phrase of 'objects being filled in visually' seems to be simply a synonym for 'being coloured', and it is hard to come up with something that is not. Furthermore, it might be suggested that we cannot understand what it is for an object to be coloured unless we have some idea of exclusion and contrast: if something is coloured it has to be a particular colour that excludes other particular colours, and this seems to invite the idea that we can understand COLOUR only if we understand the concept of being a particular colour, which might then further invite the thought that we have to have some understanding of the familiar colour concepts RED, BLUE, and the rest.

Thin prioritarians about colour might counter this line of thought with further ideas. Whatever we say about this local debate, it seems more important that those who wish to challenge thin prioritarianism about colour focus on thin prioritarians' commitment to the *genus–species* model. As should be familiar by now, this model involves two points of interest: the *genus* and the *differentia*. Once we focus on the fact that some *differentia* needs to be produced for each of the various specific colour concepts, we see that none can be given. (We saw this in the previous chapter.) It is this, rather than attention to the thin *genus*, that provides the killer blow to any two-component analysis of specific colour concepts such as RED.

Is the evaluative case analogous? No, but to the detriment of those that wish to oppose thin prioritarianism. Focusing on the *differentia* may also damage the *genus–species* case, but—again, boringly—this is the topic of Chapter Five. Our focus here is on the thin *genus*. Do we have decent understanding of GOOD and PRO prior to any understanding of specific thick concepts? Unlike the analogous questions about colour, where I have indicated that there may be something that thin prioritarians can say in their defence, our answer here is strongly in the affirmative. I have already discussed the ideas PRO and CON: we can certainly make sense of the idea of preferring one thing to another, of thinking of something as being on the positive (or negative) side of things, or thinking something better than another, and so on. Clearly such judgements strongly imply that a judge prefers something for some reason, whether or not she can articulate it. But any reasons she might offer for preferring something, say, do not seem intimately bound up with, or are simply not part of, the idea of preferring something and of thinking of something positively. These notions certainly do not seem as intimately bound up with the reasons for the positive view or preference as the specific colours might be bound up with the general concept COLOUR.

So I think it fair to say that although an interesting strategy, undermining thin prioritarianism about value concepts by looking at what happens with colour concepts is not foolproof. I think that we can make sense of the idea of PRO and CON without reference to thick concepts. But, crucially, even if thin prioritarians can make out that we have decent enough understanding of thin evaluations aside from other considerations, it is a *further* thing to establish that the best analysis of thick concepts is a reductive, separationist one that has them *constructed*, in part, from the thin. That, after all, is the key part of thin concepts being *prior*. A defence of this idea is normally missing. What could be the argument for it?

What I now do is examine three illustrative exchanges between thin and thick prioritarians. Thin prioritarians will try to show how thin concepts are prior. In contrast, thick prioritarians have to show that thick concepts play certain roles and fulfil certain conceptual needs in their own right, such that we undercut the motivation for having separationist analyses in the first place. In doing so thick prioritarians say, indeed they *have* to say, that it is the thick that comes first. No prioritarians make an appearance at the end of each exchange, emerging on top. This will take us back to Hurley's centralism.

4.7 Are Thin Concepts Conceptually Prior?

Let us imagine how the debate might go between thin and thick prioritarians, by imagining three brief illustrative exchanges. Although I have focused on thin prioritarianism, I begin by thinking about how thick prioritarians might argue.

First, thick prioritarians might challenge thin prioritarians by developing some of Williams' thoughts in *ELP*.[19] They might argue that although we use thin and thick concepts readily, thick concepts are tied more closely to our social and moral lives. Our justifications of action are more compelling if we use thick concepts rather than thin ones since we are better able to capture and describe various action types, as well as evaluate them, than if we used thin concepts alone. Our description of our social world is made brighter and clearer if we use thick

---

[19] Williams is not explicitly concerned with the issue of conceptual priority in Williams (1985). I think, however, that this extension of Williams' view is in keeping with his view of the thin and the thick. Recall that he thinks of thin concepts as more abstract concepts, where the suggestion is that they are abstracted from thick ones. I say more about this in Chapter Eight where I outline Williams' views about evaluative knowledge.

concepts. People get a better sense, a more detailed sense, of what it is to be an evaluating being if thick concepts are used. Although it is true that we can and do use thin concepts to justify actions, and to describe our social world and human agents, such uses are parasitic on our use of thick concepts, simply because of the (stipulated) merging of evaluatory and descriptive content in thick ones: they are conceptually closer to the (descriptive) world of which they are used when we evaluate.

Well, possibly. But I can imagine thin prioritarians, and neutrals, remaining unpersuaded. For a start, we need further justification that evaluative concepts are conceptually 'closer to' the nonevaluative world in a way that justifies them as being conceptually prior. An alternative picture, one amenable to thin prioritarians pre-sumably, has it that we conceive of the nonevaluative world and our (thin) evalu-ations as quite separate things, and we then have to derive our thick concepts in order to bridge the gap. (This recalls the fact–value distinction.) And, further, thin priori-tarians might put pressure on the more specific thoughts. Justifications can often be powerful if one uses no-nonsense thin concepts. Some actions are downright 'wrong' rather than the more vague and ambiguous 'beastly' or 'not on'. Thin concepts play an important role in working out the contours of our social world by marking clearly what is and what is not acceptable. They are direct, clear, simple, straightfor-ward, and unambiguous. They give us a way of thinking that thick concepts do not offer; while thick concepts can be used of wrong actions, for example, and can imply the wrongness of those actions, they work in these ways while necessarily picking out or alighting on other aspects. There is little here to persuade thin prioritarians.

However, a neutral might think differently. In defending their position perhaps thin prioritarians are merely digging their heels into their entrenched view. Where is the justification to think that thin evaluative content and descriptive content are prior in the way assumed? Indeed, we can begin to see the attractions of no prioritarianism: why not think, instead, that our thin and thick evaluative concepts are as useful as each other, that justifications of actions, and descriptions of our world and of agents, are best if we use both sorts of concept? Indeed, perhaps our judgements make sense only within a network of all sorts of evaluative concept, both thin and thick.[20]

Consider a second challenge. Imagine we think of conceptual priority in terms of learned priority. Thick prioritarians might argue that it makes sense to think that we start with certain fine-grained responses, certain ways in which we like things, or are disgusted by other things, and from that develop the more general concepts of preference, avoidance, and the like, which seem then to be translated into our developed concepts of GOOD and BAD.

But this is a difficult point to accept. For a start, if anything the psychological evidence points the other way. As babies and toddlers we begin with certain basic responses—yuks and joys—that seem to be coarse versions of thin concepts, and

---

[20] Ronald Dworkin voices this view, albeit briefly and in the context where he thinks that there is some continuum between thick and thin. Dworkin (2011), p. 183.

then, as we move about the world and learn more about it, we refine these concepts and develop more fine-grained responses, often with the help of others. These fine-grained responses are our thick concepts. It makes sense to be a thin prioritarian.

If we have to choose one or the other, we can say that the evidence favours thin prioritarianism on this particular point. However, why think that a story about how mature users of evaluative concepts learn those concepts when they are immature should decide which type of concept is *conceptually* prior? The story might indicate only what it is set out to show, namely 'temporal, learnt priority'. It indicates what sort of concept it is easier for young humans to latch onto and understand, not which sort of concept, if any, should be assumed to be conceptually prior to the other. And anyway, the assumption of a two stage process—where we begin with some thin responses that are already fully formed or become so, and *then* we develop thicker ones—seems far too cut-and-dried an account of something as complex as developmental psychology. The first thought seems to cast doubt on the general argumentative strategy. The second, while accepting this strategy, suggests that even if there are local derivative relationships based on how people learn and develop concepts, it seems better, at least as a safety-first option, to adopt a no priority view as correct for thin and thick concepts generally.

What of our third illustrative debate? Imagine any item deemed good. Presumably it will be deemed good because of certain features it has: perhaps a person is good because she has opened the door for another; perhaps the foodstuff is good because it has a certain texture and taste. Mentioning such descriptive features clearly invites a marrying of evaluative and descriptive content: the person is kind, the foodstuff succulent. So, the thought might go, if one can apply thin concepts such as GOOD, one *has* to be able to apply thick concepts. Perhaps this suggests, then, that thick concepts are prior in some fashion.

But this is clearly a poor challenge. For the challenge to be successful we need the phenomenon to show clearly that thick concepts are prior and thin ones derivative. Yet the phenomenon shows no such thing. These examples could equally well show the opposite, that thin ones are prior. After all, we might say that if one can apply a thick concept to something one *has* to be able to apply a thin one.[21] If something is deemed to be a certain thick way then it must follow that it has to be judged to be a certain thin way. If the food is succulent then, *prima facie*, it is good. If the person is gracious, she will also typically be good.

So something has gone awry here. What either sort of theorist needs in order to cement their claim is the idea that a certain sort of evaluative concept applies to an object and the other sort of evaluative concept does not apply. I find it hard to imagine a case where a thing is deemed bad and where that thing has no features that could be used to 'thicken' the thin categorization. Similarly, I find it hard to imagine a

---

[21] I examine this claim in Chapter Six, but only in a way that supports the overall suggestion that no prioritarianism is attractive.

case whereby something can be judged in a thick way and a thin concept not apply, where this case justifies the overall conclusion that the thick is prior to the thin.

Again, the possibility of a no priority view comes into view here. We do not have much positive reason to prefer it, I think, from this little exchange, aside from the fact that wherever we can apply one or more thin concepts, we can apply one or more thick concepts, and vice versa. It seems that when it comes to justifications, we can have explanations going in both directions: this is a thin way because it is a thick way, and this is a thick way because it is a thin way. The two sorts of concept seem to work together and be as useful as one another.

This is, admittedly, a fairly thin and sketchy reason for preferring the no priority view, but there is nothing in this exchange to count against it either. Hence, in the absence of any reasons to the contrary, this at least shows the view as an important contender.

Where do these three illustrative examples leave us? At each stage in our exchanges we saw that it might make sense to think of thin and thick concepts being inter-dependent. Perhaps the idea of conceptual priority does not make sense, either thinking that the thin is prior to the thick, or that the thick is prior to the thin. And this is telling. We began on this path because we wanted to undercut the motivation for thin prioritarianism, that is centralism. Even if one could make a decent case for having some understanding of thin concepts as thin concepts alone, it is another thing to say that we then must reductively analyse thick concepts partly in terms of them. Such an analysis depends on being able to provide a descriptive *differentia* for each thick concept, a topic to come. But in association with that, we can ask why someone would try to analyse thick concepts in a separationist manner in the first place. It seems curious to do so if they are used as much as thin concepts, grow interdependently with them in some evaluative network, and seem to have their own point and purpose.

Yet, notice that if we think that this idea has any merit, it is available only to no prioritarians. In saying that thin concepts are derived from the thick in some way, thick prioritarians deny the importance of the relations that thin concepts have with thick ones, that any role they play will be derived and based on thick concepts and so on. If we are to loosen the hold that thin prioritarianism might have over us, and if we do so by emphasizing the interdependence of evaluative concepts and the individual, genuine roles that they all play, we cannot do so by switching to a counter doctrine that denies just that for thin concepts. In short, the broad moral from Hurley's attack on centralism is that it is wrong to think that either sort of concept is prior to the other sort simply because such thinking is very curious and strange. The view that is forming is that thin and thick concepts are as important, useful, and illuminating as each other. Although it is tempting, trying to analyse (and partly reduce) the one in terms of the other is a chimerical and misguided aim.

After all of this, do we have a knock-down argument against separationism here, something that any reasonable thinker could accept as showing the view as implausible? I think the answer is negative. I have not exposed any sort of internal inconsistency, and I can imagine comebacks from separationists and worries about my sketched view. Some might think that there is no interconnected network of thin and thick concepts or, if there is, we should plunge deeper and show that there is this network only because the thin sits at the centre or the base. This is enough to motivate us to look for other anti-separationist arguments, even if we think that separationism is on the back foot, with its claims about the priority of the thin being exposed as weak.

4.8 Conclusion

In this chapter I have focused on the *genus* side of the *genus–species* relation. Along the way I have voiced support for a few views. I think that separationists are on safer ground if they assume the thin *genus* element in their analysis to be as thin as is possible rather than if they thicken this element up somewhat. As part of this I showed that one can thicken up thin concepts and still talk with some confidence of these concepts being thin. This itself should make us doubt that we can separate thick concepts, for then we are left with what to do with those thicker-than-bare-thin thin concepts. This doubt will be worked out in Chapter Six.

I have also shown that there is an onus on separationists to argue that thin concepts are conceptually prior to thick ones. My short discussion illustrated how difficult it will be to convince people that thin concepts are prior in the way needed.

So there is some reason already to be sceptical of separationism, but we need to think about the other side of the *genus–species* divide. As I have been promising, we now need to think about the *differentia*.

5

Disentangling and Shapelessness

5.1 Introduction

In the previous chapter I suggested that the first anti-separationist strategy fails to convince. In this chapter we focus on the second anti-separationist strategy.[1] I said in my Introduction that they can be seen as linked since both stem from the *genus–species* model. We have focused on the thin. In this chapter we now turn our attention to the *differentia*. Recall that the key idea is whether separationists can develop a *differentia* unique for each and every thick concept that will create that concept when combined with some thin conceptual content.[2]

This issue has been a key point in the debate about thick concepts and metaethics generally over the past thirty years or so. However, it has not been put in terms of *differentia* and *genus–species*. Instead, people have talked only of the possibility of evaluative concepts being 'disentangled' into component parts, and whether evaluative concepts are 'shapeless' with respect to descriptive, nonevaluative concepts. I slot the debate about shapelessness into my overall discussion of the *genus–species*

---

[1] This chapter is a shortened version of Kirchin (2010a); that article is around 21,000 words. For those interested in a comparison, in this presentation the central argument remains at the same length, but I do not have as much textual exegesis of the papers by Blackburn and McDowell, I have deleted some notes, and I have deleted material at the end of the article on reductionism. However, this chapter, for obvious reasons, situates the debate more explicitly in the wider debate about thick concepts; I comment on the relative importance of the shapelessness debate in that debate. Despite these differences, I have not changed my philosophical views significantly since writing the article, although I do emphasize here that in the final analysis the argument is not wholly convincing. That is because, in this book and unlike in the article, I am able to contrast it with a different argumentative strategy, namely that which comes in Chapter Six.

McDowell's main discussions of disentangling and shapelessness are in McDowell (1979), (1981), and (1987). Blackburn responds to McDowell in Blackburn (1981) and (1998), chapter 4 §§2–5. Wiggins discusses the hypothesis in Wiggins (1993a) and (1993b), which respond to Railton (1993a) and (1993b). My original motivation for writing on this topic was to make sense of what is, frankly, a difficult idea that receives little detailed exposure. For example, the following mention or briefly summarize the shapelessness hypothesis, and all accept it more or less without question: Dancy (1993), pp. 84–6; Hurley (1989), p. 13; McNaughton (1988), pp. 60–2; and McNaughton and Rawling (2003), pp. 24–5, to which Lovibond (2003) is a reply (Lovibond discusses shapelessness at pp. 6–8). Two notable detailed discussions and criticisms of the shapelessness hypothesis are Lang (2001) and Miller (2013), §10.1.

[2] Recall an earlier footnote in Chapter Three, note 2: a *differentia* may be united with either PRO or CON, thus creating two different concepts. Again, although I speak of a unique *differentia*, I have this corrective in mind throughout.

model because this wider discussion helps to highlight what is at stake about disentangling.

The main moral of this chapter is that while separationists are committed to there being *differentia* that play the role we have envisaged them playing, the anti-separationist point concerning shapelessness does not quite work. That is not to say that separationists come out unscathed, but just that nonseparationists should look for a further argument, or set of considerations, beyond discussion of shapelessness. That is the motivation for my discussion in Chapter Six.

In §5.2 I orientate us, laying out how the terminology of my debate links with the normal way of talking about shapelessness. In §5.3 I lay out the anti-separationist argument used by nonseparationists. In §5.4 I list a few notes that need to be made explicit, and which normally are not, in order to understand better what is going on. These take up a fair amount of space, but are important for setting up the main discussion. In §5.5 and §5.6 I get to the heart of matters and show where the argument falls short, as typically given. In §5.7 I show how the argument may be revived and what power it retains. I also deal with possible responses. In §5.8 I conclude, arguing that some other sort of strategy is needed for us to adopt nonseparationism.

5.2 Cognitivism and Noncognitivism

The disentangling debate about evaluative concepts maps onto the debate about whether the *genus–species* model accounts for such concepts. Is it possible, for any and every concept traditionally thought to be thick, to 'disentangle' it into different, component parts? And, normally, these parts are assumed to be some thin evaluative conceptual content (or similar), and some descriptive conceptual content. I prefer to talk in terms of the *genus–species* model because that lays bare the sort of conceptual priority that separationists assume, and also allows us to introduce and reflect on other traditional conceptual models, such as the determinate-determinable model.

One interesting difference is that the 'disentangling debate' was fought most strongly between cognitivists and noncognitivists. In the former camp were, notably, McDowell and Wiggins. (Although he disagreed about some things with them, especially with McDowell, Williams was also sceptical that the disentangling manoeuvre could be made.) In the latter camp were people such as Blackburn and Gibbard. To my mind noncognitivists have to be separationists. But, as we have noted in earlier chapters, separationism can be combined with cognitivism about the thin. In this chapter I focus mainly on simple separationism, although I indicate towards the end how the discussion affects complex separationism.

The disentangling argument was not so much an argument for cognitivism, as an argument against noncognitivism. The explicit claim was that a noncognitivist account of evaluative concepts could not be made to work. I retain that broad orientation, although I am more doubtful than, say, McDowell, that the argument works. I also change terminology, and label this an 'anti-separationist' argument, for this is not really a positive argument for nonseparationism. That will come in Chapter Six.

The worry about disentangling focused on the descriptive conceptual content that was supposed to be part of any thick concept. It was assumed, contrary to the noncognitivism of the day, that evaluative concepts are shapeless with respect to nonevaluative recharacterizations of them, and that this called into serious question the disentangling move. To see why this is so, and to see what is meant by 'shapelessness', I now lay out the argument, leaving behind talk of cognitivism and noncognitivism.

5.3 Shapelessness and Outrunning

The argument starts simply. We divide situations, actions, and other things into different conceptual categories: *these* things are kind while *those* things are selfish. We should take as bedrock the idea that our normal conceptual divisions are rational. In other words, there has to be some reason to the divisions we make; they cannot be made capriciously and on a whim. It is commonsensical that we should be committed to thinking that there must be *something* that connects all of the items that are grouped together using any sort of evaluative concept, such as KIND, and furthermore something (probably the same something) that distinguishes them from other things grouped together using different concepts, such as SELFISH.[3] To preserve the idea that our divisions are non-capricious, what links certain items together has to be more than just the bare fact that they *are* grouped together by people, since this criterion is satisfied if people decide on only a whim that any randomly selected two actions are selfish, say. There needs to be something about the grouped items such that it is justifiable to group them.

The next stage is concerned with identifying what the 'something' is that connects all and only all the things deemed kind.[4] This move is premised on the fact that both sides are attempting to make sense of our conceptual practices.[5] Nonseparationists argue that neither of the two elements—the descriptive conceptual content used to

---

[3] As Blackburn (1981), pp. 180–1 agrees. Notice that in order to concentrate on the shapelessness hypothesis we assume that concept use is consistent across individuals at different times and, if need be, across communities.

[4] Talk of 'the something' might suggest a particular, isolatable thing, although we will see that nonseparationists should not think in this way at all.

[5] Despite their claim that ethical judgements are expressive of some noncognitive attitude, most modern noncognitivists still wish to accommodate ethical value, truth, rationality, and the like. This is motivated partly by their aversion to ethical relativism. They could confine themselves to claiming that ethical judgements function as expressions of attitude and not care about 'consistency' in any sense. They would then not face any objection motivated by disentangling and/or shapelessness, but their position would be suspect precisely because they had not tried to accommodate this notion. This point extends from ethics and noncognitivism to evaluative elements and separationism.

pick out stuff seen to fall under the concepts, and thin evaluative elements—taken separately and, hence, 'disentangled' could, on their own, explain such practices. Hence, it makes sense to think that the 'something' that connects all and only all the kind things must be (something we are justified in calling) the evaluative feature of kindness, some*thing* that we are picking out using a (genuine, unitary) concept.

Let us take each of these two elements in turn. A thin evaluative element, interpreted cognitivistically or noncognitivistically, will be insufficient to pick out all and only all the examples of an evaluative concept. We like or hoorah or think good many, many things and these thin positive responses are alone insufficient to distinguish the kind from the just, nor will they distinguish the kind from the sublime and the humorous. We have already had a taste, in Chapter Four, of how the battle will then go. Separationists can argue that the evaluative elements can be conceived to be less than minimal, and that we can thicken them up so as to enable us to distinguish as required. I have already given pause for thought here, as to whether really specific evaluative elements of the sort suggested by Gibbard exist widely, and can be used as he wishes to use them. Other separationists may wish to employ evaluative elements that are less than specific than the ones Gibbard suggests, but which are more specific than PRO and CON. Right now we can see that *even if* this sort of path is taken, a debate about shapelessness needs to happen. For at this point the evaluative element is less specific than the thick concept being analysed. So it stands to reason that some work will have to be done by some descriptive element, some *differentia*. Hence, there is a suspicion that this descriptive element, either in tandem with some (somewhat specific) evaluative aspect, or just on its own (with some minimal PRO or CON), will be insufficient to distinguish all of the evaluative concepts as required.

Thus, from now on I focus just on that descriptive element. It is at this point that the shapelessness hypothesis is introduced. We could specify that all kind actions have the same nonevaluative feature in common, and, hence, we can characterize kindness as simply being this feature. (And the same for all selfish actions, just actions, and so on.) But what would that feature or small number of features be? I suggest that it would very hard to find anything. For example, 'having concern for others' is too loose to do the desired work. If it is interpreted in a nonevaluative manner, then we have concern for others as part of all sorts of actions, not just kind ones: ones where we act bravely for people, ones where we cruelly torture people, and so on. Interpreting this idea in an evaluative manner is ruled out, obviously. But even then it is too loose and vague to do the required work.

And, anyway, if one thinks of the types of kind action there are, then a whole host of actions suggest themselves: opening doors for people, telling the truth, telling a 'white' lie, giving someone some sweets, refraining from giving sweets, and so on. Not only is there a wide variety of descriptive features that constitute various kind actions, many kind actions have no, or no evaluatively relevant, descriptive features in common. It seems that we will move quickly beyond the idea of there being a single descriptive thing common to all kind actions. Indeed, based on a quick list of the various kind actions there are, we might think that there is a fairly long, disjunctive list of descriptive features that might make an action kind. In short, we might have something like this: 'something is kind iff it has features *a*, *b*, *c*; or features *b*, *c*, *d*; or features *e*, *f*, *g*; or . . .', where the letters indicate things or features of things picked out using descriptive language alone.

And then we have the killer thought. Supposedly, our evaluative concepts are shapeless with respect to descriptive concepts and ideas. That is, if we were to try to find a pattern between all of the sets of descriptive features that constitute kindness, without trying to view things from an ethical or an evaluative point of view (or the correct ethical or evaluative point of view), we would not be able to see it. Why so? We will investigate that in full detail below, but the idea, briefly, is that the characterization I have just given in the paragraph above can never be completed. Notice the three dots at the end. An incomplete analysis is no analysis at all.

We can put these ideas slightly differently to develop a thought that will be the focus of my discussion.[6] It is plausible to say that we could imagine a cruel situation that would turn into a kind situation with the addition of one or more features. To take a simple example, it might be cruel to refrain from sharing chocolate with a young child who desperately wants it, but it can be kind if, in addition, we are acting because there is some risk of her teeth rotting in the future. In more complicated situations it might be kinder to share, despite the risk of tooth rot, because, say, someone has hurt her feelings and she needs comforting. Or, it might be kind to offer some extra chocolate just to this one child, even if justice and fairness demand otherwise, because nothing else will stop the tears flowing and there is no possibility of any lessons being learned or of any bad behaviour becoming entrenched from such a short-lived action. We can easily imagine that situations can become more complex than this and that it is always possible that the addition of new features, or the subtraction of existing ones, will affect the situation's ethical value. Or, in other words, the chocolate case and others like it motivate us to see that the variation of features relevant to the ethical value of the situations they constitute can continue indefinitely. The key thought is that KIND might *outrun* any descriptive characterization we could give of the actions deemed kind. I will refer to this throughout simply as 'outrunning'.

Why is this bad for separationists? They wish to identify 'something' that connects all and only all the kind actions. Imagine we try to create and employ a list of disjunctive clauses of the type I have just given. This list will merely be, by definition, a summary of all the descriptive features of the actions judged to be kind up to that point. The test is whether comparison of the list alone with a new action—an action with a combination of descriptive features never before encountered—will enable us

---

[6] This is a common strategy. See McDowell (1979), §4 and Wiggins (1993b), §§IV–VII. There is no concrete example in these passages, but the idea I present is clearly expressed.

to say correctly whether the new action is or is not kind. If the above train of thought is correct, then we need not arrive at the correct answer if we employ this method. It seems there could always be a kind action that escapes being captured by our list, or there could always be an action that according to the list should be kind but which is cruel because it has new features, combined in a way that has not yet been encountered. (That is, perhaps it does have features a, b, and c, but it also has feature x that renders the action cruel. This extra information is not encoded in the list, and so we judge incorrectly.) These thoughts are often brought to life by imagining an 'outsider'—an anthropologist, perhaps—trying to predict correctly the applications of evaluative concepts within an alien community. All she can see are descriptive features a, b, and c (and x). She has no appreciation of their evaluative significance and how the 'sequence' might continue with new clauses. I illustrate more thoughts using the outsider later.

Nonseparationists typically put these matters in a positive light and say—or said—that separationism's failure is to be expected since our evaluative concepts reflect, or are an expression of, our interests and such things cannot be reduced to descriptive, nonevaluative terms, or codified using non-interest-laden terms, or similar.[7] This thought will reappear in §5.6.

There is a lot to sort out here, even from this short introduction. I now turn to a number of notes we should consider in relation to the argument. In §5.5 I think about outrunning in detail.

5.4 Seven Notes

(a) Phrases such as 'mastery of a concept' are often bandied around in this debate. A number of ideas might be meant by this. I think we should be clear that, thus far, all that the debate is concerned with is whether a theorist can map the extension of evaluative concepts, and use this to guide future use.[8] I will offer one reason to support setting matters up in this way in §5.5.[9]

(b) Note that I gave no thought as to what 'levels of description' are appropriate when considering the characterization of the descriptive features that are seen to compose the evaluative features of things, that is the descriptive characterization of the relevant evaluative concept. Are we supposed to imagine recharacterizations that include the movements of agents' limbs? Can one include the agents' intentions? Can the whole argument be run in terms of sub-atomic structures? Usually no thought is given to this question in the context of this argument. The shapelessness hypothesis is

---

[7] For example, see Wiggins (1993b), §§IV–VII, where Wiggins speaks of the 'interest in the value V', by which he means some human interest; and see McDowell (1981), especially §2, where this idea is part of the whole point of the piece.

[8] See McDowell (1981), p. 145; McDowell uses 'mastery' in just this way.

[9] I discuss the phrase more and defend my whole argumentative set-up in more detail in Kirchin (2010a), §6.

presumed to be correct for any level of description we could choose. I will proceed on this assumption, although a fuller treatment than mine might consider if the level of description affects the plausibility of either side of this debate and why.

(c) Following on from (a) and (b) a more general point emerges. Earlier on, in characterizing the debate, I made out that the challenge for separationists is to provide the descriptive element and do so in a way that summarizes all of the aspects of all of the examples of the evaluative concept. That is, separationists are typically asked to provide a summary of the extension of the concept. But, we might ask, should we not be interested in the intension of the concept and associated term, that is the concept's meaning?[10] Are we not interested in concepts that are either PRO or CON and which, in addition, are those concepts that mean such-and-such?[11]

This is a good question to ask, which is rarely raised. Although it seems as if the move I have made is odd, if not just plain wrong, it is understandable in the context of this debate.

Note that separationists, as well as their opponents, often present matters that suggest 'extension' rather than 'intension'. The wording of Gibbard on LEWD and Elstein and Hurka on DISTRIBUTIVE JUSTICE suggest conditions that need to be fulfilled in order for the concept to apply, and these conditions are given in terms of aspects of things that fall under the concept. So it seems that in order to break down the meaning of a term or the content of a concept into more understandable parts, we can get a lower level of description and in doing that we are providing more specific descriptions of parts of the things that fall under the concept. This leads us from intension to extension generally and, in any instance, by concentrating on how the concept is 'extended' or applied to various things we can be led back to the meaning of the term: 'it is these types of thing that fall under the concept, because they have these aspects, and so we can list those aspects in order to get at the meaning of the term, and associated concept'.

We can challenge this move in a number of ways. I choose not to in this study, but instead make the following point. Separationists typically think that they will be able to provide short analyses of evaluative concepts, with few clauses; just think of the amount of text that the analyses of both Gibbard, and Elstein and Hurka take up. But the key anti-separationist idea, which we have yet to evaluate, is that any analysis, for any level of description, will not be that short. Gibbard's analysis of LEWD will not

---

[10] Some may shy away from speaking of a concept's meaning, preferring to say that terms alone can have meaning. I hope my slide here does not offend too greatly. The overall point is unaffected by it.

[11] For those who do not quite get the importance of this, we can distinguish, it seems, quite sharply between a term's (or associated concept's) meaning, and the things to which it applies. We can know the one, or believe we know the one, without knowing or articulating the other. So, for example, I can identify and apply FURNITURE to various items of furniture, possibly without being able to supply a clear and exact definition of 'furniture'. Similarly, I can have a clear and confident idea of how to apply SCOUT without knowing, or being aware of, all of the scouts and being able to list all of their various features. But, beyond that sharpness, which surely *can be* and *is* exemplified by a number of examples, we may get some grey area. In some cases we may be able to get at the intension only by reflecting on the extension.

cover all of the examples we want it to cover, perhaps. (Blackburn agrees on that.) Elstein and Hurka sneakily only put in three letters! And both analyses seem guilty of employing terms in their respective analyses that are not obviously descriptive. (Gibbard's WARRANTED comes to mind, here, which has to function as more than a simple PRO.) Once we look at some illustrative analyses, we will see that short versions will be suspicious. Just think of my 'having a concern for others' example from earlier. Similarly, to give one more example, saying that 'someone is wise if and only if they employ sufficient understanding and relevant knowledge' is nowhere near up to the task. For a start, being the sort of person who employs UNDERSTANDING or who is KNOWLEDGEABLE seems to bring in evaluative content, if not employ straightforward synonyms. Also, this analysis, in pointing to the balance and inter-play between two items, gives us only vague suggestions: what exactly is 'sufficient' and 'relevant' in this context anyway? Indeed, it is not obvious that these ideas are wholly descriptive.[12] I think we can imagine with confidence that the analyses given will rely on the extension of the concept, and that these extensions may well be quite long affairs.

Having justified that this is the battleground, nonseparationists argue that when we try to create extensions in descriptive terms we encounter the phenomenon of outrunning, thus showing separationism to be wrong.

(d) We should sort out the exact relationship between the disentangling argument and the shapelessness hypothesis. What I have said reflects, fairly I think, normal introductions of the debate. Yet, there is a large hole.[13] The traditional way of construing things makes it seem obvious that the shapelessness hypothesis can be run for any evaluative concept, including thin ones. After all, just think of the many sorts of good or right action there can be. But if that is the case, then the connection

---

[12] This point relies on my view about the evaluative, on which I elaborate in Chapter Six.

[13] An exception, which explains things neatly, is Roberts (2011). (Roberts also cites Dancy (2006), p. 128. Dancy points out that McDowell's shapelessness point may apply beyond evaluative and normative concepts to any 'resultant' concept which applies in virtue of the application of other concepts.) Roberts focuses on McDowell. She agrees that he was not writing about the thick specifically, but argues that there is a way of developing his thoughts so that there is a second sense of shapelessness that may (initially) apply only to thick concepts. (The first sense is that which I develop in the main text.) In short, she imagines us sharply distinguishing the content of a concept from the things in virtue of which it applies, in the manner I suggested earlier. There may be many types of thing that are kind, but what KIND is may not encapsulate all (descriptive) aspects of all those things, or even those aspects in virtue of which the term 'kind' applies. Indeed, continues Roberts, KIND may be such that it does not encapsulate any non-evaluative descriptive content. So, even when we apply it in *one* case, there may be no way to disentangle the evaluative from the descriptive: all the 'descriptive' content is infused with the evaluative, if one continues to talk in this *faux* language of two distinct contents. But, as she admits, crucially this sense of shapelessness applies also to thin concepts, for the content of GOOD, say, seems likely to differ from the descriptive aspects of the good things in virtue of which the label applies. We are, therefore, back to trying to find some difference such that the hypothesis applies only to thick concepts—which does not seem to be achievable—and back to separating the disentangling argument from the shapelessness hypothesis as I do in the main text.

between it and the disentangling argument requires clarification. If thin concepts involve evaluative content alone, then there are no supposed parts to disentangle.[14]

Below I develop the discussion as traditionally implied, as I take it to be, and think of the shapelessness phenomenon as applying equally and strongly to thin and thick concepts. So to underline the point, I reckon that the chocolate example could be run for GOOD and there be the same philosophical outcome. But we need to adjust the traditional set up. If shapelessness is proved in the case of thick concepts, then we cannot disentangle any supposed evaluative and descriptive content. If it is proved in the case of thin concepts, then we can say that there is no disentangling argument to then be given, although we can talk of the shapelessness hypothesis leading to *an* argument (perhaps the shapelessness *argument*) and *a* conclusion that are both similar to that reached in the case of thick concepts, namely that thin concepts should be thought of along nonseparationist lines.

Going down this route adds an extra argumentative aspect. It might be that thick concepts are shapeless *only because* they have an element—a *separable* element—of them that is agreed on all sides to be shapeless, namely thin evaluative content or some thin element. That is, even if the shapelessness of thick concepts is shown, it is still an open question as to whether they can be disentangled. I will comment on this in §5.7. What should be emphasized, however, is that my prime interest here is whether the shapelessness hypothesis is correct in the first place. We need to keep an eye on how it relates to the disentangling argument, but that should not dominate.

If I had decided not to go down this route and argued instead that thick concepts are shapeless in a way different from their thin cousins, then in addition to having to argue for there being a distinction between the types of concept, I would have had to have found something in that distinction or elsewhere that supported the anti-separationist conclusion. I do not rule out such a strategy, despite the route I take, although I think that finding such a reason to identify thick concepts as different or unique with regards to the supposed phenomenon of shapelessness will be very hard.[15]

(e) At certain points I have shifted between concepts and features. I have occasionally talked of evaluative features that concepts pick out, for example. We are certainly interested in concepts, but are we interested in features?

Let me put the worry more plainly. The argument seemingly has the following broad structure. We note something about how humans use certain concepts. We argue that these concepts cannot be replaced by other concepts and there be the same extension. We then conclude that there must really exist corresponding features that

---

[14] I have suggested that some thin concepts are less thin than others. But (i) separationists may disagree and, anyway (ii) the point in the main text at least applies to PRO and CON.

[15] See again note 13. Even Roberts admits that her second sense of shapelessness applies equally to thin and thick concepts.

the original concepts pick out.[16] This last move seems a little wild. Why think that anything about human concept use implies, let alone entails, anything ontological? Are nonseparationists, through employment of the disentangling argument, committed to a type of evaluative realism?

I agree that this move seems less than innocent. Indeed, it is clear that people who have argued for the hypothesis, and those who have referenced it, have been opaque in their language. There are two things we could do. First, having noted the worry we could be strict with ourselves and previous writers. Perhaps all that we have is an argument for a nonseparationist cognitivism and we should ignore any reference to features and properties. We should sharply distinguish cognitivism—concerned with whether concepts have the possibility of referring (successfully) beyond themselves and 'encoding' knowledge—from realism, and acknowledge that even if we have established that our evaluative concepts are unitary, we leave it open as to whether they refer to anything, thus making an evaluative error theory an obvious and live possibility. This option certainly has its attractions, not least because cognitivism and realism *are* different. But why would writers have slipped into talking about features and properties every so often? Perhaps because there is a tendency to think that evaluative concepts' legitimacy as referring concepts makes sense only if one thinks that they can be and generally are used successfully. This is not to say that an evaluative error theory is not still a serious contender. But it is true that many feel awkward about it, not least because it aims to show as false such a widespread and seemingly essential way of thinking and speaking. Indeed, one might say that evaluative thinking has so many important aspects to it that it seems implausible to think that all of them are dodgy such that the whole is bogus.[17]

This leads, then, to a second way of viewing what we have. Perhaps we are being too harsh here. The conclusion of the overall argument might be better expressed as saying that our use of evaluative concepts strongly implies that we must take seriously the idea that corresponding evaluative features are, in some sense of the term, real. This need not commit us to the claim that evaluative features are as ontologically serious and proper (whatever this means) as, say, the features and properties of a supposed final scientific theory. Rather, it invites us to explore further the question of what 'real' means in this sense, and how we can make sense of the idea of real evaluative features that are real from a perspective of human evaluators; of how we can explain that there is something about the world to which we are responding rather than our evaluative categorizations being something that are

---

[16] McDowell frequently moves between concepts and features in McDowell (1981) for instance, although the features in question are often 'theoretically massaged' with the thought that they are, broadly, response-dependent in some fashion. Wiggins, although more careful in his writings, also moves between 'subjective responses' and associated properties in Wiggins (1998), essay V.

[17] See Kirchin (2010b) for an argument along these lines.

wholly a product of our 'gilding and staining'.[18] Obviously, even if the shapelessness hypothesis works, there is still much work to do in this vein, and important work at that as failure on this point will probably undermine the whole hypothesis. I will expand on these comments in my final chapter. All I wish to state is that we should not reject the argument out of hand simply because it seems to magic, by mere sophistry, some ontological rabbit out of a conceptual hat. What we can reject out of hand are those that talk exclusively of 'features' and 'properties' and who think the argument is clearly and uncontroversially an argument that establishes a metaphysical conclusion.

(f) What is the precise aim when using the shapelessness hypothesis? Here is a distinction between two readings of it. Should nonseparationists be trying to prove, from their philosophical armchairs, that outrunning does and will occur and, hence, that separationism is false? Call this the *strong version* of the shapelessness hypothesis. Or should nonseparationists claim merely that there is a reason or some reasons to think that when we carry out the necessary empirical investigation of our concepts, we will find the shapelessness hypothesis to be correct and, hence, we have reason to doubt the truth of separationism? Call this the *moderate version*. In other words, our distinction is this: when we empirically investigate how evaluative concepts work, either we will confirm what we have already shown to be true, or we will confirm what we suspected to be true.

I think neither version is correct, but later I argue, more positively, that a third option has a chance of working. In brief, the first two readings of the hypothesis assume that empirical work will definitely show that evaluative concepts are shapeless with respect to descriptive concepts. The third reading denies this: we will probably never show anything definitive in this regard. A better characterization of the hypothesis states that we are justified in supposing, in any case and after some empirical work, that the evaluative could be shapeless with respect to the descriptive. I argue that this gives some support to nonseparationism, although probably not definitive, knock-down support. I provide more detail later.

Whether or not one thinks these two readings are defensible, it is worth noting that both the strong and the moderate versions can be found in the core writings on this topic. For example, in McDowell (1979), §4 McDowell seems to imply that the argument shows conclusively that noncognitivism, that is separationism, cannot be correct.[19] His supporters are similarly bold.[20] On the other hand, in

---

[18] See McDowell (1983) for a discussion of this topic. McDowell is responding to Williams' thoughts, located in Williams (1978) for example, about the 'absolute conception of reality'.

[19] One referee for OUP suggested that my third option *is* expressed by McDowell, perhaps with this phrase in mind. I disagree, although in the broad narrative of this book this exegetical disagreement is secondary. The phrase I quote comes from the following context: we have not yet conducted any empirical work and so we can be sceptical now, but we assume that such work can be done and that the truth will out when we do this. As we will see, my third option is different from this.

[20] Sometimes it is hard to discern to what a writer is committed if they have not made explicit the distinction that taxes us, in this case that between the moderate and strong versions. However, despite their

McDowell (1981), p. 144, he thinks that the argument makes it only "reasonable to be sceptical about" separationism (that is, noncognitivism). I think this phrase, and other such phrases in the rest of the section, are meant as they stand and are not academic 'hedges'. Similarly, Wiggins, in Wiggins (1993b), §§IV–VII, thinks that he has not shown conclusively that Peter Railton's naturalistic, reductionist realism is impossible, but only that we should be sceptical about its chances.

For completeness's sake, let me state that I have not found my third option in the literature.

One last point. In introducing the argument we might wish to say things such as 'according to nonseparationists, there *will be no* descriptive match to the evaluative concept' or 'any such recharacterization *will* fail'. But, after reflection on these two readings, we might say that before we do any empirical work we should state that 'there *will almost certainly be no* descriptive match . . . ' and 'any such recharacterization *will almost certainly* fail'. Or, once we have considered my third reading, we might say something else.

This links to my last point in this section, which provides us with one reason for initially preferring the moderate version.

(g) Should we construe the shapelessness hypothesis as an a priori claim or an a posteriori claim?[21] This can be a misleading question. Clearly the claim cannot be a wholly a priori one. We cannot plausibly claim what the relationship between evaluative concepts and supposed descriptive counterparts is likely to be, let alone show what it is, through theoretical reflection alone on the nature of evaluative concepts. We have to draw on our experience of how evaluative concepts are used in order to support the hypothesis, no matter whether it is construed moderately or strongly. But saying that the claim is an a posteriori one might mislead. We might think that we can prove the claim to be true simply by going through all of the evaluative concepts that are used, or at least a central stock of them, and showing that the phenomenon of outrunning is common. Clearly this would be difficult to do to

qualifications (such as "it may be the case that"), I reckon that Dancy (1993), p. 76 and McNaughton (1988), p. 61 can be read as siding with the strong claim. McNaughton and Rawling (2003), pp. 24–5 are bolder. They assume, for argument's sake, that noncognitivism is defeated by the 'pattern problem' and that there exist normative facts.

[21] This sub-section is directed against Miller (2013), §10.1, esp. pp. 245–9. Miller goes wrong in failing to distinguish between moderate and strong versions, although it is clear that he thinks that nonseparationists (that is, cognitivists) put forward a strong version. He dismisses the shapelessness hypothesis because he thinks that McDowell—in advocating the strong version—has wrong targets. On Miller's construal those that argue using the shapelessness hypothesis will be successful only if we assume that separationists (that is, noncognitivists) claim that by conceptual a priori reflection alone one can prove that descriptive recharacterizations of evaluative concepts are possible. But, as he points out, separationists do not claim that. They claim that empirical work and substantive evaluative theorizing will reveal that evaluative concepts can be recharacterized in this way. And no a priori argument will work against that: we need empirical research to counter it. But if we introduce the moderate version, we can see that nonseparationists' aims can be different and their position less easy to dismiss. Thus, I go into more detail than Miller does about the ensuing debate between the two sides.

say the least: there are a lot of such concepts and outrunning seems to be something that will involve an awful lot of investigation.[22]

What seems to be misleading here is the assumption that we have only empirical types of justification matched with a desire to prove the strong version to be true. But nonseparationists have not gone in for such methods and, given the difficulty of proving the strong claim, even by empirical methods, this seems right. What they typically do instead is offer some examples drawn from real-life experience, such as my chocolate example, and from that reflect on the nature of evaluative concepts generally. Clearly this sort of method will not provide enough evidence for the strong version, and if we did think that this is what nonseparationists are trying to do it would be easy to dismiss their argument.

Assuming that they are not wholly misguided in what they are attempting to do, perhaps we should construe matters along the following lines: from description of limited experience, and reflection drawn from such experience about the nature of evaluative concepts, nonseparationists are aiming to show that it is likely that, if thorough empirical work were done, we would find that no, or no central, evaluative concept could be recharacterized in the manner suggested. This is clearly an expression of the moderate version.

These seven notes touch on some deep issues—levels of description, ontology, the distinction between a priori and a posteriori investigation—and, while making some positive points, for other points I have done no more than advertise them as worries and bracket them to the side. With such a subtle, sometimes obscure, wide-ranging argument this is inevitable. I hope that the reader forgives what bracketing there has been; this is necessary so that I can set up the discussion and assess the hypothesis directly. (I also hope the reader forgives the length of these notes.) With that said, then, let us now return to the main flow of my discussion. How might a more detailed exposition of outrunning proceed?

5.5 Outrunning

One idea to bear in mind as we consider outrunning is that proponents of the shapelessness hypothesis have never based their claim on any supposed epistemic inadequacy of humans. The focus is on the nature of evaluative concepts. Something about them, no matter how intelligent and imaginative humans are, is such that they cannot be captured correctly in descriptive ways by us, or are unlikely to be so.

The (supposed) phenomenon of outrunning is something that occurs because there is a gap between the extension of an evaluative concept and the extension entailed, or encoded by, some descriptive recharacterization of that concept

---

[22] I draw out exactly how much in the following section.

given in some list. What is required is some consideration of how large those extensions will be.

Imagine, for argument's sake, that there is only a finite number of ways, be it five or 20,005, in which actions get to be kind. Could outrunning then occur? Assuming that we do not have recourse to the epistemic inadequacy of humans, and assuming that we are dealing with humans who have a fair amount of time and are diligent, there seems no reason in principle to imagine that we could not produce a list that captured the finite number of ways in which actions get to be kind, even if that was a very large number. Thus, in order for the claim of outrunning to be an interesting challenge we have to assume that there is an infinite number of ways in which actions get to be kind. We can assume, for now, that evaluative concepts are infinitely complex in this way. I will examine this claim later.

Let us think instead about the list of descriptive clauses. Of course, it is highly plausible to claim that the lists that everyday humans can produce will have only a finite number of clauses, and we cannot ignore this. If KIND, say, is infinitely complex, we will not be able to capture it. But, again, this might well indicate only humans' epistemic limitations. Is there anything else to say here?

Imagine, again for argument's sake, that by some cosmic fluke humans as they are could produce lists with an infinite number of clauses. How they do so is crucial. We should recall that we are not interested solely in the descriptive capturing of evaluative concepts, but in whether this can be done 'from a nonevaluative point of view'. To illustrate, let us return to our outsider and introduce another figure, the insider. The insider is, by definition, a typical and mature user of some evaluative concept and so, in our imagined scenario, she would have the ability to convert her understanding of some evaluative concept into a complete capturing of descriptively characterized clauses. This should not unduly trouble nonseparationists. For a start, separation of thin evaluative element from descriptive feature in individual cases may be common.[23] When I judge something to be kind, I can nearly always focus on a feature or features that make it so. For example, I can say why someone's action was kind by pointing out that she gave up her seat on the bus for someone else who needed it, and approve of her action because it contains—or simply is—this. Separation in individual instances is no worry here; the whole debate is about whether we can make such a theoretical separation for the whole of the concept. Clearly the insider is converting her already existing evaluative understanding into descriptive terms, just as I can do in the bus case. The only difference between the insider as I have just imagined her and myself is that she has the fluky ability to produce lists with an infinite number of clauses. She can make the individual separations for the whole of the concept and offer a complete translation of the concept into descriptive language, something that is certainly beyond me.

---

[23] However, my line of argument in Chapter Six casts doubt on what we can class as a descriptive feature and a descriptive concept.

We now need to ask whether an outsider—who can produce lists with an infinite number of clauses—can do the same as the insider. We should tread carefully. In order for the issue to remain clear we need an outsider to remain an outsider. We cannot have an outsider doing what anthropologists typically do in real life. She cannot try to imagine what it is like for an insider, to pretend to be her, to draw on her own stock of evaluative concepts to understand the concepts of the insider's community, and so on. If we do not keep to that then we lose the point of the debate. A nonseparationist could rightly protest that our scenario does not show that the evaluative is shapeless with respect to the descriptive. What it is far more likely to show, it seems, is that if the 'outsider' (as we might now label her) has seemingly been successful in understanding the insider, then her evaluative concepts were probably not so different from the insider's in the first place and she is turning herself into an insider.[24]

We can keep to this injunction, then, but this need not mean that the outsider is at a complete loss. Perhaps she meets a friendly insider, follows her round for a while and observes how she uses a certain concept. The outsider notes down the various descriptive features of actions that the insider categorizes using the concept under investigation. Presumably, however, this will happen only for a while, and the outsider will have a list with only a finite number of clauses. The question is, given that she has the ability to produce an infinite number of clauses if needs be, will she be able to extend this list and capture the rest of the concept descriptively?

With the ground prepared we can now see that there is some chink left for the separationist to exploit that normally goes unnoticed, although I think that, in the end, it offers little support. It seems that our outsider could produce a full and correct descriptively characterized list, but only through pure chance. That is, we put our outsider on the spot and she magically produces the correct infinite list by some stab in the dark.

However, this logical possibility provides only limited support. It seems highly unlikely that such a list could be produced with no prior evaluative understanding, even ignoring the fact that we are asking for the production of an infinite list. I worry what the status of this unlikelihood is given that we are dealing with an infinite number of kind actions. (My intuitions go fuzzy here regarding probabilities and infinitude, as I imagine other people's do.) But I am content to leave this response aside. At the least, separationism's truth looks debatable if it has only this possibility on which to fall back.

A nonseparationist might object. Why allow separationists this chink to exploit? After all, it seems crazy to imagine that such a list could be produced. But I think that after a moment's reflection our nonseparationist would realize that the outsider could strike lucky. However, she might continue and wonder, more generally, whether this

---

[24] As advertised, I investigate the possibility of anthropology in Chapter Eight.

present discussion has been set up correctly. This lucky outsider would not under-stand kindness, so why think that she could produce such a list? She has not 'mastered the concept' after all. Considering this worry gives me a chance to return to §5.4(a). It is unfair for nonseparationists to state that when such a list has been produced by an outsider, separationism will be vindicated only if she is able to explain why the various clauses appear on the list rather than merely report that the presence of such features justifies a certain judgement; that she is able to say why the presence of features *a*, *b*, and *c* make an action kind, while the addition of feature *x* renders the action cruel; that she is able to explain why the action with features *a*, *b*, and *c* is a canonical example of its type; and so on. Being able to comment in such a way seems to be part of what it is to have evaluative understanding of the concept at issue. But there is no reason to expect that the outsider will be able to comment in this way, since the outsider is being challenged to do something without evaluative understanding. Why think that she can produce the list with no understanding and expect that, from such a position, evaluative understanding over and above the ability to capture the concept's extension will then follow? How is full evaluative under-standing to be magicked from none? This sets the bar too high for separationists, surely. This is why the debate should be restricted to discussion of the extension of concepts. That is enough of a challenge anyway.

Something deeper might motivate separationists. So far we have been discussing disjunctive lists. Some nonseparationists might question whether we can seriously think that such things legitimately represent KIND. I have little sympathy with this move.[25] As we have just seen, even if we do not normally think of evaluative concepts in these terms, it seems possible for an *insider* to produce such a disjunctive list, be it finitely or infinitely long. That is as legitimate as it needs to be for our purposes.

I am being hard on nonseparationists here. Even if we acknowledge that our outsider can *have* and *produce* a correct list, if she does produce a correct list she does so only by good fortune. The worries that I imagine some nonseparationists airing show us starkly how lucky the outsider has to be. After her travels with the friendly insider have finished, the remaining number of ways in which actions get to be kind have to be made up by the outsider, or they have to pop into her head, or similar. It is, I hope, clear both that this is possible, but also how extremely unlikely it is. Indeed, additionally, it seems that the real worry is with descriptions popping into the outsider's head, and it is not so important whether the list that has to be produced is infinite or just a very, very long finite one.

The debate could proceed from this point with us discussing other things about the points of view of the insider and the outsider, and whether this can be used to nonseparationism's advantage. I will do this later. For now, let me recap this section. We have shown that in order for the claim of outrunning to convince, we need to

---

[25] At least in the context of this debate. In Chapter Six I think about what it is to characterize using only descriptive, nonevaluative language.

imagine that kindness comes in an infinite variety of forms. If we do that, we need to ask whether someone could capture it nonevaluatively. Even if someone has the ability to produce infinitely long lists, she can do so 'normally' only if she is an insider. If she is an outsider, she can do so only by pure chance, and this gives little support to those that oppose the shapelessness hypothesis. We now have to ask whether we have reason for thinking that supposed evaluative concepts are infinitely complex.

5.6 A Prejudice

Let me comment briefly on my phrasing, for clarification. I have talked of evaluative concepts being 'infinitely complex' and, more strictly, of there being an 'infinite number of ways in which actions get to be of a certain evaluative sort'. This is in contrast to there being an 'infinite number of actions of a certain evaluative sort'. There might be an infinite number of kind actions, but the nonevaluative feature or features that are crucial to their being kind might come in only a limited number of forms. In which case, there might be no reason in principle why humans could not capture what it is for something to be kind in nonevaluative ways. What needs to be established is not just that there are, or are likely to be, an infinite number of kind *tokens*, but that there are, or are likely to be, an infinite number of kind *types*.

What reason have we for believing that outrunning will occur? Let us start with the strong version of the shapelessness hypothesis. Recall that, in this case, the conclusion nonseparationists are aiming to show is:

(A)   Evaluative concepts cannot be recharacterized in descriptive terms unless one has full evaluative understanding of them.

Recall that (A) was earlier supported, in §5.3, by the positive light in which nonseparationists saw things:

(B)   Evaluative concepts are essentially 'human-laden' (in a special way): they reflect our interests which receive expression in ways that can be codified only in evaluative ways.[26]

But what reason have we for believing (B), and (A) for that matter? At this point in our discussion all we have is (C):

(C)   There is an infinite number of ways in which actions get to be a certain evaluative way. For example, there is an infinite number of ways in which actions get to be kind.

---

[26] I include the caveat in parentheses since arguably all concepts are 'human-laden' in the sense of reflecting our interests. The claim relevant here is that the human-laden nature of evaluative concepts results in uncodifiability with respect to the descriptive.

But to what can we point to support this claim? I can think of nothing except the chocolate example and similar cases. Recall that we supposedly conclude that the value of the action could always alter following the addition of new features.[27] But this assumption seems motivated *only because* we assume that the evaluative cannot be recharacterized in wholly descriptive terms, or that ethical concepts are essentially human-laden and reflect our interests that are expressed in uncodifiable ways. Indeed, we are assuming that evaluative concepts are special concepts where out-running occurs, as opposed to other concepts—such as 'is a line'—where we assume this does not happen, since we assume that there are only a finite number of types of way to exemplify the concept, even if there are infinite tokens.[28] All that we have standing against our accepting that there is only a finite number of ways in which actions get to be kind is some pessimism about strategies involving descriptive recharacterizations. If this is true, then nonseparationists who employ the shapeless-ness hypothesis are guilty of begging the question.

That is one way of expressing that there is an unjust prejudice at work. A different way is this. Instead of accusing nonseparationists of smuggling their conclusion into the premises, we might worry that (A), (B), and (C) are merely different ways of phrasing *the same* idea and, hence, none can be used in support of the other two. In the terms of the present debate, what it is for something to be noncharacterizable in wholly descriptive terms is just for it to be essentially human-laden. Similarly, 'nonrecharacterizability' is just an easier way of saying 'there is an infinite number of ways that an action can get to be kind, say, and hence it cannot be represented in descriptive terms'.

So the strong version of the shapelessness hypothesis is really only an expression of the (controversial) initial anti-separationist hunch. We certainly do not have an *argument* here. Talk of outsiders trying to understand the value of various actions involving the giving or withholding of chocolate might make the anti-separationist hunch more vivid, but does nothing to strengthen it or add to it.

Well, that is the strong version of the hypothesis. What of the moderate version? We might think it is in better condition. Claiming only that evaluative concepts are *likely* to resist recharacterization in descriptive terms commits us to less than the strong version; we could be wrong about the definite claim, but the balance of reasons still favours us being right in advance of doing some investigation. If the moderate version seems good, then the onus shifts to separationists, which is no mean feat.

However, this is not quite right. Our rejection of the strong version exposed the fact that our evidence for believing it was only the initial anti-separationist hunch.

---

[27] Which, of course, would result in slightly different actions each time. We are concerned with the value of the general action type of giving chocolate.

[28] This comparative judgement is here for illumination of the evaluative case. We could challenge the claim about 'is a line' and worry about rule-following generally. That does not strictly affect the claims about evaluative case: is there or is there not uncodifiability here?

It is not as if we have acquired only a little evidence aside from belief in nonseparationism, and concluded that it is too little to base so strong a claim on. It is that we have no evidence beyond the anti-separationist hunch. With that in mind, the moderate version is in no better condition. Of course, the weaker claim allows for the possibility that evaluative concepts might be captured from a wholly descriptive perspective. But we are still, then, saying that the phenomenon of shapelessness is more likely than not. However, what justifies this? Only again some thumbnail sketches of various evaluative concepts whose characterization is infected with anti-separationist bias.

Some might think I am being harsh on the employment of the shapelessness hypothesis here, and specifically the moderate version. After all, many might feel the force of the anti-separationist hunch and they might think the thumbnail sketches fairly true to life. (I do, as it happens.) But some have intuitions that go the other way. Opponents might instead feel the force of the thought that scientific work over the past centuries has explained various phenomena in all manner of ways. Parts of scientific investigation embody the hope that one can explain phenomena that seem united as a type only at some higher level of description and which are disparate and seemingly unfathomably complex at some lower level of description. And, relatedly, science has explained the unified nature of phenomena at lower levels that at higher levels seemed disparate, and will continue to do so. Even if nonseparationists cannot convince their opponents, they might need to offer more to convince neutrals who, as yet, might be caught between both intuitions.

As I have said, the hypothesis can be rehabilitated a little. I am being hard here since I want a defence of the anti-separationist view to have a better chance of standing up to critical scrutiny. Shifting simply to the moderate claim invites the worries that (i) we still have only prejudiced reasons for believing the supposed likelihood; and (ii) one could easily reject the claim based on opposing prejudices. Nonseparationists who wish to use the shapelessness hypothesis against separationism need to think a little harder.

5.7 A Third Option

There is a third way we can understand the aims that lie behind the shapelessness hypothesis.

What the strong and moderate versions of the shapelessness hypothesis share is that both make claims about what we will discover when we investigate how evaluative concepts work. We can claim from our limited experience either that something is or is likely to be the case. What they both leave unquestioned is the epistemic position of the people doing the investigative work and what they will and should think when a lot of that work is done.

So what if we consider that? Consider the outsider again. After she has finished following the insider around she has a finite list of clauses. We then challenge her to predict how an insider will view a sample of new actions that we will present. We can imagine that the sample will be a mix of actions that have many of the same features of previously judged examples, as well as those that have very few. Based on previous thoughts we can accept that there is a possibility that the outsider will get every case correct. But how confident will she be of doing so and how confident will we be in her abilities?

The answer depends in large part on how bright she is. If she is dim and slow-witted, then she might stumble along attempting to make her judgements, and sometimes get it right and sometimes get it wrong. She might not reflect on this and simply shrug her shoulders when she goes wrong. If she is brighter, then her experience might teach her that she is not doing as well as the insider and that this change of scenario has exposed her as being less than competent with the concepts under investigation. If she is brighter still she might reflect on her experiences and imagine cases such as the chocolate example. (Or perhaps she is simply knowledge-able and has read about shapelessness.) We might imagine that seeds of doubt are sown in her mind. She might, first, doubt that she will ever be able to capture the concept under investigation descriptively. But, second, on reflection she might revise that for the (better) doubt that she could capture the concept in this way, but that she will never be able to tell if she has done so. She will always wonder if a configuration of nonevaluative features is possible that does not appear on her list but which is such as to be deemed kind, say. I think it plausible to say that our outsider's confidence in her ability with the evaluative concepts under investigation will diminish, possibly significantly. And I take it that this will reflect our confidence in her abilities, given our previous thought about how likely it is for her to get things right every time.

What position are we in when we judge? If we follow through this train of thought we can imagine that seeds of doubt are sown in our minds also. We have been introduced to the shapelessness hypothesis, made vivid by some examples. We might think, 'Well, that could happen to me and the concepts that I use, and any new ones that I try to understand. Perhaps I won't be able to latch onto an exhaustive descriptive pattern. Or [the better doubt] even if I can, perhaps I won't know that I have.' It seems that if this train of thought is correct, we should start to be unsure about our concept use and lose confidence in our abilities. A different way of putting the idea is this. Before we started to doubt we might have considered ourselves to be insiders rather than outsiders, that is if we could have accepted this distinction without buying into all of the doubts. But now, after reflection, we might not be so sure whether we are insiders or outsiders. Insiders are people that pretty much understand their concepts.[29] They can be confident that their extensions are pretty much consistent. Even if they get some individual examples wrong, they can be

---

[29] Even if we cannot articulate the necessary and sufficient criteria of application of a concept, or even get close, we might be able to apply the concept well enough, and manipulate it and reason about it in individual cases.

confident that they will understand why that is, after time and reflection anyway. They might question their use of a concept on an occasion; they might debate with others and change their mind. But this is from a base of being confident with the concept and related evaluative concepts overall. Yet perhaps we are not like this. Perhaps we are more like outsiders. Perhaps we might come across some new cases and fail by some margin to get things right and, further, be ignorant of our failings and fail to realize that someone could challenge what we think.

But this train of thought seems pessimistic. An interesting contrast is provided by the fact that many of us *are* confident in how we use our evaluative concepts. Certainly we might get things wrong every so often but, as I remarked just now, that is consistent with being an insider. We do not normally think of ourselves as dim or reckless when it comes to our use of evaluative concepts. We can participate in everyday evaluative discourse and can argue and reveal ideas in ways that people find agreeable and unsurprising. Indeed, furthermore, we normally think that we are able to understand other people and their initially alien concepts. Anthropological research is based on such confidence.

It could be that we are being dim or reckless. Perhaps we adopt an air of confidence because we prefer to be optimistic, even if this has no basis in reality. But that seems a little implausible. At the very least, I could imagine a neutral agreeing with what has been said so far.

Why is this bad for separationists? If we have confidence in our concept use, then it shows that we have found some pattern of items in the world that we categorize in the same way, and it shows that we are happy that we have, pretty much, immediate access to the (rough and ready) contours of the pattern, such that we could consistently extend it to new cases. If the shapelessness hypothesis has any power, then the thought will be that for evaluative concepts this pattern will figure in our deliberations strangely if we think of it, on reflection, as a descriptive, nonevaluative pattern, as separationists suppose. We may not have latched onto it, and even if we do, we will not know that we know it; we cannot conceptualize it as 'the pattern of kindness' if separationism is correct. So how can our everyday confidence in our concept use persist? Why is our confidence justified? This looks like a curious state of affairs, and suggests a strange state of mind.

This contrasts with the nonseparationist thought that the pattern is evaluative. We might not be able to articulate the whole pattern in nonevaluative ways, but we seem to be fairly confident in our application and understanding of kindness, say, as the pattern of kindness. Or, in other words, the 'something' that links all and only all the kind things is the feature of kindness, or the fact that they are kind, or some other, similar phrasing. We are able to latch onto this pattern with none of the bother that separationism seems to entail.

Hence, we can provide a mirror claim to that given for the strong and moderate versions. The precise aim of the shapelessness hypothesis is to claim that the evaluative *could* be shapeless with respect to the descriptive. The difference between this and the moderate claim, with its 'likely' or 'strongly likely', is that we will never be able to know whether shapelessness is a real phenomenon, whereas the moderate version says that it is likely that empirical work will show the hypothesis to be correct. This epistemic point should make us question whether our natural, everyday confidence in our concepts is undermined by the separationist account of evaluative concept use. Cases such as the chocolate example are not designed to justify something being the case, either to us now or once we have done the necessary empirical work. Rather, they get us to think about whether we could ever know that the necessary empirical work was complete and whether we could show conclusively that appropriate descriptive characterizations were forthcoming.

How might separationists challenge this? They could argue, first, that we are deceiving ourselves and that our confidence is misplaced. This is a possibility, although condemning most people like this does not seem an attractive strategy. Besides, there are other more interesting responses, (a)–(d).

(a) One obvious response—perhaps *the* obvious response—is to agree that we are confident in our use of evaluative concepts and, hence, agree that this is probably because we are picking out some pattern. However, separationists can challenge and ask why this cannot be a descriptive pattern. The idea from above is that we cannot capture and articulate such things. But, goes the response, the existence of descriptive patterns and the articulation of them are separate issues; it might be that we can articulate such patterns only feebly at most.[30] So it might be that separationists cannot prove that there are suitable descriptive charaterizations available, but it might also be that nonseparationists cannot prove that there are not.

Can nonseparationists respond? It is true that they cannot conclusively prove that such descriptive characterizations are not forthcoming. But nonseparationists could adopt a piecemeal strategy and attempt to convince neutrals. They could give a battery of examples such as the chocolate case. Then they could alter the descriptive features of each a few times to show how the applicable evaluative concepts might change. By going through this process they cannot show that it will happen every time, mainly because of the nature of the debate: 'infinite or finite?' But they can show that it can happen a fair amount, in each family of cases. They could then move the discussion on. It is certainly true that they cannot prove that this process will not stop. Yet, given that examples have been continued some way, then perhaps the onus is on separationists to show why we should continue to believe what they say. If we have an awful lot of continuation, why not think that the default is to imagine it will continue unless proved otherwise? In effect, what nonseparationists do is shift our argument so that they are not trying to show that separationism is wrong, but to argue that the onus is on separationists to prove otherwise. This might be enough to convince a neutral to back

---

[30] See Blackburn (1981), p. 167. I comment on this in Kirchin (2010a), pp. 11–12.

nonseparationism, at least as a 'safety-first' option. Perhaps this onus-shifting move is the best way of articulating the force of examples such as the chocolate case.

But it must be said that this is no knock-out argument, even if separationism does not emerge victorious either. (If nothing else, my discussion shows this *contra* all commentators on the debate.) This line of thought may do little to persuade separationists; I am not sure how neutrals will respond. That alone should incline us to look elsewhere for a way to defend nonseparationism and query separationism, although there are a few other thoughts I have let slip in this chapter that require questioning anyway. And, of course, it affects what we say in the overall discussion of how important this strategy is in showing separationism to be incorrect.

Before we get ahead of ourselves, though, what other separationist responses might there be?

(b) A separationist might wonder about the chocolate case and other examples.[31] I have provided only a snapshot of how this case might go. We could argue about how long that case could continue, but let us imagine it could continue a lot. More interestingly, a separationist might ask whether the new examples would be that surprising, or rare, or cause us to rethink what we have been doing previously with the concept. After all, that seems to be where these examples bite. In short, the challenge is to think whether we could summarize an everyday evaluative concept descriptively based on some examples, and from that be confident that nothing too surprising will then emerge. If so, our confidence will be enhanced.

The response to this is to recall some previous thoughts. Think back to the outsider. She merely notes down the descriptive information that has gone before. Her future judgements are a function of this. It is no part of this noting down that she is able to discern which features of a case justify the application of the relevant concept, unless the insider tells her. Similarly, given my set up, she will be at a loss to notice that a feature pops up more times than others or, at least, she will be at a loss to explain what, if any, evaluative significance is carried by this statistical fact. With that in mind we can say that she will be surprised by a lot of things that to us, as everyday users, would be unsurprising. For example, some insiders start to talk about kindness with reference to chocolate being shared between children. But then they start talking about teeth and pain. And then they start to talk about tears and upset children. And then the insiders are not so bothered that the children are upset because the thing that is causing the upset is trivial (which is then further specified). But now the insiders become more curious because they learn that the thing causing the upset is not so trivial because of some further thing (again, to be specified). And so on. It could be that at no stage are we, as everyday users, surprised. But the outsider might well be. And, I think, this reveals a theme of my discussion.

---

[31] Here I respond to a nice point from Daniel Elstein.

I have tried to be fair-minded when dealing with separationism, particularly on the issue of 'mastery of a concept'. The bar cannot be set too high. But here we reveal the limits of the separationist interpretation. Simply because separationists' ambitions for the outsider are just for her to follow and articulate the extensions of concepts, it seems unlikely that such an outsider will be confident that she can continue on her own, since the features themselves will not reveal any pattern. This could be what the whole debate turns on: the rival conceptions of what an evaluative concept is; when push comes to shove: something *sui generis* or something that can be characterized in other terms. According to the former conception of evaluative concepts, many new features and situations will not be surprising. But, in accordance with the latter, every new situation, no matter how trivially different it seems to us as readers of this book, has the potential to be surprising to users. Or, in other words, the challenge to separationists is that separationism characterizes us all as being outsiders.

Of course, we start as philosophers by thinking about what our everyday use is like. Perhaps the idea of shapelessness might not get off the ground unless we found that new situations came along that surprised us with unexpected features. But I reckon that is fairly common. It is certainly common when we are first learning to use a concept: one's first case of a cruel action that is also kind can be a revelation. Similarly, working out exactly what sorts and mixtures of furniture, clothing, and musical style are kitsch or classy can be surprising. But this phenomenon applies even to mature users. Such changes in concepts (or, rather, conceptions) do not, I think, mean that we should be low in confidence in our use of evaluative concepts. Indeed, an awareness that you might not have got all of it right and have room to grow can add to your confidence. The key is that one is recognizing patterns in the instances that one is picking out using an evaluative concept, one can manipulate it and can connect it with other concepts, and so on. None of this is going on in the mind of an outsider.

(c) Recall that I said, in Chapter Two, that it was never part of the classic presentation of the disentangling argument that separationism should reflect our phenomenology. Separationists might argue that our rejection of their position is driven by worries about their theory not reflecting everyday phenomenology. After all, we have a case where we supposedly feel confident in our everyday evaluative concepts that their theory says we should not have. But, separationists might claim, we should not dismiss a theoretical treatment of a phenomenon if that treatment does not accurately reflect the phenomenology of it.

I think that that final claim is right. A mismatch between theory and phenomenology does not and should not spell the end of a theory straightaway.[32] However, what sort of mismatch do we have here? It is not just that the phenomenology is not accurately reflected in the theory. We have the theory and phenomenology standing

[32] See Kirchin (2003a) where I argue that 'phenomenological arguments' *alone* in metaethics cut no ice. Moral phenomenology is useful only when allied to certain metaphysical, epistemological (etc.) arguments.

opposed: the theory says that we are picking up on a descriptive pattern when we categorize evaluatively, while the phenomenology not only is, supposedly, free of such patterns, but could never be sure that one had captured such a pattern even if one had. Even then we might say that in some cases this does not dissuade some philosophers from adopting certain theoretical positions. (Certain approaches to inductive knowledge come to my mind here.) But we might want to say that if a separationist raises the issue of phenomenology, she should be prepared to argue that there are clear benefits, and even clear benefits overall, for adopting her position despite the drastic mismatch between theory and phenomenology. Yet, although it may have some *prima facie* merits, we have already seen, in the previous chapter, reasons to worry about separationism, and in the next chapter we will encounter some more. So, a defence based on short-circuiting the supposed phenomenological motivation for our worry is suspect. And this is so particularly because the opposing position, nonseparationism reflects the phenomenology pretty well and continues to do so after theoretical reflection on the precise matters discussed in this chapter.

(d) One last discussion in this section introduces a more complicated response. I promised earlier I would address how this argument worked against complex separationism. The choice of label reflects something that seems to be an advantage here. We have a more complex analysis of evaluative concepts, with some evaluative element being used within some general descriptive element. This is advantageous because we are supposing that evaluative concepts are complex and so we may be able to capture them better. But this is a false hope. The supposition on the third reading of the shapelessness hypothesis (and similarly with the other two come to that) is that there is some reason to think that the evaluative is so complex that it cannot be separated into component parts. Any attempt to make a separationist analysis more complex will do nothing to stop the scepticism that we have now, finally, captured the concept. And note that when it comes to details, Elstein and Hurka's analysis of DISTRIBUTIVE JUSTICE included just one role for some evaluative element to affect the concepts' extensions, and INTEGRITY included just two. This is hardly ramping up the complexity of the analysis very much.

In a similar vein we can close off an earlier avenue. I do not see how making the thin evaluative element thicker than a PRO or a CON will help fend off this challenge. We are thinking about nonseparable or 'uncapturable' complexity. Even if we make the evaluative element more specific (yet not so specific as to make us worry that we have a thick concept introduced on the sly), I am unconvinced that this will do the required work. There will still be an *assumed* gap between the materials and the extension of the evaluative concept, and that is all that is needed to generate the worry I have voiced.

But in returning to this position we can see a different challenge emerge. Recall that in §5.4(d) we reflected on the relationship between shapelessness and disentangling. Perhaps thick concepts are shapeless, but what drives the shapelessness of the thick is only the shapelessness of the thin and, so, thick concepts can still be disentangled.[33] This seems to be an option only for cognitivist-separationists: their noncognitivist cousins will not want to say that thin concepts, such as PRO or GOOD are shapeless. I take it, crucially and to repeat, that what has been said about kindness goes for goodness: the chocolate case and many others will work in the same way for the thin and the thick.

So what of cognitivist-separationists? They might be happy with PRO and GOOD being shapeless (or, rather, 'appearing to us to be shapeless because we can never be sure that we have captured their shape nonethically'), and happy for (disentangled) thick concepts to be shapeless but only in virtue of their thin, evaluative element. This might be a victory of sorts for the McDowell–Wiggins nonseparationists, but at most a half-victory, and almost certainly a moral defeat.

A response to this brings us back to earlier ideas. We need some reason to think that thin concepts should be conceived as being conceptually prior at this point, and we saw that even if separationists were not definitely wrong about this matter, there is a large question mark hanging over their position. We can extend things a little here also. The specific position under consideration right now is the idea that thick concepts are shapeless only because thin elements within them are shapeless. What is the motivation for that view? If we think that the chocolate case will carry on changing such that we will carry on switching our judgements about its variations from good to bad and back again, then why not think that the cause of the changing in the case of the thick is the same as with the thin, rather than the cause being only the thin itself? All of the features mentioned in relation to the chocolate case—dental health, learned behaviour, being upset, features that are trivial (perhaps the upset is because the chocolate bar is the child's favourite), features that are not (it is the child's birthday; the bar reminds them of a relative they hardly see)—seem to be intimately connected with kindness in this example in a way that is the same as in the case of goodness. Although not a cast-iron, unquestionable point, it seems telling that when we justify something as kind or cruel or brave or mean we look and consider the features themselves in a way that is unmediated by whether these features are good- or bad-making. Is it so obvious that the thin should be assumed to be conceptually prior? There may be no further way of expressing this point. But maintaining the opposite view—that only the thin is shapeless—seems to me to maintain a theory for its own sake, despite the evidence to the contrary.

I think there are too many question marks hanging over this envisaged retreat. If we were to accept that the thin is shapeless, it seems justifiable to accept that the thick is too. Of course, we could deny that the thin is shapeless. Or, as a reminder, we could deny that we will ever be certain that the thin was not shapeless. But the chocolate case and others like it, married with the argument earlier in this section, seem to favour our holding out against this, at least as a safety-first option. The onus is on

---

[33] Thanks to an anonymous referee for encouraging me to comment on this idea.

those that oppose the nonseparationism of evaluative and descriptive content to provide clear and unambiguous arguments that either show that evaluative concepts, thin and thick, are shapely with respect to the descriptive, and that we can know when we have a correct analysis; or show that the thin is shapeless, while the thick is not.

There are worries with this proposed retreat, then, such that we can confidently dismiss this avenue.[34] But we should not forget my earlier cautiousness. The disentangling argument, with its employment of the shapelessness hypothesis, does not deliver a knock-out blow to separationism. This position might still be correct. The most we can say, even if we accept that no separationist counter that I have considered works, is that we can never know if separationism is correct and that this scepticism does not chime with the state of mind that separationism suggests.

I am inclined to think that there is a tension between our normal state of mind and that suggested by separationism. Yet, I am prepared to think that others will disagree. Furthermore, there is lack of directness about this argument: it is a suspicion, but separationists might push the point that I earlier sidelined and argue that we should not be as confident as we are. Or, if we insist on such a confidence, then that simply shows that there *is* some nonevaluative pattern to our evaluative categorizations.

Aside from these points, we can now see that the two strategies we have thought about—the one that concentrates on the *genus* and conceptual priority, and the one that concentrates on the shapelessness of the *differentia*—work together, and not just because we have two parts of the *genus–species* model in play. They work also because at various points, as we have just seen, we are left questioning whether, for example, the thin *genus* really is prior. Furthermore, then, separationism is left with question marks hanging over it, even if there is no decisive victory against it.

5.8 Conclusion and a Pause

In this chapter we have dissected in lengthy detail one of the key arguments, if not *the* key argument, that has been raised by nonseparationists against separationists over the past thirty or so years. The claim is that the evaluative is shapeless with respect to the descriptive; no descriptive-only analysis of evaluative terms and concepts will work. Putting it in the terms I have favoured in this book, there is a grave suspicion that the *differentia* cannot be specified such that we can conclude that thick concepts are *species* concepts.

I have raised doubts about the shapelessness hypothesis and disentangling argument. I do not think it works as it has normally been given. A third way of understanding it has merit but, as an overall move against separationism, both this strategy and the first may leave us wanting more. There is no point in my discussion

---

[34] In Kirchin (2010a), p. 23 I discuss this avenue in a little more detail.

where we can say with confidence that separationists should be worried and that nonseparationists can claim victory. We have not really got to the heart of some of the debate against separationism. It feels as if there is more to uncover about thick concepts.

The argument of this chapter revolves around the idea that we cannot reduce the evaluative to the descriptive. The strategy employed takes these two types of thing and shows they are different. But that sort of strategy assumes that we have two distinct types of thing in the first place. As I expressed in Chapter One, one of the reasons thick concepts were originally a focus of such interest was that they held out a hope for some thinkers that it was not so clear that the evaluative and the descriptive were different, or if there were clear examples in each camp, it was not so clear where the one domain stopped and the other started. In the next chapter we think about that idea.

Before that, a pause. I have said that I wanted to understand the terrain and get under the skin of separationism in the first few chapters. Much of my tone may have been negative. However, we have uncovered a number of positive ideas. Here I list the major ones as they will help ease us into Chapter Six.

(i)   In Chapter Three I started to make the case for evaluative flexibility. We saw that it may seem odd to postulate a large number of separate concepts, such as ELEGANT-PRO and ELEGANT-CON, when we can just have one concept, ELEGANT, that holds within itself more than one 'pointed evaluation'. In Chapter Six I return to this idea and show how it connects with nonseparationism.

(ii) In Chapter Four I argued for the idea that concepts that are typically labelled as thin can come in a range of thicknesses, or at least can be more or less specific than one another. PRO is different from GOOD and RIGHT. GOOD is different from ETHICALLY GOOD and AESTHETICALLY GOOD, not just in content but in specificity. Yet it is not unreasonable to think of all of these examples as thin or as 'simply' evaluative. If so, then it seems as if it is reasonable also to think that we should investigate more the notion of what it is for something to be evaluative, given that all of these examples are treated as evaluative concepts.

(iii) Although suggestive only, in Chapter Four we saw that 'no prioritarianism' might be at least as viable and plausible a position as both thin and thick prioritarianism.

(iv) Finally, we have just seen that nonseparationists may make no convincing headway, ultimately, if they argue only that evaluative and descriptive conceptual content are intertwined in some way that suggest they cannot then be separated. The emphasis here is wrong. Nonseparationists need to focus on questioning the assumption of there being a split or separation in the first place. If they do this they open up a different way of defending their view and of characterizing the evaluative.

PART II

A Positive View

6

Thick Evaluation

6.1 Introduction

In this chapter I get to the heart of the debate about thin and thick concepts and, in so doing, reveal two very different pictures about them. The positive nonseparationist picture I draw understands evaluation in a way different from how evaluation is understood by separationists. My overall argumentative stance against separationism and for nonseparationism should therefore be understood in this light. Recall from Chapter One my argumentative aim. I do not show to devastating effect some fatal incoherence in separationism, or similar. Indeed, I believe that there is no such flaw. Instead, I aim to show that nonseparationism understands and casts thin and thick evaluative concepts in a better light than separationism and, further, that in the end separationism emerges as strange and curious. Recall also my hope that neutrals will be persuaded to side with me; it may be that some separationists will question their allegiance also, but I do not expect many to do so.

There a number of ideas at work in this chapter and I now list them. Most are repeated from earlier adverts in the book.

(a) In this chapter one aim is at the forefront: to persuade people that there is a notion of the evaluative at work in everyday thought and language that goes beyond notions of positive and negative stance (pro and con, and even pro-in-a-way and con-in-a-way), even if it also encompasses them. Further, such thick concepts cannot be separated into component parts. We may cast this position in various ways, using terms such as 'entangled', or describing thick concepts as 'unitary' and perhaps as 'basic', 'non-derivative' and the like. Whichever terms we use to flag up particular ideas, the central notion I expressed in the first sentence of this paragraph is clear. And it can be amplified by another central idea mentioned in Chapter One also: thick evaluative concepts are as wholly or purely evaluative as thin concepts are, even if some evaluative concepts are more specific than others. This claim then invites us to reflect in detail on what our conception of the evaluative is.

(b) Following on, then, and to hark back to labels introduced in Chapter One, in this chapter I am motivating the liberal view of evaluation, and showing the conservative view to be unattractive. *Liberals* think that some concepts can be categorized as evaluative even if some instances of their use have no positive or negative view conveyed, no pro or con stance to them. *Conservatives* think that there must be such a stance in each and every instance for a concept to be an evaluative concept. (I provide more detail of each position later.) So according to liberals we can apply a concept such as MACABRE legitimately on some occasion where its use does not convey any positive or negative stance or view (the judge may not intend any, the audience does not infer any), and yet the concept overall can still be called an evaluative concept and it can be taken to be used evaluatively in this instance. I aim to defend the possibility of this position through reflection on many examples of how we use concepts, and make it obvious that we assume such a position in the first place.

A quick note. How does the liberal–conservative disagreement intersect with the separationist–nonseparationist disagreement? They are different, after all. Clearly I am a liberal-nonseparationist: I believe that our everyday notion of evaluation is not exhausted by notions of pro and con, and I believe that thick concepts cannot be separated into component parts. The special nature of my position, I suppose, is that I think the best version of nonseparationism has the liberal notion of evaluation at its heart. As I have said before, to say that thick concepts unite (thin) evaluation and descriptive content is to give away too much to separationists already. We need a notion of evaluation that they simply do not typically presume is on the table. This then takes me to the next possible position. All of the separationists we have met are conservatives, since they implicitly assume all the time that evaluation just is positive or negative, pro or con, although they typically use the language of good and bad. What about other possibilities? A conservative-nonseparationism is certainly coherent, but I believe it is vulnerable to attack by separationists. One thinks of thick concepts as unitary concepts, yet what is united is evaluation and descriptive content as separationists conceive them. (This was my worry expressed at the end of Chapter Five, and noting the vulnerability of this position leads to the liberal outlook I defend.) Liberal-separationism appears to be a very strange position, verging on the incoherent. A person occupying this position assumes that we should characterize evaluation as being something that is not exhausted by pro and con stances, something that appears to be (as I take it to be) neither descriptive nor pro-or-con-only, yet is also something that can be separated into component parts. Perhaps someone could make this work, but I would want to know what one would be separating this evaluation into: what *are* the component parts? For reasons of brevity, in what is going to be a lengthy chapter anyway, I will ignore this fourth position from now on.

(c) Having sorted out some positions in logical space, I should make clear a different aspect of my view that will occupy much of my time in this chapter, and again I have raised it before. I argue that although there may be clear examples of descriptive, nonevaluative concepts, and also clear examples of evaluative concepts—that is, evaluative concepts *as separationists understand them*—I also argue that there are many examples of concepts that do not fit neatly into these two camps. Furthermore, I argue that such concepts deserve to be thought of as evaluative concepts by theorists and, from what I can tell, are routinely thought of in this way in everyday thought and activity.

Let me pause so that we can take this in, for it may seem confusing. The phrase in italics in the previous paragraph is key. I think that there are many examples of evaluative concepts, and that many concepts can be classed as evaluative, probably more than separationists think. That is because I have a more liberal view of evaluation, something that is not exhausted by the conveyance of either pro or con stance on any and every instance of the concept's use. So, I do not think there will be much dispute between myself and most or all separationists that KIND is an evaluative concept. (The analysis of it will be different, but that is another matter.) However, there is very likely to be different reasons for our view that it is evaluative. Whereas separationists will think it evaluative only because it is normally used to convey pro views, I think that while such a concept can and is used in this way, it is used to do other things as well. That extra thought leads me to think about many other concepts also, and mount the case for them being classified as evaluative.

There is a further part to my view that may well muddy the waters even more. In this chapter and book I do *not* provide conditions, let alone necessary and sufficient conditions, at some exacting level of detail that any and every concept has to satisfy in order to be evaluative.[1] This is because I think there is strong reason to believe there is a grey area between those concepts that are obviously evaluative and those concepts that are obviously nonevaluative. Or, in other words, I think that there is strong reason to think that there is no hard and fast dividing line between the evaluative and the nonevaluative. I believe this is shown by many examples. This view may seem counterintuitive and indeed downright gnomic, if only for reasons of logic and English: we have two clear categories—evaluation and nonevaluation/descriptive— that are clear negations of each other, so surely any concept must be one or the other. We cannot have any third category, grey area, or anything else. I aim to show, instead, that when we reflect on a range of examples, we can see the possibility of this grey area and, therefore, what we might well wish to give up is an adherence to the strict, unbending idea that we have two mutually exclusive categories which exhaust the field.[2]

So my focus on various examples will attempt to press two main, interrelated ideas. First, that an evaluative concept can be evaluative (overall, and in any particular instance) and not convey a positive or negative view in every instance of its use. Second, even if there are clear examples of descriptive concepts and clear examples of evaluative concepts by separationists' lights (perhaps concepts that are exclusively used to convey positive or negative view)—and, to stress, I do believe there are clear

---

[1] There is another reason related to that in the main text. Recall also the cute but important thought expressed in note 1 in Chapter Two. It may be difficult, to say the very least, to try to describe necessary and sufficient conditions for a concept being descriptive or nonevaluative in language that does not beg the question as to what it is for concepts and terms to be evaluative and nonevaluative.

[2] To avoid confusion, some clarification. I phrase the last idea as 'I believe there is strong reason to believe that...'. I do not think I have any clear-cut, knockdown argument for my view. But I believe the examples and reflections I offer make the view highly attractive and there are strong reasons to believe my suggestion.

examples of each type—there are many concepts 'in between'. Their character is such that we at the very least may wish to extend the notion of what an evaluative concept is, simply because we are stretching our notion of the evaluative (in effect, the first point just mentioned). We may also wish to call into doubt whether there is a clear and fast dividing line between the evaluative and the nonevaluative in the first place, strange as that may initially sound.

(d) Recall another important part of my view, namely that I think of thick concepts as being essentially evaluative. By this phrase I mean that a thick concept has the ability to convey evaluation because such evaluation is a central, necessary—that is, essential—part of its nature. Indeed, talk only of conveyance of evaluation misses something. These concepts *just are* evaluative, and this is partly expressed because they can convey evaluation, such as pro and con views. The opposing view says that such concepts, while they may be able to convey evaluation at times, do so only accidentally or contingently, because of one's tone of voice, linguistic context, or other matters external to the nature of the concept itself.

In this chapter I am motivating the liberal view. So much of that view, in fact, relies on the notion of evaluation I am suggesting being an essential part of the concept. It is not just that pro and con views are conveyed, but that the concept's very nature is to have a variety of functions and to be a certain way. (Hence my 'just are' qualifier in the previous paragraph.) These various functions and aspects may be influenced by situation and tone of voice, certainly. But all of this malleability is something that is also part of what the concept is; anything that changes should not automatically be thought to be only accidental to the concept and a contingent feature of context.

So, although this chapter motivates the liberal view, my defence of my position continues into Chapter Seven where I consider an important, recent challenge due to Pekka Väyrynen. Recall my brief summary from Chapter One. In essence Väyrynen questions whether many of our concepts that are seen as evaluative and used in evaluative ways are essentially evaluative, rather than having evaluative uses that are only accidental. (He phrases the question by asking whether concepts classed as thick are 'inherently evaluative'; I comment on this terminological difference in Chapter Seven.) MACABRE is one of many examples that Väyrynen will have in mind, but he also worries about pretty much all the concepts routinely accepted as thick and evaluative. He holds a conservative view of what it is to be an evaluative concept. Considering his position is important. If we assume that this present chapter is successful and that I can persuade people that what evaluative concepts have is not exhausted by pro and con stances, then this may still leave a doubt in people's minds that evaluation could be different from how conservatives think, and yet still be accidental to thick concepts. Reflecting on Väyrynen's arguments and attempting to rebut them reveals more of what my view entails.

(e) Here are a couple more ideas, and the chapter structure, before we begin. First, I have used a number of examples in this book thus far. I have used KIND,

ELEGANT, and JUST plenty of times, along with infrequent uses of other concepts such as INTEGRITY and WISE. I have used other concepts as well, but perhaps there have been too few exciting examples. Concepts I have in mind include MACABRE, as well as MUNDANE, JEALOUS, DULL-WITTED, HUMANE, JEJUNE, DEFIANT, TANTALIZING, STIMULATING, KITSCH, CONTORTED, DISARMING, SCINTILLATING, SINISTER, HONOURABLE, RIDICULOUS, GENTLE, PICARESQUE, SLOB, ANTAGONISTIC, TANGLED, TRANSCENDENT, STRAIGHTFORWARD, BOLD, MARVEL-LOUS, TASTY, DIABOLICAL, and many more examples that this list suggests.[3] As mentioned, by working through examples such as these, I am to show the plausibility of my views. I am aware that someone could easily question whether some of the concepts above are evaluative or thick. They might accept GOOD and RIGHT as evaluative, and perhaps JUST and BEAUTIFUL, but draw the line at STIMULATING and TANGLED. They might certainly baulk if we focus on the qualifiers in phrases such as essentially or inherently evaluative: 'Is TANGLED really *essentially* evaluative?' Such a worry is understandable, but I think it is wrong, and that is the point of this chapter.

Second, this chapter is somewhat complex. In service of the main themes mentioned above, it gathers together a number of ideas, some of which have been mentioned before and some of which are new. I hope that the structure I have chosen helps to relate those points to each other and builds a clean narrative rather than adds to the confusion.

In §6.2 I carry on from the last chapter by diagnosing why the disentangling argument fails to convince. I then begin the main story. I do not dive straight into discussion of the liberal view but instead build to it slowly. I think it important to put the reader in a mood to be receptive to it. First of all, then, in §§6.3–6.5 I encourage us to see how thick concepts have a number of different functions. I focus on Williams' characterization of thick and thin concepts in order to do this, and go quite deeply into it. I think Williams goes wrong in an interesting way in his account of thick and thin concepts or, as I think it more accurate to say, a slogan associated with his view misguides us. I illuminate why this is by thinking about Ryle's account of thick description.[4] In discussing Ryle I outline his view of concepts generally. All of this will be important background and motivation for my view.

Having discussed Williams and Ryle, I put forward my view across various subsections of §6.6 by thinking about a number of examples and drawing morals from them. I round off the discussion with thoughts from Foot. In §6.7 I return to separationism and compare its picture of thick and thin concepts with mine. In §6.8 I lay out some possible challenges to my view which set the agenda for the final chapters. In §6.9 I conclude.

---

[3] And why stop at adjectives? We can also talk of nouns such as PEST, WIT, POSEUR, ADVOCATE, PRAT, CURMUDGEON, and ZEALOT. Later on in the main text I discuss the verbs CAJOLE and GOSSIP.

[4] The sections on Williams and Ryle are a rewritten version of Kirchin (2013). I also compare and contrast ethical, aesthetic and epistemic concepts more in Kirchin (ms).

6.2 Previous Arguments

The disentangling argument and the employment of the shapelessness hypothesis are not downright hopeless. Any nonseparationists should agree with the spirit of the overall claim: the evaluative is shapeless with respect to the descriptive, and one cannot disentangle thick concepts into component parts. But writers seem to fixate on the idea of shapelessness and they typically give scant regard to asking in a deep way why it is true, assuming it is. This is wrong, to my mind: it is absolutely imperative that we ask why shapelessness is true and use this result as the opportunity to think about the nature of the evaluative. In the absence of the sort of questioning that I think is necessary we end up by saying—or at least I did—that the best version of the argument is an 'epistemic' version. This can cause discomfort for separationists but it does not seem fatal.

There is therefore important motivation to consider the ideas of this chapter. Furthermore, if nonseparationists are not careful, they will be open to a fatal attack. The point is to argue that evaluative concepts cannot be separated into component parts, and that they are essentially evaluative. In arguing for this claim, supposedly, anti-separationists will point to the shapeless nature of evaluative concepts. But what happens if the supposed shapelessness nature of evaluative concepts does not show them to be essentially evaluative and, by implication, distinctly different from other concepts? Indeed, the reasons why they are shapeless may have nothing to do with the fact that they are evaluative, essential or otherwise. Väyrynen puts forward this challenge and articulates it nicely.[5] He argues that the shapelessness hypothesis cuts no ice against his view that thick concepts are not essentially or inherently evaluative. Consider OLD. This is a context-sensitive concept: an object can be considered to be old in one context (or in comparison with a range of other objects) and yet considered young in a different context. There is both a strong suspicion that there is no way of capturing OLD in 'non-OLD terms', and that the context-sensitivity of OLD is what explains its shapelessness with respect to the non-OLD.[6] (A listing of examples in non-OLD terms of the object-groups to which items considered OLD are compared may very well fail to capture OLDNESS fully and definitively.) In addition, it seems plausible to think of OLD as a descriptive concept. We can use it to convey pro or con evaluations, such as when we insult someone by calling them old with a certain tone of voice. But mature users of English know this evaluation is not core to the concept. (Think of FAT and CHAIR from Chapter Two.) We can use OLD and many other examples to then cast doubt on thick concepts. Many thick concepts seem to be context-sensitive, and perhaps it is this that explains their shapelessness. Or perhaps there is some

---

[5] Väyrynen (2013), pp. 186–202.

[6] Presumably we can capture OLD using synonyms and other related concepts, such as AGED, NOT YOUNG, and LONG-LIVED. What precisely is meant by 'non-OLD terms' need not hold us up; I take it that we have enough sense of this in order for the point to go through.

other reason than context-sensitivity that explains the shapelessness. What does not explain it is something special about the evaluative, that these concepts are essentially evaluative in a way that other concepts, such as OLD, are not.

Here is a quick link back. In §5.6 of Chapter Five we encountered claim (B) which talked of evaluative concepts being essentially 'human-laden' (in a special way) since they reflect our interests. But this is bluster, for many concepts, not just thick ones, can be described in these terms. Väyrynen thinks that nonseparationists who use the shapelessness hypothesis have to articulate the crucial difference between the evaluative and the descriptive, so as to show why the evaluative—or the shapelessness of the thickly evaluative—is different such that it justifies the evaluative and thick concepts as being treated as fundamental to our thought. He is sceptical that this can be done.

I return to address this in Chapter Seven. For now we can agree that Väyrynen's is a good worry. In addition we can contrast his challenge with the challenge I set myself. Instead of assuming that there is some dividing line between the evaluative and the descriptive, and then being caught trying to articulate what that difference is, I prefer to cast doubt on there being a dividing line in the first place.

What of the first argumentative strategy I built to in Chapter Four? The quick debates at the end of that chapter were concerned with whether thin or thick concepts were conceptually prior to the other. These may be instructive, although we saw through my illustrative exchanges that pretty soon the debate may run out of steam. I bring out a different point now in relation to this present chapter with a simple question: why think that the thin is conceptually prior when you have not given thought at the start to what the evaluative is? The assumption running though the first few chapters is that the thin just is the evaluative, and the thick is evaluative-*plus-something-else*, with the debate about priority being presumed (either implicitly or explicitly) on those terms: do we add something to evaluation that exists prior, or do we take something away from the more complicated concept to reach simple evaluation for all thin and thick concepts? What I am doing now is explicitly thinking about the terms upon which this debate is built.

I pursue that task now and start by thinking about the work of Williams and Ryle.

6.3 Williams' Distinction

The aim in this section and the next is to introduce the idea that standard thick concepts have a number of functions and roles, and that we should not narrowly pigeon-hole such concepts in the way that people sometimes do. As mentioned, this will, I hope, warm us up for later thoughts to come later on.

Recall that Williams, in *ELP*, draws the distinction between thin and thick concepts differently from how I and others draw it. He thinks of thin concepts as being wholly action-guiding, and thick concepts as being both action-guiding and world-guided. This *summarizing slogan*, as I refer to it, is used by both Williams and others to capture his views.[7] Yet, his views are more subtle than this as I show. However, even accepting that there is more detail to his view than the slogan captures, I believe both that the slogan is a good way of capturing the foundational point of ethical concepts, but also that this slogan is a bad way of capturing thin and thick concepts in general, across many domains, and that even in the case of ethics it hides important points.[8] Williams may have been led to say what he says because of his focus on ethical concepts, but even with that acknowledged we need to correct the view that the slogan strongly implies. In doing so we begin to see what is going on with the evaluative generally.

Let us consider the three main passages in *ELP* where Williams defines what he means by a thick concept. In a first passage he discusses the fact–value distinction, where he is arguing against Hare and other prescriptivists.

What has happened is that the theorists [i.e. prescriptivists] have brought the fact–value distinction to language rather than finding it revealed there. What they have found are a lot of those 'thicker' or more specific ethical notions I have already referred to, such as *treachery* and *promise* and *brutality* and *courage*, which seem to express a union of fact and value. The way these notions are applied is determined by what the world is like (for instance, by how someone has behaved), and yet, at the same time, their application usually involves a certain valuation of the situation, of persons or actions. Moreover, they usually (though not necessarily directly) provide reasons for action.[9]

Later he says:

Many exotic examples of these [thick concepts] can be drawn from other cultures, but there are enough left in our own: *coward, lie, brutality, gratitude*, and so forth. They are characteristically related to reasons for action. If a concept of this kind applies, this often provides someone with a reason for action, though that reason need not be a decisive one and may be outweighed by other reasons ... Of course, exactly what reason for action is provided, and to whom, depends on the situation, in ways that may well be governed by this and by other ethical concepts, but some general connection with action is clear enough. We may say, summarily, that such concepts are 'action-guiding'.

At the same time, their application is guided by the world.[10]

Lastly he contrasts thick with thin concepts.

This brings us back to the question whether the reflective level might generate its own ethical knowledge.... [I see] no hope of extending to this level the kind of world-guidedness we have been considering in the case of the thick ethical concepts. Discussions at the reflective level, if

---

[7] For example, see also Tappolet (2004) which casts Williams' work in this way. Williams himself indicates this slogan in the second quotation we are about to consider in the main text.

[8] I admire Williams' work a lot. Even if I differ in some respects, I agree with much of the spirit of his writing. I leave to others to decide whether he would have agreed with some of the points I make here.

[9] Williams (1985), pp. 129–30.　　[10] Williams (1985), pp. 140–1.

they have the ambition of considering all ethical experience and arriving at the truth about the ethical, will necessarily use the most general and abstract ethical concepts, such as 'right', and those concepts do not display world-guidedness (which is why they were selected by prescriptivism in its attempt to find a pure evaluative element from which it could detach world-guidedness).[11]

Certainly the summarizing slogan is not a wholly incorrect way of characterizing Williams' view. He considers thick and thin concepts to be different, and the latter to be wholly action-guiding and to display no world-guidedness. Yet, there is more to say.

Here are three brief points that indicate the detail. First, we might have to think hard, in a way that Williams' writing often invites us to, about how and when concept-application will provide us with reasons to act. Williams seems to accept, in the second passage, that because concepts 'often' provide people with reasons to act, then they sometimes do not despite his insistence on the characteristic point of them. Following on from this we can, second, think about Williams' first passage. How is it that concepts offer or embody reasons 'directly', there and then in a situation, and how and when do they guide action only indirectly? Perhaps indirect guidance is provided when a type of action is described in a steady drip-drip sort of a way, and action occurs only when the context is right. Third, and relatedly, we will also have to think hard about the nature and character of the reasons that the application of ethical concepts creates or embodies. This links in an obvious way to Williams' much-discussed distinction between internal and external reasons.[12]

Even if the summarizing slogan is a decent summary of Williams' views, we can see already that, as is often the case with summaries, it leaves much that is interesting unsaid. That takes me to the next section.

6.4 Where the Slogan Goes Wrong

Williams clearly thinks of 'action-guidingness' as the central and foundational characteristic or point of both thin and thick concepts. But his summarizing slogan is misleading because it hides one qualifier he explicitly makes: thick concepts *often* provide reasons for action, not that they *always* do so. The slogan would lead someone to think that Williams thinks the latter, but clearly it is the former he advocates, and he is surely sensible to do so.

Indeed, we can see that as regards other sorts of evaluative concept, not only do they sometimes not provide reasons for action, Williams thinks it is unwise to see

---

[11] Williams (1985), pp. 151–2.
[12] Williams (1981). For commentary on the tension between his work on thick concepts and his work on internal reasons see Heuer (2013) and Wiland (2013).

them as being characteristically related to action. Elsewhere in *ELP*, earlier than the passages quoted above, he criticizes Hare for characterizing all evaluative concepts along prescriptivist lines.

> In saying that anything is good or bad, admirable or low, outstanding or inferior of its kind, we are in effect telling others or ourselves to do something—as the explanation typically goes, to choose something. All evaluation has to be linked to action.
>
> This result is not easy to believe. It seems false to the spirit of many aesthetic evaluations, for instance: it seems to require our basic perspective on the worth of pictures to be roughly that of potential collectors. Even within the realm of the ethical, it is surely taking too narrow a view of human merits to suppose that people recognized as good are people that we are being told to imitate.[13]

The worry Williams has is that if all evaluation is linked to action then it reduces the idea of evaluation to choosing, or promoting, or recommending, or *doing something* beyond (or as part of) the act of categorization.[14] When it comes to aesthetic concepts, are we to assume that if we praise an outfit as glamorous, say, we are expressing our desire and intention to wear it, or telling people to wear it, or anything else similar? Clearly we do use aesthetic concepts in this way, but we do not always do so.

Let me continue in this vein by detailing my previous sentence. First, no one should doubt that we do use aesthetic concepts to guide action. It is not as if aesthetic concepts exist in some 'pure realm' devoid of any connection to what we do. We make choices and act on the basis of aesthetic categorization all the time. I choose to wear an outfit because it is eye-catchingly beautiful, while you decline because you think it is garish. We can also disagree about which people are attractive and swop various evaluative concepts in our discussion. (Recall Betty and Frank from Chapter Two.) Despite our disagreements about clothes and people, we may both decide not to buy a certain novel because we have read a review of it that describes it as naive and clunky. And so on.

These are contexts where a direct, unmediated choice is forced upon us, but action-guidance can occur indirectly as well, even in the aesthetic realm. There may be no intention in my mind at the time I categorize something using an aesthetic concept, but there is no reason to think that a reason to act may not come later. My evaluation of a book can lead you in future, when a direct choice faces you, to spend your money in one direction and not another.

Yet, Williams is right in the passage to draw attention to the fact that we often do not use aesthetic concepts in this way. We can pass judgement on outfits, novels, and many other things with no intention at all to express our desires about them, or get

---

[13] Williams (1985), p. 124.
[14] The types of action I give are all positive. I could easily have listed refraining and dismissing as well, for example.

people to do things in relation to them. We simply wish to categorize them in a certain way. Further, we use certain aesthetic concepts to explore what we think about them and, indeed, to reveal their nature better. 'Well, why is it naive? Mainly because the set-pieces, though probably decent in the abstract, were too clunky and came too thick and fast to allow the characters room to breathe.' We also use aesthetic concepts to contrast one thing with another. Action-guidance might come, but it might not. The link between concept-application and reason-giving might be so weak and tenuous that it is misguided to speak of there being any link at all, even something indirect.

An advocate for the literal application of Williams' slogan for all evaluative concepts could counter by claiming that action-guidance will come at *some* point, no matter how indirect. I am not so sure that it will. But even if it does, this objection takes us down the wrong argumentative track. The present discussion is *not* concerned with whether we can find counter-examples to show that an evaluative concept can be applied with no consequence at all for the guidance of action. The debate is whether talk of 'action-guidingness' should be seen as the best way of characterizing the *fundamental* nature of aesthetic concepts and, more broadly, all evaluative concepts. On that point, just imagine that when reading *ELP* you had come across this summarizing slogan: 'thin aesthetic concepts are action-guiding, while thick aesthetic concepts are both action-guiding and world-guided'. I suspect any reader would have been a little unnerved. This surprise would have remained even after digging beyond the slogan and acknowledging the qualifiers about the frequency and directness of the action-guidance provided. It just seems wrong to think that aesthetic concepts are primarily concerned with the guidance of action and that casting them in this way reveals something fundamental about their nature. Williams himself saw this.

That is enough for us to stop and say that Williams, or at least his slogan, was wrong to characterize *all* thin and thick concepts in terms of the guidance of action. As I have already said, perhaps his focus on ethical concepts led Williams to say what he says about all evaluative concepts. But, beyond this, might we worry also about ethical concepts? Notice that in the fourth passage quoted, although the focus is on aesthetic concepts, Williams mentions ethical concepts at the end in the same regard.

I think there is a difference of degree between typical ethical and aesthetic concepts. (The qualifier 'typical' indicates the fact that I do not think we can be too precise here.) Ethical concepts are more frequently and pointedly related to action than aesthetic concepts are. Ethics seems to have at its core how we interact with other people: how we treat them and how we respond to what they do. It seems to involve the giving of guidance, the organization of our lives, and decisions about what to do. It also covers the area of our lives where we categorize and decide what we do for ourselves. (The overlap here with prudential concepts is obvious.) This is why Williams' summarizing slogan in a book about ethics does not surprise in the way I imagined an 'aesthetic version' surprising us. There is nothing bad about saying that ethical concepts are characteristically related to action, assuming that in doing this we are drawing a contrast with those evaluative concepts that are not characteristic-ally like this.

Yet, I stress that even in the case of ethics we should not think that any sort of problem is solved and that we can carry on blithely using the summarizing slogan. The slogan hides Williams' qualifier about reasons for action only often being provided. If there are cases where no reasons are provided, then those concepts must have some other function or functions, at least on those occasions. And, probably, they have this other function or functions on occasions where reasons for action *are* provided. Indeed, it is obvious that ethical concepts can be used to categorize and shape our view of things in a way that is unrelated to any attempt to influence action. We just want to understand better in an ethical way what the thing is like, and what our view of the thing is like. How does it compare with those other things and how complex is it? Evaluative concepts allow us to do all of this, and ethical concepts are no exception.

To drive the point home we can think about evaluative epistemic concepts such as WISE, KNOWLEDGEABLE, DULL-WITTED, IGNORANT, GULLIBLE, CLEVER, SHREWD, and NAIVE. Just as in the case of ethics we can describe these concepts as related to the guidance of action. We choose one dictionary rather than another because we believe it is more comprehensive, and we listen to the views of one person rather than another because she understands better what is going on. But talking of action-guidance is too broadbrush here, for it is obvious that there is a certain class of actions—if we call them that—that epistemic concepts typically apply to. These concepts are characteristically related to the formation of beliefs and the development of under-standing. So if we were to form a summarizing slogan for epistemic concepts, we might talk of 'belief-formation' or (the ugly) 'understanding-enabling', say, rather than 'action-guidance'.

However, as should be clear, I think we should try to resist the temptation to form any such summarizing slogans. As in the case of ethics and aesthetics, epistemic concepts do more than merely give guidance as to what beliefs we should form. We also use them to categorize things in ways related to this aspect of our lives. Someone may be described as knowledgeable without there being any intention that we should go to her when we want to ask a question. And a scientific method may be described as reliable merely so that we can distinguish it from its rivals. The moral here is that it is a mistake to think that all evaluative concepts should be thought to be wholly about the guidance of action or wholly about something else. Evaluative concepts have a number of different roles, even those from within areas such as ethics or aesthetics. If we *are* tempted to use summarizing slogans, we need to make clear that they are just starting ideas from which we can extend our knowledge and which need to be rethought in the light of further reflection.

Having said all of this, a reader might worry about my tendency throughout this book to speak of thick concepts as being both evaluative and descriptive. I happen to think these two labels are broader than Williams'. But the spirit of the charge may still stick: being wedded to these two labels rules out certain sorts of function that are important when it comes to thick concepts. Indeed that is true. Ironically, the idea of action-guidance is not obvious from talking of 'the evaluative'. But to deflect this charge the reader should realize that this whole book is an extended reflection on what is meant by 'the evaluative' and 'the descriptive' in this context, and as I hope is clear, I am happy to be generous and open-minded about what sorts of action or function are encompassed by 'the evaluative'.[15]

What of the other part of Williams' slogan? Thick concepts are world-guided, while thin concepts are not. This seems odd, at face value. Imagine the everyday application of concepts and terms to the world. (Even separationists will be able to entertain the idea that, at first glance, evaluative concepts can be and are legitimately applied to things.) At this level it seems obvious that people can be honest and horrible, and that actions can be good and bad. The use of these concepts and terms seems guided by how things are in the world, for there are many things in the world to which these concepts and terms apply.

So the slogan has to be implying more than what it says simply on the surface, that thick concepts are world-guided while thin concepts are not. As mentioned in Chapter One, Williams thinks of thick concepts being more important than thin ones. (He is the best example of a thick prioritarian.) The clue is in the fact, mentioned in Chapter One, note 11, that Williams does not refer to 'thin concepts' by this label in *ELP*, but instead talks of the "most general and abstract concepts", as in the third passage above. Extrapolating, but only a little, we can form Williams' view. Thick concepts give us a way of categorizing things. (Indeed, we might say that the *stuff* of the world becomes isolatable and understandable as separate *things* partly in virtue of our categorizations.) They are specific and relate to, and help to pick out, aspects of individual things to which our attention is drawn. We note that some things bear great similarities to each other, and when we apply a concept to one thing we apply that same concept to another thing. And, in fact, concepts develop partly on the basis that similarities are noticed by us. Crucially, for Williams' view, some evaluative concepts are very specific. Some less so. The really specific ones relate, we can imagine, to only a few examples. The less specific the concept, the more likely it is that it will apply to more things.[16] We form less specific concepts often by abstracting from the really specific concepts and the things to which they apply.

---

[15] A small note about my argumentative strategy. Someone might be suspicious that in pushing this generous account of what evaluative concepts are, I am simply helping myself to the liberal notion. Clearly if this is what I was doing, then it would be suspect. However, what I take myself to be doing is to show that it is good to be generous and open-minded about what thick evaluative concepts are since, later on, we will see that it helps us make better sense of what they are like.

[16] Note the qualifiers. There are possible worlds where there are few good things but many wicked things, but that need not mean that GOOD is more specific than WICKED. Despite such examples, I think the general identification I make in the main text holds in this world, by and large.

So, to take a family of examples I have already used, we can distinguish actions by marking them with concepts such as SYMPATHETIC, EMPATHETIC, COMPASSIONATE, and THOUGHTFUL. Despite the differences between these concepts and the examples they apply to, most or all actions categorized with these concepts can be categorized using KIND. Williams' guiding thought is that thin concepts, such as GOOD and RIGHT, sit at the top of our 'abstraction tree'.[17] They are the end point of many abstractions and, as such, have little or no important connection with any of the things they are used to categorize. They do not generate or ground the sort of evaluative knowledge that can be used by a community to ward off any threat of relativism. They provide little understanding of the world because they are so abstract and removed from what the world is like. In short, they are not world-guided, but are merely thin content formed from other, more specific concepts.

In conclusion, Williams' detailed prose is, as one might well imagine, nuanced and reflective. His slogan does not do his thoughts justice. I have no criticism to offer of the slogan's use of 'world-guided' in the way in which I criticized 'action-guidance'. I say more in Chapter Eight about evaluative knowledge picking up on my comments just now about the 'abstraction tree'. I think that Williams is too pessimistic about thin concepts and sees them only through the prism of thick concepts. The reason for me talking about world-guidance now is so that I can introduce Ryle's work on the idea of thick description. This allows me to reinforce my criticism of the slogan: concepts, both individual concepts and concepts of a certain particular type, have a variety of functions. Conveying this idea has been the main task of this section and the one previous. Looking at Ryle will help us to broaden our understanding of what is going on. This is all with a view to understanding the evaluative better.

6.5 Ryle on Thick Descriptions

I have three aims in this section. First, to understand Williams in the light of Ryle. Second, to introduce the suggestion that thick concepts are a type of thick description, that is that they are a simple subset of the larger group. While this idea is partly correct, matters are not as straightforward as they seem. Third, to set out Ryle's view of concepts. This takes us to §6.6 where I lay out my view of the evaluative and defend it.

We can think about the idea of a thick description by starting with one of Ryle's examples from Ryle (1968). He thinks about how we distinguish different sorts of wink. He imagines a succession of boys who wink in different ways and for

---

[17] I would go further if I were Williams and say 'PRO and CON', but that is a small point. Aside from which concepts sit at the top of the tree, Williams was also interested in criticizing fellow philosophers' obsession with thin concepts, mainly GOOD, RIGHT, DUTY and the like. More in this day than in the mid-1980s, PRO and CON seem appropriate focuses of this criticism, at least of some parts of our philosophical community.

different reasons.[18] The first boy has an involuntary twitch. The second winks conspiratorially to an accomplice. Yet he does so in a slow, contorted, and conspicuous manner. The third boy parodies the second in order to give malicious amusement to his cronies. He acts clumsily, just as the second did, but he is not himself clumsy. This third boy is later imagined in a different setting, and so becomes a fourth example: he practises his parody and so rehearses for a (hoped-for) public performance. This boy is later imagined in another setting, thereby creating a fifth example. When winking he had not been trying to parody the second boy, but had been "trying to gull the grown-ups into the false belief that he was trying to do so".[19]

Ryle asks what is common to these examples. The obvious answer is the thinnest description, such as 'the boy contracted his eyelids'. Ryle thinks this applies to every case, and we can say of each that there is a physical movement. However, he presses two points. First, in order to distinguish the boys' actions—note, not just their physical movements—we need to employ thick descriptions. This need (which is my word) is not just a matter of ease of language, that thick descriptions act merely as summations of various (separable) elements that could be expressed without them if only we had the time and patience. We need particular descriptions rather than others because some actions are so complex that they cannot be separated into parts that can be described separately. We can see this through a second point. Ryle argues that the boy who winks conspiratorially does not do, say, five things that should be treated as separate from one another: (i) winks deliberately, (ii) to someone in particular, (ii) in order to impart a certain message, (iv) according to an understood code, (v) without the cognizance of the rest of the company. For Ryle it is better to describe the boy as doing one complex thing, something with a number of aspects, rather than saying that the boy is doing five separate things at one and the same time. In some cases of a particular action described in a particular way one can be successful (or fail) in one aspect only if one is successful (or fail) in other aspects. Ryle refers to clauses such as those just expressed as embodying 'success-and-failure' conditions, and this is a key point for him. Actions such as winks and conspiratorial winks are to be distinguished from physical movements, such as involuntary twitches, because the former have success-and-failure conditions, which in turn guide us in our descriptions or, better, are embodied in our descriptions.

We can elaborate. Imagine an example one step on from Ryle's list. A boy is both parodying a fellow pupil, with the complexity familiar from above, *and* is trying to win a girl's heart. On some understandings of this description we can have a case where not all aspects of the action stand or fall together: the success-and-failure conditions are separate. The boy can parody the other pupil without trying to impress the girl and he can impress the girl in all manner of ways. In the sort of understanding I have in mind of this case it seems right to say that our winker is

---

[18] The examples are introduced in various ways across pp. 494–6 of Ryle (1968).
[19] Ryle (1968), p. 496.

trying to do two things. In this case one part—'trying to win a girl's heart'—can be dropped. That would change the action as described previously, but it seems as if we have two actions that were conjoined anyway, all along, and dropping the one aspect will leave the other intact and unchanged.

We could have had a different description—one that some readers may have in mind—where aspects of the action might well stand or fall together: the boy is trying to win the girls' heart *by* parodying his fellow pupil. Perhaps someone corrects the previous description: 'No, Eric isn't parodying Ernie *and* trying to win Vanessa's heart. He's trying to impress her *by* impersonating his friend.' Here I think it plausible to say that the winker is doing only one complex thing.[20]

This shows how and why the description is paramount for Ryle. As we might term it, there is the physical movement, which in this case is the contraction of the eyelids, and there are the various actions. Each individual physical movement can be picked out with the same thin description: 'the boy's eyelid contracted'. But for Ryle there seems to be no one core thing that is the action in his examples which then gets added to separable aspects, or to which separable aspects are added in order to create more complex actions. So, to finish with my two cases just given, while in the first case (the one that employs '*and*') dropping the part whereby Eric is imagined to be winning the girl's heart will not change the part or action where Eric is imagined to be parodying Ernie, in the second case ('*by*') it is not obvious at all that a subtraction of the former aspect will leave the latter aspect intact and unchanged.

We can generalize. If there is a range of similar actions such as Ryle's range of winks, described using related but different thick descriptions, then for Ryle there need be no core that all has in exactly the same way. This is true even if we imagine that the core is 'the boy winked'. For a start, it will not cover our first case, of the involuntary twitcher. But also the ways in which people wink are different and embody different success-and-failure conditions. There is no reason to think that we have one thing, winking, which is exactly the same thing at the core of each action to which we simply add separable aspects that do not change it in any way as we move from case to case. This is why I talk of Ryle in this book. It is clear to me that this idea of his is nonseparationist in outlook, even though we must grant that it is not developed using or applied to evaluative concepts.

These points can be hard to see when it comes to winking simply because 'wink' is often used colloquially to describe the physical act of contracting the eyelid. It is easier to see the thought with the activity that is Ryle's prime focus in his (1968), namely thinking, for thinking is not colloquially thought of as a physical activity. There are many types of thinking: pondering, meditating, coming to understand,

---

[20] The final remark of Ryle (1968) shows this perfectly. "A statesman signing his surname to a peace-treaty is doing much more than inscribe the seven letters of his surname, but he is not doing many or any more things. He is bringing the war to a close by inscribing the seven letters of his surname." The word 'things' at the end of the first sentence is key to understanding Ryle's point.

and so on. These examples are exemplified in many ways: mental arithmetic, writing on a piece of paper, chatting with others, arguing with others, manipulating some wood, playing notes on a piano, picking food from a shelf, and so on.[21] Are we confident that there is one separable core activity called 'thinking' common to all these examples that we could isolate and that stands revealed as the very same thing in each instance? Can we also, therefore, imagine that we would then be left with one or more separable element for each action that would be our remainder? The answer is surely not an obvious yes, and, I think, we would and should be inclined to say no. For Ryle, when we describe an action with a thick description, we are labelling something that is a unitary thing.

Of course, in one sense all the examples of winking and thinking have something in common, namely the former are all cases of winking and the latter are all cases of thinking. But this simple, innocent point can lead us astray. It would be wrong to move from this thought to think that there was a core, narrowly construed action of winking or thinking that was divorced from all its instances and which was conjoined with all the various aspects to create those individual instances. Instead, those aspects of acts of winking and thinking help to us appreciate what winking and thinking are, in a fuller way. This is why there is no simple subtraction from actions of certain aspects that leaves the act of winking or thinking intact as before. From this we can generalize, again.

In short Ryle thinks that we understand a concept only through its applications and uses.[22] Furthermore, we can make a point not just about us understanding concepts, but a point about what concepts are. A concept is the abstraction from words and phrases used in all manner of ways in various contexts.[23] The various inflections of meaning and the (sometimes) subtle differences in meaning across context are such as to affect our appreciation of what a concept is and what an associated term means, and all of this appreciation reveals to us what the concept is. Think again about THINKING. For Ryle we appreciate what it is to think only if we understand the various exemplifications of the concept, which things count as thinking and which do not. Someone playing on a piano fiddling around to find a tune can very well be thinking, and this sort of thinking differs from the thinking we

---

[21] Some of these examples are from Tanney (2009), p. xviii. I categorically do not wish to suggest that every instance of, say, playing notes on a piano is a type of thinking, just that some are. To elaborate these examples: the physical activity is not something separate from the thinking. It is how the thinking is exemplified and how an idea, some inspiration or frustration, say, is worked through.

[22] The resemblance to the later Wittgenstein on this point is striking, but I do not detail it here.

[23] This applies also to technical words for Ryle. To take a much-used example, we might say that it is discovered and *stipulated* that water is H_2O. Fine. But non-scientists rarely encounter H_2O. What most people typically encounter is H_2O with impurities of various sorts. Does that mean we should not call the stuff in the bottles on our desks 'water'? Do we have to say that it is just a shorthand? Do we have to say that we have one word 'water' that, strictly, stands for two related concepts: the technical one and the everyday one? These are options. Another option is to say that, despite first appearances, WATER can legitimately be applied to more than just pure H_2O.

typically experience in a philosophy seminar between two disputants trying out an idea on one another or arguing with all guns blazing. It will also differ from idle fiddling around on a piano when someone is not thinking about anything even a tune, but is just, well, fiddling. Appreciating the similarities and differences of these and other examples is simply to appreciate the contours of THINKING and how it can be applied and withheld correctly and incorrectly, creatively and foolishly. Of course, once we do that we will appreciate what THINKING stands for. So just on this basis it would be wrong to say that there is no fixed meaning for THINKING. THINKING means whatever our investigation of its uses reveals. However, once we accept that there can be all manner of different things that can be categorized as THINKING, with no core element that THINKING stands for, we should appreciate that new uses will appear, present uses will disappear and, therefore, that the concept itself, and not just applications of it, can change.

Of course, one could say that thinking just means any sort of general mental activity. But that seems only to give a definition by (trivial) synonymy. What we are after is something deeper than that, something that allows us to apply and withhold properly, something that allows us to connect it in meaningful, plausible ways to other concepts. In order to do so, we have to get a handle of some of the uses familiar to us and understand all aspects of acts of thinking.

Despite the claim that we can understand concepts only if we understand the many and various contexts in which the concept is used, this is not to say that we have wild and frequent changes in concepts' meanings across such uses, at least for every concept. (In the case of a supposed single concept, that might well point to us having different concepts to cope with.) Instead, we can talk of there being a common root, and rock-solid commonality, and other such things. Philosophers are important because they can point out this fact and map the ways in which different concepts work and their implications, as well as pointing out mistakes that fellow philosophers have made.

All of the foregoing is no straightforward argument for Ryle's view. But it is central in the picture I am building for thick concepts. In brief, I think Ryle's view about how concepts and language work is right, and it will be key as we go through other ideas. In short, I think that thick concepts are such that (i) we understand them only through understanding how they are used, and (ii) the content of thick concepts, and the meaning of thick terms, is given by how they are used. For now, two topics are left for this section.

First, what of Williams in relation to Ryle? Quite simply, despite the suggestive and interesting nature of his qualifiers, in my view Williams does not pay enough attention to the ways in which various evaluative concepts are used, and from that the various trends that become apparent. While many ethical concepts have success-and-failure conditions that guide action, they often have conditions that do not provide reasons to act at all. Williams I think is guilty of paying too much attention to how some ethical concepts work on some occasions and not enough to the success-and-failure conditions that they and other evaluative concepts have. (This is ironic given how much Williams bemoans modern philosophers' fixation on the narrowly moral concepts associated with duty and obligation.)

So, for example, a concept such as HONEST can be used to guide action directly.[24] But it can also be used to guide actions indirectly, and it can be used to evaluate with no thought of the influence of action, and action to be guided in the future. It can be used to compare. It can be used to voice hope, express relief and joy, and many more things. It can be used of people, of actions, of institutions. It can indicate a narrow judgement about a particular piece of language. It can be used of a document and what is said between the lines. It can also be used of the intentions of speakers and writers, and of their wider spirit of personality. Despite all of these various uses, we typically are able to get a handle on the concept through some process of abstraction, even if people will have different conceptions of that concept.

Discussion of Williams and Ryle is therefore instructive. We have talked through the idea that evaluative concepts can have a variety of functions and roles. We have also seen suggested that many concepts, not just those regarded as straightforwardly evaluative, can be understood through their uses. Such uses reveal that there is no narrowly construed idea of a concept that, when it is applied, is applied in separation from other aspects of the action that it is describing. Those other aspects enable us to capture a mature understanding of the concept in question.

A second thought ends this section and sets up the next. A tempting idea moves into view. Are thick concepts a type of thick description? It seems straightforward to answer in the affirmative. Thick descriptions are specific descriptions or, as we can say with a little licence, specific concepts. Thick concepts are a type of specific concept, namely specific evaluative concepts. Therefore thick concepts are a type of thick description.

Now, it is not as if this is a terrible idea. But as with Williams' summarizing slogan, it requires pause for thought since it may hide important points. Talk of thick evaluative concepts that are a type of thick description implies, strongly or weakly, that there is a type (or there are types) of thick description that is (or are) not evaluative. This talk of types may imply, strongly or weakly, that we can easily divide the evaluative from the descriptive or nonevaluative along a neat line. It is this implication that worries me and which we need to uncover and reflect upon. How confident are we that we can divide in this way? In the next section I suggest that we should be highly wary of being able to do so. We may not wish to commit to any division at all or, if we do, we should be wary of thinking that it lies where some writers think it does and wary that we can pinpoint its location with confidence.

---

[24] I owe this example to Sophie-Grace Chappell.

6.6 Evaluative Concepts

We now examine some ideas that move beyond the appreciation that concepts can have a variety of functions. In the discussion of ethical, aesthetic, and epistemic concepts we assumed that some function or functions other than the guidance of action would still involve some explicit pro or con stance within the evaluation, be it implied or just inferred. Yet, if we can now see that evaluative concepts can do a few things, why think that the giving of, and the embodiment of, pro and con stances and views is exhaustive of their nature?

I begin this section with some examples and then draw some morals.

(a) *Some examples.* Chapter Four saw us run through various concepts accepted as thin which we saw come in a range of thicknesses. Even if we might accept that all of these concepts are always used in pro or con ways—although I will come to that in a little while—it is clear that the labels of the 'simply' or the 'purely' evaluative cover more complexity than is acknowledged by separationists. And if we are comfortable with that idea, we should consider if other concepts can be called evaluative, even if they differ from each other and differ from the traditional diet of thin concepts. So we need to motivate the idea that various concepts (not just thick ones) function in the ways that those concepts routinely labelled as thick function. We then need to think about the character of these concepts.

No one doubts that JUST and KIND, BEAUTIFUL, and WISE are thick concepts. Separationists may offer an analysis of them that I think is wrong, but that is a different matter. They are not treated as descriptive concepts first of all.[25] We can move on a little. Many theorists also routinely accept that KNOWLEDGEABLE and ELEGANT are thick evaluative concepts. They clearly pick our specific features of people and objects in the way that thick concepts routinely do. They are also often used in straightforward pro (and con) ways.

Is a concept such as ELEGANT so different from concepts such as GROTESQUE and MACABRE? We can certainly apply MACABRE in a way that indicates positive or negative appraisals. We can praise a story for the macabre atmosphere that it creates, given that we want something to spook us; Hallowe'en is no time for sugary fairy tales. But we can also damn by calling something macabre: its sinister nature chills us when we require something to soothe and comfort. We can also apply this concept and be offering no obvious pro or con evaluation. We may call a thing macabre and be trying to articulate its nature, either to others or to ourselves. We may also be using this word to compare and contrast it with other things: 'No, that is not fun, it is macabre' or 'What fun! How macabre!' Furthermore, we might be explaining things: 'It is terrifying because it is macabre.' Calling something macabre seems to

---

[25] At the very least, they are treated as descriptive concepts that often or always carry some pro or con element with them.

pinpoint the nature of something in a way that is more specific than calling it terrifying, for example. This is also what we do with ELEGANT, I suggest. Although we can praise the elegant, and often damn because something is elegant, we can apply this concept simply to categorize, to compare, and to give conceptual shape to the thing we are trying to understand.

Although I am often wary of looking at dictionary definitions in philosophical contexts, the *OED* entry for 'macabre' mainly lists synonyms such as grim, horrific, and repulsive, all of which are suggestive of something negative. But, as we know from LEWD and from human psychology, sometimes we can revel in the grim and some people are drawn to things they conceive of as being repulsive.[26]

Similarly, consider GOSSIP. We can talk in a variety of ways and gossiping is one of them. It is certainly more specific than COMMUNICATION, say, and something more than and different from the idea of 'sharing information'. Furthermore, we can damn a piece of information as gossip, or revel in the loveliness of gossip, as well as enjoying the piece of gossip we have just heard. The *OED* has: "... idle talk; trifling or groundless rumour; tittle-tattle. Also, in a more favourable sense: Easy, unrestrained talk or writing, esp. about persons or social incidents." We see here, as with MACABRE, the reliance on synonyms, and also the switch from negative to positive. There is no clear 'good' or 'bad', let alone 'pro' or 'con' mentioned, but no competent speaker of English could fail to latch on to the positive and negative associations that occur in general with the concept when it is used. And, similarly, we can classify and categorize some conversation as GOSSIP, with no explicit pro or con point, in order to categorize it in a particular way.

The same is true of CAJOLE: it is a way of asking someone to do something and is, to my ear, a little more specific than persuasion. We can persuade in many ways: with threats, with explicit incentives. And cajoling, while it may use implied threats and incentives, is something different. Importantly, we can praise a piece of persuasion by calling it an instance of cajoling, and damn it as well. We can also, plainly, use it as a way of indicating what the action was.

The *OED* has this, as a verb, "To prevail upon or get one's way with (a person) by delusive flattery, specious promises, or any false means of persuasion." Later, however, it also defines it in a more neutral way: one can persuade by flattery, with the 'delusive' dropped.

I am building up the case that the difference in function and nature between the routine diet of thick concepts name-checked by writers and these others concepts is slight; indeed it might be non-existent. It is so slight, if it exists at all, that it does not offend to call MACABRE, GOSSIP, and CAJOLE thick. Indeed, I reckon that before my discussion we would have called them thick anyway.

---

[26] That last comment takes us into deep waters, where we have to think about people being attracted to the bad. I do not wish to wade too far in. I do not know about being attracted to the bad (rather than attracted to things that one thinks others think are bad), but I do think that people can be (counterintuitively) attracted to the repulsive and not just attracted to that which they acknowledge repulses others.

Consider two more examples mentioned above. If we work only with concepts such as JUST and KIND then it would be understandable to class an adjective such as CONTORTED and a noun such as MEDITATION as nonevaluative, descriptive concepts. However, we do use such concepts with explicit pro and con views in mind, even if we do so in fewer cases than we do with JUST and KIND. Poems and dancers can be damned for being contorted, but they can also be admired for the same reason. Some academic can praise another for work that has come out of some serious meditation on a problem, and praise the activity of this special sort of thought itself. We can also bemoan the meditation and endless thinking going on when what we really want is action.

Again, the *OED*'s definitions are interesting here. For 'meditation' we first of all have "to consider thoughtfully", and "to consider deeply", and later on "serious continuous contemplation". It is not obvious to me that these ideas are wholly nonevaluative. We can say similar things about CONTORTION: the idea here is of something that is uncomfortable, strenuous, and unusual. These words are not neutral: they have strong negative associations. But they have positive ones also: sometimes it is good to make ourselves uncomfortable, both physically and mentally.

Yet more concepts are worth mentioning. Gibbard's analysis of LEWD employs what, to my mind, is an example ripe for the same treatment, namely WARRANTED. (I mentioned this niggle in passing in Chapter Five, §5.4(c).) When we categorize a piece of behaviour or a belief as warranted we are saying that it is the sort of thing that is allowed and authorized. By implication we are saying that the thing is good in a certain sort of way. So it is not just good *simpliciter*.[27] Similarly, when we say that something, for example a belief, is justified, we say that there is some special link between it and some piece of evidence that shows the belief to be a good one to hold in some way.

Yet more. Earlier in this study I said that someone who was wise had sufficient understanding and relevant knowledge. Words such as 'sufficient' and 'relevant' are in the same boat as 'warranted'. We are marking out a certain sort of understanding as sufficient, just the right amount (of understanding) to allow us to categorize something in a certain way (a person as wise, say). When we call something relevant we are saying that it is linked to the thing in which we are interested in the right sort of way. And, we can further specify 'right way' depending on the things in question: something can be linked to something else such that it is relevant because it illuminates the thing, or is useful for the thing, or something else. Importantly, it is not just right *simpliciter*, but is right in a particular way, for a particular reason, a reason that may be explained only using other concepts that (I suspect) are evaluative. Knowing when something is relevant will involve the exercise of judgement.

---

[27] Dancy (1995), §VIII mentions this point and discusses and extends it in a way similar to how I do: introducing the notion of the good or right sort of way immediately takes us back to the evaluative and the thick.

It seems we can talk in this way at will. We can say that if something is relevant to something else we think it is good in a way, a way that may be illuminating and useful. Similarly, if something is useful, it allows us to do something that we want to do. Also, if something allows something else, it permits or eases the path of that something where before there may have been barriers of a kind. And so on.

In all of these cases, and many more, we have concepts and ideas that are sometimes used in overtly pro and con ways and sometimes not. There may be some variation between these concepts as to how frequently they are used in pro and con ways, or the significance of those occasions when they do so, and what types of instance of concept application are considered canonical and exemplary.

One last line of examples. Let us go back to those concepts thought to be thin or fairly thin: DUTY (or DUTIFUL), OUGHT, ACCEPTABLE, APPROPRIATE, and the like, concepts that easily shade into JUST and FAIR. We will often use such words to praise and to indicate something positive, and their antonyms are used negatively. But often we just report that something is someone's duty or that someone is being dutiful, or that something because it is appropriate fits well in the situation or with other things. Such uses have the potential to lead to praise or to negative judgement, but they need not be used in this manner directly and immediately. They operate in similar ways to the other examples of this section.

(b) *Some morals*. There was a lot going on with these examples. Let us draw matters out slowly over the next few sub-sections. I start with our big themes.

(i) *The liberal view of evaluation*. One more reminder. The *conservative* view of evaluation categorizes concepts as evaluative concepts only if those concepts are used routinely in an obviously pro or con way. The *liberal* view of evaluation views evaluation as encompassing pro and con, but it does not confine the nature of evaluation to such matters. It allows that a concept can be an evaluative concept and yet, on certain instances when it is used (sincerely and straightforwardly), there be no positive or negative stance as part of its use and this not threaten the fact that it is an evaluative concept, either overall or in that particular instance of its use.

In cases where we have a term being used with no obvious positive or negative view at all, conservatives are likely to say one of two things: either that we have the same word, but a different concept in play; or that we have a single concept across these different uses, but that the concept is not evaluative, and when it is used evaluatively such pro and con evaluations are accidental to the concept, contingent add-ons conveyed through tone of voice for example, and implied and inferred through conventional means.

Note that I am not arguing that any concept used in an evaluative way in an instance can be, or even that it has to be, an evaluative concept. I am interested only in negating the conservative view. I think that concepts can be evaluative even if at times they do not convey some pro or con view at all. Note also two more extreme views that I do not favour. The *radical* view says that a concept can be an evaluative concept and there be no instance of its use that has a simple, obvious, pro or con stance to it. The *crazy* view says that an evaluative concept must not have any instances that have any pro or con stances to them. I use these as contrasts to underline the fact that I think that there must be some clear instances of pro and/or con use for a concept to count as an evaluative concept. I explain why later.

So why hold the liberal view? To motivate it, consider those two options conservatives have to take when it comes to our examples above. The first says that all of these examples are not evaluative. This does not hold water. Not only can we see that these examples are routinely used to indicate pro and con views (even if they are not used in this way every single time), we can also see that those fairly thin concepts such as DUTY and OUGHT are used in this way too. Does it seem useful or plausible to restrict our notion of what an evaluative concept is simply to GOOD and RIGHT, or just PRO and CON?[28] I suggest that it is not, and that we do not treat examples from above in this way.

Second, conservatives could say that words can cover a range of concepts, given with different tones of voice or similar—our familiar MACABRE-PRO, MACABRE-CON, and MACABRE-NEUTRAL—and that only some of these concepts are evaluative, those with the –PRO and –CON suffixes. (The same can be said for DUTY-PRO and DUTY-CON, of course.) Does this stance hold water?

We saw when discussing Williams and Ryle that concepts may do many things: predominantly guide action and judgement, categorize objects, and express positive and negative stances. Further, I outlined Ryle's view that the nature or content of concepts is constructed from the ways in which we use and apply them. We get a sense of what the limits of acceptability are and what things are relevant to what other things only through understanding the types of example which fall under the concept and the ways in which the concept and associated term are employed across many instances. The mastery of a concept comes when we appreciate the point of the concept, how it can be used and what various parts of the concept really stand for. I agree that we should take a holistic approach to such understanding. When I say of a novel that it was macabre, and do not intend praise or blame or anything else positive or negative, I am still offering evaluation of it (that is, there is still evaluative content), because my categorization of it in this instance relies on, or is an expression of, an understanding that encompasses times and instances when there are explicit types of praise and blame or other positive and negative reactions. The content of macabre—what this means and how it applies—relies on all sorts of instances. If I cannot understand when to offer and withhold the concept, when it can be used creatively and foolishly, when it can be used positively or negatively, and *why*, then I do not understand what it is for something to be macabre. Aside from this instance, I might be asked to explain what MACABRE is and doing so will require my drawing on an appreciation from a number of different examples.

---

[28] It is at this point in the argument that my consideration of Vayrynen's argument in Chapter Seven is relevant.

I think that all of this tells strongly against the conservative option that we should restrict 'the evaluative' to a very small number of concepts such as GOOD and BAD, and for all the rest multiply concepts in the manner indicated. It seems far better to start with the view that some or many concepts will have a variety of functions, even if not every single use is exemplified in every instance. Given how important it often is for some concepts, such as MACABRE or SHREWD, to convey pro and con stances, then this is enough to call them evaluative overall.

Furthermore, this idea leads to the following crucial point. All the foregoing tells in favour of there being some special evaluative content that is not exhausted by pro and con views. One's understanding of what it is for anything to be MACABRE, and the meaning of 'macabre' and what 'macabre-ness' *is*, seem to be based on a variety of uses, and one's understanding synthesizes and encapsulates them (or at least those uses we think of as significant, core, and exemplary). When nonseparationists talk, perhaps too loosely, of there being intermingling that offers us nonreductive, non-separable conceptual content, perhaps it is this idea to which they point. Partly through those uses of MACABRE that convey pro and con stances, the whole of the concept exemplifies or is something evaluative. Likewise, partly through the particular uses that have no obvious pro or con stances we can appreciate the special nature of why and how something MACABRE can be thought of in a positive or negative way. Sure, this concept is more specific than GOOD, but it is evaluative all the same.

One further note. This explains why I do not favour the crazy and radical views, mentioned earlier. I think that one has to have some instances of clear positive and negative usage for a concept to count as evaluative because of my reliance on one's use of the concept across many instances.[29]

---

[29] This is probably the best place for me to discuss Debbie Roberts' view. In Roberts (2013) she outlines a very similar view to mine, where she makes the case for the 'Inclusive View'. The Inclusive View is the view that thick concepts have or just embody completely (in my terms), nonseparable evaluative content. Roberts and I are in broad and deep agreement. However, there are some details that *may* indicate disagreement, although in the end they do not. Two notable ones are worth drawing attention to. (Note that Väyrynen (2013), p. 210, note 51, highlights the first point as a potential difference, although this is because he does not go into detail and sharply distinguish the views I have called 'conservative', 'liberal', 'radical', and 'crazy'.) (a) I am happy to say that on some if not many occasions thick concepts can be used to convey some pro or con stance. Furthermore, I think that the possibility of them being used in this way is something essential to how it is that they are evaluative concepts. And, relatedly, I use this idea to motivate why they can be thought to be evaluative concepts and why this content is special. This is all consistent with thinking that thick concepts' evaluative content is not to be exhausted by PRO and CON. But I do wish to turn my back on the crazy and radical views, as indicated in the main text. What of Roberts? In Roberts (2013) she sets out a view that thick concepts have content that one can call evaluative and where "a plausible case can be made that they do not encode particular thin evaluations in their content" (p. 79). Is this a clear difference between us, particularly with her talk of 'encoding' and my extended discussion that stresses the appreciation of concepts across many instances? On paper this difference may be only a matter of emphasis rather than clear opposition anyway, but in personal correspondence Roberts said that she found my position attractive and hoped that what she said in Roberts (2013) did not count against my position. (b) She focuses on the question of what it takes for a concept to be evaluative. For example, she considers essential contestability. This could be, and has been, misinterpreted. For a start, many of the conditions she picks out may not work. (Väyrynen, (2014) is a pretty good examination and

Of course, one obvious challenge leaps out from this. How can we tell when a concept is evaluative and when it is not? Is it because of the number of times in which it is used with pro and con point? Perhaps. Is it because of the significance of those uses to how we understand the concept? Probably. Despite my comments, can we really think of CONTORTED or SIMILAR as evaluative? I think we should. But my point here is that such classifications will be matters of judgement, debate, and reasoning across a community of mature concept users.

All of this discussion—in this sub-section and perhaps the whole book—may be frustrating for some readers. They may acknowledge that I am arguing against a particular view of evaluation that is characterized in terms of pro and con stances, and they may understand my claim that the evaluative is more than that. They may even agree to a greater or lesser extent. However, the frustrated cry may still go up, 'But what *is* your view of evaluation? If it isn't pro or con, of exhausted by these stances, then what is it?' I can appreciate that there may be some frustration, but such a worry starts from a wrong assumption. The worry is predicated on the idea that in articulating a different view of evaluation, my task is (and has to be) to replace one definition—'to be evaluative a concept must express a pro or con stance'—with another, where that replacement gives a definition in terms of a similarly grained term or set of terms. Or in other words, one may think that the task of this whole study is (and has to be) to fill in the schema 'evaluation is or equals x' where x is at the same conceptual or terminological level as 'pro or con stance'. However, this is not the task in this study at all. I do not believe that this is the only way to articulate a positive view in general, nor is it what I do here. Positive accounts of ideas can be cast in these ways. But sometimes—and certainly here—a view can make a positive advance both by showing that a way of casting some central term or idea is not the full picture, and by showing people what else is part of that picture, even if what is then put forward as the replacement is not a definite thing or term. Furthermore, I strongly believe that evaluation cannot be articulated as a specific thing or things (such as pro and con stance) that can be treated as different from itself such that a meaningful characterization is produced. My whole, positive view of what it is for a concept to be evaluative is that such concepts have multi-various functions: they

---

attack on the condition of essential contestability being a necessary condition of the evaluative, and there is a general discussion of such marks in Väyrynen (2013), pp. 208–13.) But, more importantly, use of 'marks' may suggest that Roberts is interested in providing necessary and sufficient conditions that help to fix what it is for a concept to be evaluative. I have explicitly set my face against this strategy, and in personal correspondence Roberts has said that she is also not interested in doing this. That is why she chose the term 'marks'. Unfortunately, Väyrynen clearly thinks of these 'marks' *as* necessary and sufficient conditions. Terminology is always difficult here. If I had to pick any one term to try to summarize some of the aspects that evaluative concepts typically have and which nonevaluative concepts may not have, I would use the word 'trend', or even the phrase 'broad trend'. Whatever term we pick, Roberts and I agree that it is essential for the sort of position we defend that it is stated explicitly that one should be wary of being sucked into a philosophical game of trying to define that which cannot be defined at a particular level of detail in an exact and specific manner.

encompass the ability to praise and blame, and express positive and negative stances, certainly (and with that they can motivate and provide reasons for action), but they can also simply offer specific understandings of how the world is that do not have to cast the world in obviously positive and negative ways. When we call a concept 'evaluative' we have in mind a looser sense than separationists, say, typically give. Separationists, among others, are guilty of fastening onto one aspect, albeit an important one, which evaluative concepts have. Evaluation and evaluative concepts are fundamental sorts of understandings or characterizations of the world and its parts, characterizations which I do not believe it is helpful to pin down exclusively to an expression of clear positive or negative stance. So, if put on the spot and asked what I think evaluative concepts are, I would say that they are fundamentally evaluative concepts. What links all of the examples I have been discussing in this chapter and elsewhere is the fact that we treat and use them as evaluative because they help to articulate particular ways of viewing the world. To get a better sense of what 'evaluative' means here one has to see how the terms and concepts typically treated as evaluative are used in many different situations, rather than trying to offer a definite term with defines evaluation. There is no magic x here with which I wish to replace 'pro and con stance'.

It is time to move to a different related discussion. Much of the above leads us to think about whether there is a supposed dividing line between the evaluative and the rest. After all, there are many ways of specifically understanding the world. Surely not all of them can be evaluative?

(ii) *The evaluative and the descriptive*. I repeat again that I think there are some concepts that are clearly and essentially evaluative by separationist lights; presumably this camp includes GOOD and BAD. Some separationists may now wonder if DUTY and OUGHT and APPROPRIATE should be included. Imagine they do. They may also think of JUST and FAIR as being initially evaluative concepts, but they will not treat such concepts as essentially evaluative since they can be separated into component parts. And on the other side of matters, there are many, many concepts that seem ripe to be classed as descriptive, nonevaluative concepts. CHAIR has been my favourite example in this study, and such an example suggests many, many more. Nouns such as AEROPLANE, PEN, COMMITTEE, BOOK, HEAD, ENTROPY, and ELEPHANT; verbs such as CHARGE, SHAKE, JUMP, EAT, and SPEND; and adjectives such as BROWN, METALLIC, and LARGE. I just want to make the case that there are some concepts that can be seen as evaluative, and by their nature call into question the idea that we have a sharp dividing line between evaluative concepts and others.

This raises a few questions. First of all, we can call into question a (deliberate) identification I have made through this study. I think that when focusing on other matters it is perfectly fine and philosophically innocent to treat as synonymous 'the descriptive' and 'the nonevaluative'. But right now we are considering the categories as a whole and thinking what, if anything, stands opposed to, or at least is different from, 'the evaluative'. To treat as central the label of 'the nonevaluative' in this regard invites the accusation that my thinking is muddled, for I am labelling the different camp of 'the evaluative' with a label that indicates a polar opposite and which assumes a difference in kind. I have turned my back on this type of clear division.

Let me make something clear. I *do* think it is philosophically fine and innocent to begin by treating as synonymous 'the nonevaluative' and 'the descriptive', if only to get us into the right frame of mind to realize that there is an interesting question to be considered about how these categories relate to the evaluative and what the character of thick concepts is. But an innocent labelling should not be enough to stop the position I articulate here. The real action concerns what lies behind the labels, namely the character of the examples we consider. We should not confuse labelling for argument, either an argument against my view or an argument for views I oppose. Indeed, it is clear that one should use these labels only after one has thought about the character of the concepts that one is putting into each camp, and thought through whether one wants to support or oppose a clear and exact division between the camps.

And this brings me to the examples I laid out above. Moving from RIGHT to JUST to ELEGANT to MACABRE to TWISTED to SIMILAR to ALLOW should invite us to question whether we have such a clear and exact division between the camps of the evaluative and the descriptive, even if, as I keep on repeating, we think there are obvious examples of both sorts. I want to call into question, through my reflection on the examples above and many other points made in this study, whether the difference between them is so clear and exacting. I doubt that it is. The only sound basis for there being such a clear and exact division, it seems to me, is to take some very conservative line that only a concept that is used in a clear pro or con way in every instance deserves the label of being an evaluative concept. That has the philosophical virtue of being simple and clear. Yet, I think my examples throw doubt on this view for we simply do not treat concepts in this way.

This idea that we have some difference but no clear and exact difference or division (or whatever it is one calls it) may seem strange. But I am not the only one to think it to be perfectly acceptable. Hilary Putnam casts doubt on what he calls the fact–value 'dichotomy' (which is what I am doing, in effect) in part by drawing the historical threads that led to its adoption, from classical empiricism, through Kant's discussion of the analytic and the synthetic, and to logical positivism.[30] For Putnam, to adopt a dichotomy is to do something far from philosophically innocent. It is to make a metaphysical and/or conceptual decision that the two items that one marks as different are polar opposites and that they, therefore, exclude one another, with no relevant example being able to occupy both camps. His recurring phrase is that the fact–value dichotomy assumes an "omnipresent and all-important gulf", and he reaches the same conclusions as I do, that there is no real argument for this gulf,

---

[30] Putnam (2002), especially chapters 1 and 2. I also referred to this in Chapter One.

and that our practices do not bear it out anyway. At one stage he concludes, when thinking about how we should classify the principles of mathematics and how they seem unlike both paradigm examples of analytic truths and descriptive truths, "This illustrates one difference between an ordinary distinction and a metaphysical dichotomy: ordinary distinctions have ranges of application, and we are not surprised if they do not always apply."[31] We might distinguish the evaluative from the descriptive, but there will be many examples where a (sharp) distinction does not apply and where our categories may fail us, if we assume that they have to be sharp.

To make clear, in the above discussion I have assumed not just that there is a grey area, but that there is enough in our examples to justify us calling many examples evaluative. If arguments from authority hold any weight, then it worth noting that although he does not go into detail about many examples, when thinking about scientific practices and concepts Putnam does assume that COHERENCE and SIMPLICITY are evaluative concepts.[32]

This takes me to some more examples. Think about the examples named as obvious cases of descriptive concepts at the start of this sub-section. Now recall OLD. At the start of this chapter I used as OLD as an example of a descriptive concept in order to make a point about context-sensitivity. But we might ask whether it is so different from RELEVANT. Both seem to be applicable because of the context in which they are used, both enable us to compare one item with another or more. Both can be used to convey pro and con points. So are these descriptive, evaluative, or what? Perhaps annoyingly I am not going to be drawn into making a definitive pronouncement, although my hunch is that RELEVANT sits more towards standard evaluative concepts than OLD does. I think we need to look at how people use these concepts, how often and how significant clear pro and con points are conveyed, how often they are used alongside evaluative concepts to help reinforce a judgement overall, and so on. In short, whether something is an evaluative concept is a matter of communal judgement. There are no necessary conditions that can be articulated to decide definitively that something is evaluative.

(iii) *Evaluation all the way down*. Notice that when giving those *OED* definitions we saw other thick terms making appearances. That has happened every so often through this study. This takes us to an important idea. Some people think that evaluative concepts go 'all the way down'.[33]

A standard model of thought might be that we have thin evaluative concepts at the top, with thick concepts coming next. Perhaps the former, plus some descriptive content, help to form the latter. Perhaps thin concepts are simply abstracted from the latter. Whatever story we adopt, it is tempting to think that there is a level below the

---

[31] Putnam (2002), p. 11.   [32] Putnam (2002), p. 31.
[33] Jonathan Dancy has shared this view with me in conversation. See also Griffin (1996), chapter III, although he focuses on properties and supervenience.

thick. In this level are wholly descriptive, nonevaluative concepts. This account can be challenged, however. Is it so obvious that we can eventually get to some rock-bottom regarding our concepts, where this final level is understood as a place where there are no evaluative concepts whatsoever? It may be possible to exorcise all reference to PRO and CON, but that may be a different matter.

Consider yet another example. In Chapter Five §5.5 I gave the example of a kind action in which someone gave up a seat on the bus because an old lady needed it. What is it to need something? In the example it does not stretch a point to imagine that in everyday speech we would say that an old lady might need a seat on a bus, particularly if we give more detail to picture her as somewhat frail and carrying heavy shopping bags. But it is not as if she will die if she does not sit down, in my example at least. She would just have to endure some discomfort for a fifteen-minute bus ride. Clearly NEED is a context-sensitive concept: while it may be true in one context, or compared to one standard, that the old lady needs to sit down, when compared to another standard and set of concerns, she does not *need* to sit down even though it may be nice if she does so. Despite our recognition that the concept works contextually, that does not stop us from thinking that NEED here is in an evaluative fashion. The general meaning is clear and unambiguous, no matter what the standard: if we need something then that something has to happen otherwise something serious (or relatively serious) will occur, and that serious thing is typically unwanted. But SERIOUS looks as if it is a qualifier that works in a way similar to RELEVANT and SUFFICIENT.

To take us back to the main track, in our explicit definition of NEED we are highly likely to have to refer to other concepts that can be considered to be evaluative in the same sort of way and for the reasons outlined previously. If we try to redefine SERIOUS, say, then we will encounter exactly the same situation, and we will find that the evaluative goes all the way down or, what amounts to the same thing, that it is inescapable.

When I previously discussed this example in the context of the shapelessness hypothesis, I said that we can easily separate a one-off instance into evaluative and descriptive elements; the debate is whether we can do so for the concept as a whole. But that assumption is now being questioned. When we take away the bare approval of the individual action, we are left with elements of a situation that themselves, or the concepts use to categorize them, seem evaluative.

We can refer back to make an important point. I find Elstein and Hurka's take on DISTRIBUTIVE JUSTICE from Chapter Two to be a bit of a cheat. They have 'blank' placeholders for the supposed descriptive conceptual content that Rawls or Nozick (and their supporters) will use to fill out their definitions. But what would Rawls and Nozick plug in for X, Y, and Z? Rawls might have: is a distribution 'chosen under conditions of fairness'. Yet, that introduces an obviously thick term. What about 'chosen under conditions of ignorance of one's place after the resources are distributed'? Well, that is better, but it is not as if a person has to be ignorant of everything about themselves according to Rawls, nor would that be a good idea, I think. It is only relevant and significant pieces of information that someone has to be ignorant of. And that introduces two concepts that I am suggesting can be conceived to be evaluative. Also, for that matter, what sorts of resource are going to count? The relevance of the knowledge is intimately related to the resources to be distributed in Rawls' system, and perhaps any liberal system such as his. Similar thoughts affect the choice facing Nozick and his supporters. What counts as an acquisition? As Nozick's comments about labour-mixing show, for him it has to be something obtained by someone in the right sort of way for the correct reason in the appropriate circumstances.[34] Specifying the right sort of way and the appropriate circumstances can be done only with reference to other suspiciously evaluative concepts such as RELEVANT, IMPROVEMENT, and ENOUGH.

All of this highlights a contrast. I have been talking of the right sort of way, or good for a particular reason. The contention behind this is that there is no way of characterizing what is going on unless we employ a thick concept: the rightness of the way and the reason for it are united and, in fact, a single unitary item with two aspects. In Chapter Two Elstein and Hurka's proposals were characterized as indicating that we could pick out some (separable) descriptive content to include in our analysis of a concept if we approved of it, that is if there was approval *simpliciter*. But talk of approval *simpliciter* is a fiction in this debate. We need to be able to specify the reason why, and we either think we can (be certain that we can) specify this completely in descriptive terms—which I have argued is not straightforward by any means—or do so in obvious thick terms.

We need to pause here to highlight the point of all this discussion. My overall aim in this book is to argue that thick concepts are unitary concepts, and that we can speak justifiably of there being nonseparable thick evaluative conceptual content. I have suggested that the domain of the evaluative seems to stretch further than one might initially think and, moreover, that the evaluative-descriptive boundary is a grey one. In order to undercut all of this, my separationist opponents need to be able to analyse concepts as products of distinct elements. But at each turn we have seen doubt cast on the idea that we can analyse thick concepts in terms of some thin or (supposedly) pure evaluation plus some nonevaluative conceptual content. It is not clear at all, and indeed very doubtful, whether we have the sorts of nonevaluative conceptual content to do the job, content that allows one to map fully the large variety of evaluative concepts that we use. CHAIR and the like will not be sufficient in the slightest. We need concepts such as ALLOW, SUFFICIENT, NEED, and TWISTED. If they operate, as they seem to, like ELEGANT, MACABRE, BENEVOLENT, and SHREWD then it is highly unlikely that we can separate thick concepts in the manner envisaged by my opponents.

Alongside this it seems right, to my mind, to make the extra leap of categorization and classify thick concepts, and their content, as evaluative, that is as purely, wholly

---

[34] Nozick (1974), pp. 174–8.

evaluative. We saw an inkling of this in Chapter Four. The range of thin concepts—
which may differ slightly in their thick–thin specificity—are all routinely thought of
by philosophers as purely and wholly evaluative. Why not say the same about the
thick concepts in this chapter? The fact that these concepts also alight on and help to
pick out features of the world should not blind us. We should move away from the
thought that to be purely evaluative is something that is exhausted by an expression
of positive and negative view. An appreciation of such views and when and why to
express them is something that is core to what it is to appreciate and use an evaluative
concept. (This was part of the moral from Ryle.) Furthermore, collecting together
certain features and viewing them *as* a collection is part of what it is to express an
evaluative view of the world. It is not just any set of concepts that can be joined
together, and joined together with a certain positive or negative view. (We saw this
just now when discussing Elstein and Hurka.[35]) There is, of course, the extra point
that at some level of description we may be alighting on features that themselves may
well be evaluative, features such as the fact that someone needs something, or that if
I do something it will allow someone to do something else.

In short, when one scratches the phenomena surrounding thick concepts and their
use, there is little to persuade one to adopt a separationist stance. In contrast, there is
much to persuade one of the merits of nonseparationism, and a particular version at
that, one that takes seriously the idea that it is worth calling such concepts purely and
wholly evaluative. It is just that this occasions serious thought about what 'the
evaluative' is or could be.

(iv) *Evaluative flexibility.* In Chapter Three I indicated some initial reason for
adopting evaluative flexibility. Now I indicate final support for this view by showing
how it knits with other ideas I have put forward.

The link is a clear one. I believe that the best strategy that nonseparationists can
adopt is one that questions what the evaluative and the descriptive are in the first
place, rather than simply agreeing with the separationist terms of the debate that
these two sorts of content intermingle in some way. If they do that, then we have to
think about what the evaluative is and they have to motivate the case that thick
evaluative content is nonseparable. I think that the best way to do that is to think
hard about the various uses that concepts can occupy and to show that there are
various uses. In which case, embracing evaluative flexibility helps and strengthens the
overall case, for all that this view says is that a single concept can have pro, con, and
neutral uses across a range of instances, just the sort of thing that nonseparationists
need to employ to motivate the best version of their view.

This view is to be found in Dancy (1995). In this Dancy considers Blackburn's
claim (from Blackburn (1992)), that separationists (that is, noncognitivists) have an
advantage: they can accommodate the idea that a concept can be employed in

---

[35] Below I underline this point with thoughts from Foot.

different situations with different evaluative points—variations on PRO and CON—whereas nonseparationists cannot do this because they are stuck with the idea that each concept has *an* evaluative point, which has to be an essential part of the concept and so must remain fixed. We have already seen, earlier in this book, that strictly separationists cannot deal with the evaluative flexibility of a single concept, for the evaluative element floats free of the descriptive.

In brief Dancy's reply is that it has never been part of nonseparationism (for Dancy, cognitivism) that there be a narrowly defined and conceived evaluation. All that matters to the nonseparationist is that, in some way, evaluation is mixed with description. (And, Dancy further hammers home the idea I have expressed that we can question if we have separate evaluative and descriptive elements to mix in the first place.) There is no reason to suppose that the evaluative part of a thick concept has to be conceived to be a single attitude. Instead, Dancy thinks, competence with a thick concept can involve competence with a range of attitudes associated with a concept, in a way I have also discussed.[36]

(v) *Conceptual change.* Although not central to my case, I think it worth considering the phenomenon of conceptual change, in part because I mentioned that Ryle thinks concepts, or the terms that express them, can change their meaning and in part because it links to other points I have made.

Thick concepts can clearly change. Blackburn approvingly quotes a nice example due to Quentin Skinner. At the end of the sixteenth century in England, words such as 'vocation' and 'calling', which had previously been applied only to religious positions, began to be applied to other jobs and roles partly to justify certain economic activities.[37] A number of other ethico-religious concepts suggest themselves as good examples: SANCTUARY, CHASTE, SINFUL, and NAUGHTY.[38]

Why does this happen? Let us think about some examples. Gibbard's account of LEWD employs two things that catch the eye. First, there is the vague idea of an activity 'passing beyond certain limits'. Exactly what the limits are and what it takes to pass beyond them is open to dispute. The number and type of cases that might be categorized by such a concept will differ from person to person and across time

---

[36] Dancy (1995), p. 270.   [37] Blackburn (2013), pp. 124–5, quoting Skinner (2002), chapter 8.

[38] In Williams (1996), pp. 29–30, Williams thinks about CHASTE (strictly, CHASTITY) and makes a related but different point, namely that a concept can be lost as time moves on, even if the word remains. In addition, concepts change as well as being lost. 'Sanctuary' as both noun and verb now straightforwardly means a safe refuge and to take safe refuge (as well as being part of a church), but in early times it referred specifically to taking refuge in a holy place and, even more specifically, doing so if one was a debtor or a fugitive from justice. Shakespeare straightforwardly uses 'naughty' to mean 'wicked' in *Macbeth*, Act III scene ii. Many religious and ethico-religious concepts have changed since medieval times in the West, for obvious reasons. In order to deal with other issues, I leave in the background the question 'At what point does the change of a concept introduce a brand new concept, rather than a new version of the same concept?' I am assuming that we are dealing here with the case of the same concept changing, and we need to understand why this happens. It is clearly relevant to my discussion to decide when a new concept emerges, but I put it aside here. That issue is a whole other book.

periods. The vagueness involved in the concept invites a range of cases; the 'elasticity' of the concept is set up for this. Over time the range and numbers of case to which the term is applied might change so much that the concept itself changes. (Or, in other words, the extension of the concept might change over time so much that this leads to a change in the associated term's intension.) People see *this* case as falling under the concept description, and *that* case as being similar to the first case, and *this third* case as being similar to the second and . . . And, before you know it, you have an *nth* case that bears similarities to the cases that have gone before and is not wholly miscategorized, but which also is not quite in tune with the first case or the original idea of the overall concept.[39] The vagueness that is built into the concept is not enough to allow for the range of cases that people end up grouping under the same banner. So, for example, what once would have been categorized as naughty, because it is truly terrible, heinous behaviour going beyond certain acceptable limits, is now thought not to be naughty, simply because this categorization is now typically reserved for a lower-level type of bad behaviour. NAUGHTY occupies some of the same conceptual region as CHEEKY, MISCHIEVOUS, and DISOBEDIENT, and is now not as associated as it once was with WICKED and EVIL.

We can underline this first point by returning to THINKING. Eschewing simple synonyms, such as 'mental life', we can imagine change happening. Earlier eras may have defined THINKING by relying on what went on in the (literal) head and that which controlled action and emotion. But given what beliefs, moods, calculations, and other things might be prompted by and exemplified in thought, we may see a change in such a definition. Earlier in this chapter I talked of people thinking while fiddling on pianos or when choosing ingredients for a meal. Similarly, the 'extended mind' hypothesis, whereby the mind is seen to extend beyond the physical brain and be inhabited in all sorts of tools that we use to store information and knowledge, gives credence to the idea that THINKING is open for revision.[40] What counts as thought can change, and this might cause change in the concept itself.

(c) *Foot.* Consideration of Foot's work helps to summarizing many of the previous ideas as well as helping me to underline others.

In Foot (1958) and (1958–9) she, like Williams, takes Hare's prescriptivism, and noncognitivist theories of the day generally, as her targets. In both papers she is worried that there is a lack of appreciation by noncognitivists about how arguments work and what reasoning looks like. (I believe her arguments apply to separationism generally.) Foot accuses noncognitivists of assuming that moral argument works thus: a person accepts certain premises and from them reaches a conclusion. There is a noncognitivist assumption that there is a strict and unbridgeable divide between

---

[39] That was brief, but I hope the idea is clear enough. Other things can pull at the contours of a concept, such as one-off momentous events.

[40] See Chalmers and Clark (1998).

facts and values. So some of the premises will be factual, while some will be evaluations of the facts. At the end of the argument, in which a moral conclusion is reached, an opponent to our original protagonist can *simply* reject some or all of the various evaluations given and so the argument—if that is what we call it—between them breaks down.

Foot complains that this is too coarse a way of understanding argument and is based on faulty theory. How is the opponent imagined to be rejecting the idea? What reasons have they themselves given? She worries, in Foot (1958), about a situation she takes to be analogous. Imagine a man being shown all that could be shown about the roundness of the Earth, and then asking (simply) why he should believe it was round. "We should want, in such a case, to know how he met the case put to him; and it is remarkable that in ethics this question is thought not to be in place."[41]

This sets the scene for her article. Foot wishes to understand how it is that people understand others and the shape of how they reason in ethics: what do they count as evidence for their beliefs and why? Foot worries that in the noncognitivist account of reasoning there is no link between statements of fact and statements of value. Because of this, each disputant makes his own decision as to which things count as evidence and which do not, and nothing can be said by others against him if they disagree.

Foot seeks to undermine noncognitivism and uses RUDE to do so. Calling some behaviour rude can be a way of condemning it and trying to stop it happening. It is clearly an evaluative word. But she notes it can be used only when certain types of features are in place. It cannot be used of just any action, or used on just any occasion. Foot says that it can be used only when a certain kind of behaviour "causes offence by indicating a lack of respect".[42]

How does this help? Foot thinks that once we use a word such as rude to categorize an action or thing, we open up other categorizations, such as 'offence' in this case. If a disputant says that a man has caused offence (or someone thinks that offence has been caused), yet our disputant denies that the man has been rude, we need to know why it is that the behaviour is not rude. What reasons for exemptions are forthcoming? What sorts of thing does our disputant consider rude? Foot considers certain answers—'a man is rude when he behaves conventionally', or 'a man is rude when he walks slowly up to a front door'—and thinks that in such a case our disputant has left behind the concept RUDE, assuming that no further explanation is forthcoming.[43]

Foot assumes, perfectly reasonably, that everyday ethical disagreements are awash with thick concepts. When such concepts are used, there are fairly well-accepted criteria of application and definition. Because of this, we cannot apply concepts willy-nilly. But, when applied, and when seen to be applied, certain sorts of evaluative point follow.

There are points on which to challenge Foot. For example, a disputant might refrain from agreeing that a piece of behaviour was rude simply because she does not

---

[41] Foot (1958), p. 503.   [42] Foot (1958), p. 507.   [43] Foot (1958), p. 508.

wish to condemn it. (Think again about Betty and Frank from Chapter Two, and the various concepts they employ to describe people who are bigger than the average.) But, in response, although that is an issue, Foot says towards the end of her piece that disputants have to work within an accepted tradition and, by implication, a conceptual environment. We cannot choose to apply and withhold concepts as we wish for we must respect certain traditions and norms. If someone has explicitly insulted someone to their face and made them cry, say, it would have to be a surprising piece of reasoning to conclude that the behaviour was not rude. And that is Foot's point. Evaluative concepts shape our argumentative landscape and there is not the freedom to attach and detach evaluative point from descriptive content as noncognitivists might think.

Foot repeats her argument, more or less, in Foot (1958–9). However, in this paper she labels and makes explicit an important idea, namely that of an 'internal relation' between object and evaluation. Evaluation cannot apply to just anything. And, further, specific sorts of evaluation cannot apply to just any sort of object. Or, again, if someone does do something creative when judging, we require further explanation, and if this explanation is accepted we can classify the use *as* creative, rather than as bizarre or downright wrong. In Foot (1958–9) she uses the feeling of pride as her main example. We do not see just anything as worthy of pride. It would be odd to look at the sky and feel a sense of pride, as if one had stopped the sky from falling, or if one had laid one hand on another.[44] Again, we can make sense of this if there is some special background. Perhaps someone's arms are injured, and so it is rational to take pride in his 'finally managing' to put his hands together. Foot continues in this vein. It is simply strange to think that just anything can be pride-worthy or dangerous or any such thing, at least rationally.

This shows the importance of Ryle. My use of 'finally managed' just now is meant to be significant. It is with these sorts of description that we can fill out the background in the right sort of a way in order to make sense of how it is that the movement of hands can be considered to be worthy of pride. If we do not bother about which description we use, then we cannot make sense of what is happening.

Further to this, I want to underline a key point that is riddled throughout all of my discussion. What is absolutely central is the idea that mature users of concepts use evaluative concepts while appreciating the point of their use: why they are used in a certain way, and why certain sorts of activity and object are linked together (and occasion positive and negative views, reasons for action, and the like). That may be accepted by many, even some separationists on some understanding of the claim. (We saw in Chapter Two that even simple separationists can claim that the thin evaluation helps to determine the extension of the concept.) But the importance here is that appreciation of such matters is part of the concept itself, and that goes

---

[44] Foot (1958–9), pp. 86 and 87.

especially for those occasions when we use concepts with positive and negative view. As we use concepts and language, we know that not just any evaluation, in general and on some particular occasion, can help with the application. Certain features of the world go with certain sorts of evaluations, according to a certain reason and logic that is socially special, and that is something that any account of the evaluative and the thick must accommodate. In Foot's view, which I share, it also must be central to any account.

So ends my tying of a number of related points. But what of our overarching accounts?

6.7 Separationism and Nonseparationism

Separationists restrict the idea of evaluation to PRO and CON. (When they try to extend it, as Gibbard does, we see problems.) Doing so seems curious. The types of definition or analysis that are then given for individual thick concepts rely on a clear and obvious separation between the evaluative and the descriptive that seems, after exploration, to be fictitious. What are we to say about ideas such as WARRANTED, USEFUL, and ALLOW, as well as all of those important qualifiers such as RELEVANT and APPROPRIATE? Are we just to think of them as some descriptive material—completely value-free—with some pro or con evaluation added? This is worrying on two counts. First, it ignores the complaint that we do not simply approve of something, but do so for a reason. This seems inevitably to invite thick concepts back in, as I indicated with some examples. Second, it denies flat out that there is anything to Foot's insight that certain internal relations have to hold if the norms of our everyday conceptual use are to be respected. It is only in respecting such relations that we give structure and reason to our evaluative practices.

We saw, in Chapter Four, the first inklings of what was wrong with separationism. Separationists wish to separate thick concepts into something descriptive and, typically something thin. But as we saw, there are a number of different sorts of thin concept and there seems to be a range of thicknesses among them, albeit a smaller diet than is found across thick concepts. Yet, we see no harm in calling these concepts thin, whether we wish to indicate a difference in kind or degree from thick(er) concepts. And, further, we saw that separationists probably need this diet of concepts to express different ideas. In this chapter we have simply expanded this suspicion. Separationists find it hard to justify their assumption that the thin is one thing and the thick a divisible other, simply because the thin does not seem to be a unified single sort of thing. It is certainly true that thin concepts typically carry (or essentially carry) a pro or a con evaluation in a way that typical thick concepts do not. But the fact that thin concepts come in a range of specificities should open our eyes to the possibilities of thick concepts. It should also open our eyes to the idea that just as thin concepts might still be thought to be 'simply' or 'wholly' evaluative, so we might think of thick concepts in the same way, once we have thought about what conceptions of the evaluative are available.

In short, separationism seems curious because it has a limited view of the phenomena it is trying to account for. Separationists attempt to divide, isolate, and sharply categorize that which cannot be treated in this way. It may go nicely with some distinction between facts and values, but the phenomenon of thick concepts calls into question that very assumption. That was what Foot and Murdoch were doing all those years ago, and the moral still holds.

6.8 Some Objections

(a) *Essentially evaluative*? As advertised, there could be a fatal weakness in what I have said in this chapter. I have laid out the positive view that concepts can be essentially evaluative and yet, on occasion, not be used with an obvious pro or con point. However, it is possible to draw a different conclusion from the phenomena: that any concept that is used on occasion without a pro or con point is not essentially evaluative. Those uses where it is used with pro or con point are the odd ones, even if they statistically predominate, for such pro or con uses are accidental to the concept and not an essential part of it. In brief, MACABRE and CAJOLE are a lot more like CHAIR than they are like GOOD. They are descriptive concepts with accidental evaluative uses, rather than essentially evaluative concepts. In short, the conservative view of evaluation is still correct.

Chapter Seven sees me examine and attempt to rebut an argument for this line by Väyrynen.

(b) *Understanding others*? Part of my position, and a traditional part of noneparationism, has it that people master a concept only once they understand its point and how it can be used. Some seem to think that this implies that people have to share the evaluations that are the point of the concept in order to understand it. This raises an interesting issue, which seems as if it could prove fatal to the whole position. We routinely think that anthropologists, for example, can understand other people and their culture. Indeed, we routinely think that they can understand the concepts, including the evaluative concepts, that these people have. Sometimes this may take a while and much effort, but we certainly think it is possible. But how is this possible? Do anthropologists sincerely have to share the concept that they are investigating? This challenge threatens not just the possibility of anthropology, but of understanding anyone who is different. The challenge then is to articulate what is involved in understanding a concept that allows us to master it and yet not share it sincerely.

In Chapter Eight I articulate a way of setting up and thinking about this problem that indicates what nonseparationists should say. As advertised, I also tie this to

Williams' pessimism about the possibility of evaluative knowledge. I have left hanging the status of thin concepts: I think of them as separately understandable but not conceptually prior to the thick. I comment more on this also.

(c) *Evaluative realism*? In Chapter Five, §5.3, I mentioned the idea that if we are committed to there being unitary evaluative concepts, then it implies that these concepts refer to something. And if they refer, it looks as if we are committed to evaluative realism. I have made some progress in addressing this issue already, but in Chapter Nine I review where we have got to and articulate, briefly, what it would be to be a nonseparationist and not be committed to an outlandish realism. Furthermore, we have to be confident that there is some way in which we can distinguish legitimate, decent, genuine thick concepts from illegitimate ones.

I use this as a way of offering a conclusion for the whole book. Every so often, including §6.7 just now, I have mentioned the fact–value distinction. I suspect that it is a fear in losing this that motivates some people to worry about evaluative realism. I briefly address this idea in my final chapter.

6.9 Concluding Thoughts

I began this chapter by diagnosing the failures of the disentangling argument. I then moved on to the failures of Williams' slogan and how it disguised much of his thought. The moral of the story is that evaluative concepts seem to do more than Williams' famous slogan has them do, something that even he acknowledges. I then isolated what had gone wrong by thinking about Ryle's thoughts about thick description. This opened up the thought that not only can evaluative concepts do more than guide action, they may do more than categorize in an explicitly pro or con manner. I worked through that idea in a number of ways and in so doing elaborated a view of how concepts work. This took me on to articulate and defend my particular version of nonseparationism. Along the way I hope to have shaken up and cast doubt on assumptions that separationists make.

Having sketched the positive view, I now work my way through the three objections just mentioned.

7

Essentially Evaluative?

7.1 Introduction

In his *The Lewd, the Rude and the Nasty* Väyrynen puts centre stage a very important question:

> Evaluation Question (EQ): How are thick terms and concepts related to the evaluations they may be used to convey?[1]

Väyrynen is to be applauded for concentrating our minds on EQ. As indicated in the previous chapter, his view is that while thin concepts can be and should be understood as inherently evaluative (his phrase), thick concepts need not be at all, and indeed we should assume that they are not. The assumption that thick concepts are essentially or inherently evaluative is absolutely key in the whole debate about thick concepts, and Väyrynen is right to focus on it. Not only does this assumption affect the particular concerns of the last chapter, it affects other matters too. For example, if thick concepts carry evaluations only 'accidentally', as I have labelled the idea, then they are quite different types of thing from thin concepts, and the whole question of whether conceptual models such as the *genus–species* model are applicable to their relation falls away.

Straightaway we need to appreciate something about Väyrynen's position. He is asking a question before we even get to the debate between separationists and nonseparationists, the debate that has occupied us thus far. He agrees with separationists that thick concepts are not inherently evaluative, but while most separationists think that this is because they can be disentangled into evaluative and descriptive aspects, Väyrynen thinks it because he denies they are evaluative in the first place, at least inherently so. His key positive contribution is to argue that the evaluative aspect of thick concepts is something pragmatically given, by tone of voice and context, and is not part of the semantics of the concept. (So one could be a separationist and think the evaluation is part of the semantics of (some complex) concept, even if it is something that can be separated from the descriptive parts.) Emphasis on the pragmatics of evaluation is something he shares with Blackburn, although it is fair

---

[1] Väyrynen (2013), chapter 1.3.

to say that Väyrynen in his work has given the most meticulous and careful treatment of this idea to date, hardening it into a thoroughly worked-out position.[2,3]

There are some things Väyrynen and I agree about. For example, although in the end I am inclined, unlike him, to think we can make out some difference between the thin and the thick, we both agree that more attention should be paid to the assumption that some binary distinction exists. We also think there is a deep and misguided assumption in the literature that all thick concepts work in the same way. I also agree with him that we understand a lot about thick concepts by putting EQ under the spotlight. However, we disagree about the answer we give to EQ, and this disagreement is significant.

I start in §7.2 by commenting on our different phrases: Väyrynen's 'inherently evaluative' and my 'essentially evaluative'. This sets the scene for my argument. In §7.3 I summarize Väyrynen's view and the main arguments for it. (This is condensed as his answer to EQ occupies his entire book.) In §7.4 I counter his arguments. In §7.5 I conclude.

7.2 Inherently or Essentially Evaluative?

Looking at philosophers' labels can sometimes be a blind alley. It can appear that much hangs on some term or phrase, but sometimes less is revealed than is predicted. I am not sure how much Väyrynen's language reveals about his intentions. But I can say, confidently, that it reveals something about *my* thinking.

There is a difference in English between 'inherent' and 'essential' even though it is small. The idea of inherence is that there is some quality or some attribute or some something that exists quite inseparably and essentially in another thing. That seems to capture nicely a lot of nonseparationist talk about thick concepts. We have the idea of something being inseparable and essential, and we can remain quite neutral on how to characterize the thing credited with these qualities. It might be an element or it might be an aspect, and this echoes my discussion early on in this book about these two terms.

Yet, even though Väyrynen's language is not completely misleading, it does still assume, however implicitly, that evaluation is thought to be a quality or aspect of the whole of the thick concept. We have one thing—the evaluation—*in* the thick concept. This phrasing, however well-intentioned, still buys into and underscores the idea that evaluation is something that is apart from the concept as a whole. For evidence, see his use of phrases of thick terms and concepts 'containing' evaluation and of

[2] How Blackburn would place himself in relation to this matter is an interesting question, but I leave it aside here.

[3] I could have started this whole study by rebutting Väyrynen's argument, and followed that with the debate between separationists and nonseparationists. But given the historical significance of the ideas in that debate, and given that some of my arguments against Väyrynen rest on my own view, I introduce his view only now.

evaluation 'being built' into the meaning of such terms and concepts.[4] By use of this word, then, perhaps Väyrynen shows his assumption about what evaluation is.

My use of 'essential' is supposed to bypass this worry. The key thing about thick concepts is that they are evaluative and are so essentially. That is all. I leave it open, at the beginning, whether the evaluation is an essential part or aspect of thick concepts, or something else, such as the idea that the thick concept *just is* something that is evaluative. Of course, I argued for this latter view in the previous chapter: our familiar thick concepts simply are forms of evaluation. 'Inherent' shuts out this important option.

I did speak of 'aspects' early on in this book, and I have run everything in terms of evaluative and descriptive content, thus implicitly emphasizing some clear difference of kind. But I turned the spotlight on this in the previous chapter and questioned this type of talk. This is not to say that I disown all of my set up and see it merely as a vehicle for ideas before we get here; a necessary journey before Nirvana. We can still talk of thick concepts having descriptive and evaluative aspects. But that sort of talk should invite questions and reflection into what is meant by 'aspect' and whether the evaluation should, in the end, be seen in such-and-such a way. It should not indicate a settled matter as we move onto other questions. Talk of thick concepts being essentially evaluative is supposed to make us question how close talk of 'evaluative and descriptive aspects' is to talk of 'evaluative and descriptive elements'. For me there is a world of difference. Further, I think we are better off characterizing the best sort of nonseparationist position in terms of 'essential' and not 'inherent' evaluation.

From now on I switch between 'essential' and 'inherent' as necessary, in order to stay faithful to Väyrynen's expression of his view.

7.3 Väyrynen's View and the Arguments for it

Väyrynen uses linguistic evidence and theory to discuss how thick terms are used in everyday contexts. He claims, correctly, that not enough attention has been paid to language in the debate about thick concepts and, further, that we can draw interesting conclusions about concepts from what happens to their associated terms.

As mentioned, Väyrynen's answer to EQ is that thick concepts do not convey or carry evaluation inherently, and he criticizes those that think it does. He further specifies this idea by saying that to think of a thick term, and concept, as inherently evaluative is to think that it has evaluation or evaluative content as part of the literal meaning of the term (and associated concept), as used in a normal context. In contrast, he thinks that evaluation is best understood as something that speakers imply or suggest in using thick terms and what hearers typically from their uses, in normal context, and such implications and suggestions are conveyed by the context,

---

[4] Väyrynen (2013), p. 32, which echoes p. 9 and p. 31.

by the tone of voice, and the like. According to him, pro and con evaluations are not very reliable constraints on literal uses of terms in normal contexts, since such evaluations do not behave as a semantic entailment is supposed to behave once we consider many different linguistic phenomena. This is true even if we assume, as he does, that the relationship between evaluations and thick terms is fairly robust across different contexts. It is just that he prefers that this should be explained pragmatically rather than by assuming that the evaluation is secured as part of the semantics of the terms. He assumes a fairly clear and strict division between pragmatics and semantics.[5]

In contrast, thin terms and concepts are understood by him to be *the* paradigmatic type of evaluative term and concept; throughout the first two chapters the question of whether evaluation is inherent in thick terms and concepts is run in terms of whether and how they convey good and bad evaluations.[6] The following establishes his view of what he means by 'evaluation':

My suggestion for characterizing evaluation without reference to *pro tanto* value is to understand is as information that is somehow positive or negative in favour. This needn't mean the sort of bare 'pro' or 'con' assessment exemplified by the proto-emotivist understanding of evaluative judgement as an expression of a 'boo' or a 'hurrah'. Evaluation might rather be understood as information to the effect that something has positive or negative standing—merit or demerit, worth or unworth—relative to a certain kind of standard. If we say further that the relevant kind of standard must be of the kind that is capable of grounding claims of merit or worth, this would explain why claims of merit and worth are often expressible by the sorts of attitudes that we associate with evaluation, such as praise, admiration and criticism. (A standard may be *of a kind* to ground claims of merit or worth without actually succeeding in grounding them. Even if calling something lustful, for instance, implies a negative standing relative to a standard that the speaker regards as grounding a claim of demerit, it is a further question whether counting as lustful is in fact a demerit . . .)[7]

He goes on:

The characterization I offer is ecumenical in nature. It can allow the relevant kind of standard to be vague, indeterminate or controversial. For instance, what counts as morally good, or even as a good philosopher, is controversial and may be vague. The characterization is also flexible regarding the strength of the relevant kind of standard. The relevant kind of standard can concern *pro tanto* value, the characterization allows also standards that ground evaluations as

---

[5] This is very condensed. Across Väyrynen (2013), chapter 5, having dismissed semantic entailments (which I focus on below), Väyrynen also considers that evaluation can be cast as something else (for example, as conventional implicatures, conversational implicatures, etc.) before settling on his particular pragmatic view. For reasons of space I ignore these discussions.

[6] See also Väyrynen (2013), p. 208 as a summary: "I assumed [throughout this book] that what distinguishes the thick early on from the thin is that thick terms and concepts somehow hold together evaluation and nonevaluative description whereas thin concepts are purely evaluative. And I assumed that the evaluations to which thick terms are concepts are most closely connected are claims to the effect that something is good, or bad, in a certain way."

[7] Väyrynen (2013), pp. 29–30.

good (or bad) in some other sort of way. To say of someone that she is a good assassin, or a good football player, or good at cooking, is to say that she is good in some particular way or respect. In this sense such claims are no less evaluative than claims to the effect that something is morally good, or admirable, or just. On this view of evaluation, information that someone is a good assassin counts as evaluative because it is information to the effect that she is good in a particular way. Of course, some things will be bad in certain ways, such as morally, if they are good in certain other ways, such as assassinating. But this is perfectly coherent if standards may be relativized in ways that this view of evaluation allows.[8]

Standard thin terms may be employed in larger expressions, for example, 'good assassin', and those expressions can end up having evaluative points different from those that are usually associated with the terms on their own. This is to be explained by the standards that apply to certain terms or phrases in those different contexts. Similarly, a certain sarcastic tone of voice might alter 'good' to mean 'bad', but that is easy to understand and ubiquitous. (Indeed, it seems right to say that the term 'good' said sarcastically is used to convey BAD or CON.) We can imagine that someone could agree with Väyrynen and take this phenomenon on one step, and argue that concepts such as JUST and WISE are inherently evaluative. Sure they can be transformed by tone of voice and be used to convey con evaluations, but such instances are comparatively rare. We could infer, following further investigation, that because of the character and frequency of the transformations, such concepts are inherently (positively) evaluative. That would make sense of the idea that such concepts are fairly close to standard thin concepts and may even be classed under this heading. However, despite this possibility, it is clear that Väyrynen accepts only a few examples into the group of inherently evaluative concepts.[9]

More insight into Väyrynen's views on evaluation comes from a view he sets aside as extreme.[10] This view states that a term or concept is evaluative if it has *any* evaluative connotations. (Again, by 'evaluative' he means pro and con evaluations.) He acknowledges that some linguists do think this, citing Adrienne Lehrer.[11] In her discussion of wine, she counts terms such as 'buttery', 'sweet', and 'woody' as evaluative. Väyrynen rejects this view since it is obvious that a term can be used in this way and yet not be inherently evaluative. Just think back, again, to my example of CHAIR in Chapter Two, or to OLD from Chapter Six; we might feel uncomfortable in saying that CHAIR or OLD were evaluative concepts even if on occasion we use them to convey some positive or negative view or attitude. Just because there are a few examples of contexts where a term or concept carries evaluative connotations, this does not mean such a term or concept is inherently evaluative.

---

[8] Väyrynen (2013), p. 30.
[9] He never says as much, although it is a clear implication of the whole book and, as I read it, is *supposed to be* a clear and direct implication of the whole book. However, the final paragraph of Väyrynen (2013), p. 185 is relevant. Here he discusses the possibility of 'distributively just' being classified as thin, just as 'ought' is.
[10] Väyrynen (2013), p. 33.   [11] Lehrer (2009).

That, then, is his view. He has three main arguments for it: (i) thick terms can be objected to, in a way I set out momentarily, and the evaluations supposedly inherent in them project to other contexts in a way that other semantic parts do not; (ii) thick terms' evaluations are far too defeasible in a way that semantic entailments are not; and (iii) other features that supposedly support the view that thick terms are evaluative are better accounted for in ways that show these evaluations to be given pragmatically.[12]

(i) It is routinely assumed in linguistics that if parts of a term or phrase are to be considered part of its semantics, then they should not 'project' when that term or phrase is embedded in certain contexts. We can use one of Väyrynen's favourite examples to introduce the idea. Imagine people saying these:

(1) Madonna's show is expensive
(2) Nah, Madonna's show is not expensive.[13]

When we say (2) the embedding means that we unambiguously say that Madonna's show is not expensive. The core meaning of the term 'expensive' is that something costs a relatively large amount of money and by saying (2) someone clearly rejects the view that it does. Or, in other words, embeddings such as (2) easily and unambiguously cancel core semantic entailments. When we say that some part of the term or phrase, some implication, 'projects' then we are saying that it survives such embeddings and remains uncancelled in some way.

What about thick terms? Väyrynen introduces the notion of an 'objectionable' term (or concept). This is any term that one could take objection to because, one thinks, the pointed evaluation that is most closely connected with the term does not fit those items that are typically classified using the term. Väyrynen uses 'lewd' as his main example and I construct the following scenario to illustrate his point.[14]

Imagine that Huey thinks Madonna's show is lewd. Dewey disagrees. He thinks the show is within appropriate boundaries. But the key point about them is that they are both prudes: they typically go around saying that things are lewd, and praise certain non-lewd things for their decency, and do so sincerely. They think that categorizing things as lewd is important, illuminating, appropriate, and the like. So in that broader sense they are in agreement, despite their disagreement about Madonna's show. In contrast, a third person, Louie, objects to the term 'lewd'. He objects to it being employed pretty much anywhere and everywhere, in part because it classifies certain sorts of activity as bad that he does not think should be classified as bad. He thinks that using 'lewd' is itself a bad or unjustified or silly (or . . .) thing

---

[12] The first and second arguments are in Väyrynen (2013), chapters 3 and 4 (especially 3.3 for the first, and 3.4 for the second), while the third (comprising a range of considerations) comes in the following chapters, particularly chapters 7–9. See also Väyrynen (2009) for an earlier statement of the first argument.

[13] To be really clear, (2) does not express a double negative. The 'Nah . . . ' is supposed to reflect everyday speech patterns.

[14] For simplicity, I focus on negations, but Väyrynen also considers questions, epistemic modals, etc.

to do.[15] So Louie disagrees with Huey because he does not think the show is lewd. But he also lacks the broad agreement that Huey and Dewey share.

To understand what is happening, consider:

(3)   Madonna's show is lewd.

(4)   Nah, Madonna's show is not lewd.

Huey says (3). Dewey says (4), but that might be a little unsatisfactory if we are capturing real life. We can imagine that Dewey could and would offer some reasons for asserting it. He might say something such as:

(5)   Madonna's show is sexually insinuating alright, but it's not lewd because no private parts are exposed.[16]

From this Väyrynen says:

What the speaker of (4) [i.e. Dewey] isn't naturally heard as denying are some such evaluations as the generic claim in (6) or the singular conditional in (7):

(6)   Overt displays of sexuality that transgress conventional boundaries are bad in a certain way. (Read as meaning: bad in a distinctive way that typical *lewd*-users regard them as bad.)

(7)   If Madonna's show involves overt displays of sexuality that transgresses conventional boundaries, then it is bad in a certain way.

So it is reasonable in the context primed above the speakers of (4) [i.e. Dewey] accepts something like (6) or (7).[17]

Or, in other words, (6) and (7) are plausibly construed as implications that Dewey accepts.

So what? Imagine a normal conversational context. Väyrynen imagines that Dewey could happily say (4) while Louie cannot, at least without offering further explanation of his view. Louie is liable to be misunderstood and there will be some ambiguity in the situation. So he may be reluctant to assert (4) straightforwardly, even if he can do so meaningfully.[18] How come? It is because, says Väyrynen, that Louie does not accept (6) and (7), or similar ideas, and people such as him typically do not succeed in denying (6) and (7) by uttering (4). (Indeed, Louie's reluctance might be because he knows that this is how everyday communication and arguments work.)

This then gives us Väyrynen's proposal, which is to treat evaluations such as (6) and (7) as implications of utterances of (3) and to see them as implications that

---

[15] More specifically, he may reject the particular *conception* of LEWD that Huey and Dewey employ with that associated term. But to keep things simple we will ignore this wrinkle, even if it is important in real-life situations.

[16] Väyrynen (2013), p. 62.   [17] Väyrynen (2013), pp. 62–3.

[18] Louie's situation is just like mine when I say, 'That table is not blogon' and where I think BLOGON is not a meaningful or useful concept. When I deny that the table is blogon, I am saying something meaningful and something I take to be true, but I could be taken to be a (sincere) blogon-user, who would happily say, 'While *this* table is not blogon, *that one* over there is.'

project. They should be treated in this way because they are not cancelled simply by uttering (4). (Remember, even if he is reluctant to say (4) in many conversational contexts, Louie can still meaningfully say it.) And so if (6) and (7) are not cancelled simply by being embedded in a context such as (4), then we should not treat them as part of the semantic core of the term.

We need to realize that this generalizes. *Any* thick term (or concept) can be an objectionable thick term (or concept), for there may be someone who rejects its presuppositions and implications. An objector objects to a certain collection of features being grouped in a certain way with either some pro or con evaluation conjoined to it. 'Lewd' shows this well, and many people do not wish to be prudes. Derogatory racial and sexual epithets show the phenomenon even better, since many people object to and reject such terms. But we should realize that any thick term or concept can be challenged: ELEGANT, WISE, and all the rest.

(ii) Väyrynen's point about defeasibility is easier to state.[19] Consider this:

(8) Whether or not Madonna's show is lewd, it's not bad in any way distinctive of explicit sexual display.[20]

In short, if the con evaluation of 'lewd' were part of the semantic core of the term, then we would find (8) to be semantically improper. But we do not, says Väyrynen, for (8) seems reasonable to say. So it is better if we do not treat the con evaluation as part of the semantic core of the term, but instead assume that evaluations can come and go more freely, and be offered and understood pragmatically.

(iii) In addition to these two arguments, Väyrynen considers a range of considerations that have been given to support the view that thick terms are inherently evaluative. These considerations include: evaluations help to drive the extensions of thick terms and that one cannot understand the extensions without understanding the evaluations; that thick terms are supposedly shapeless with respect to nonevaluative terms; and the idea that evaluative and descriptive aspects are inseparable. He argues, instead, that his preferred pragmatic view can easily explain these phenomena. He then wields (a generalization of) Grice's razor, that other things being equal it is better to adopt the pragmatic view because it assumes fewer semantic properties.

7.4 Responses

(i) I use a suggestion from Debbie Roberts to help meet Väyrynen's first argument.[21] The first question—a revealing one—to be asked is whether a thin term or concept

---

[19] However, I am summarizing and ignoring many of the interesting details Väyrynen works through, again for simplicity's sake.

[20] Väyrynen (2013), p. 70. This is numbered (23) there.

[21] Roberts (2015), especially pp. 3–4. Roberts also raises the general question of whether other things *are* equal when considering Grice's razor, which I mention in my response to the third question, although I put forward points different from those she does.

such as 'good'/GOOD can be objectionable in the same way. That may seem a startling question. After all, who could possibly imagine that 'good' could be objected to? But, as Roberts notes, Väyrynen himself opens this avenue even if he does not pursue it with as much vigour as she and I would want. Specifically he considers whether JUST can be objected to and rejected in the same fashion as above, and references Thrasymachus and Marxism.[22] Alongside these people, we can think about Milton's Satan, at least on some readings. One may find it difficult to imagine these as serious, real-life cases; and even if one accepts it for JUST one may find it hard to imagine if for GOOD. (Väyrynen himself notes this worry but mentions the phenomenon of imaginative resistance in support of us being open-minded about objection.) And, further, we have to remember that GOOD can and is objected to by people, certainly if by this we mean MORALLY GOOD (and if we recall from Chapter Four that we can distinguish between GOOD and PRO). We do not even have to think about Marxists and Nietzcheans, but more philosophically mainstream people such as moral error theorists, and artists and political agitators of various stripes through the years.

So let us assume that there is enough motivation for GOOD and similar thin concepts to work in the same way as LEWD and thick concepts. Louie, or someone like him, may feel reluctant to enter a discussion in which others are debating whether something is morally good, simply because he rejects the whole notion. In which case, we then have to conclude that the pro or con evaluation that is seemingly part of 'good' and GOOD is also detachable, and that thin terms and concepts such as these are not essentially evaluative either. That seems like a crazy conclusion. If you worry that running the worry in terms of GOOD is too far-fetched, then even running this in terms of the slightly more specific MORALLY GOOD seems to result in a crazy conclusion. Are GOOD and MORALLY GOOD really not going to count as inherently evaluative? Are the only inherently evaluative concepts PRO and CON? Too much has been proved and the situation or phenomena are more complex than Väyrynen makes out.[23]

Roberts argues that we need to make a key distinction between conceptual evaluations and substantive evaluations. The former concerns the evaluation or evaluations that are part of the concept, the latter concerns the evaluations that one can make of the concept, its evaluative point, and how it is used. In the cases of GOOD and MORALLY GOOD, the conceptual evaluation is clearly something pro. Most people will then also have a positive, substantive evaluation of these concepts, but a few people will not. They may reject them for many different reasons but at the core will be a rejection of some positive assessment of ways of acting in some moral fashion, where 'moral' is understood along some social or psychological lines that

---

[22] See Väyrynen (2013), p. 150. I worry he is a little too dismissive on this point. His main response to the consideration he raises is that the pragmatic account he forwards explains things better anyway.

[23] A quick observation. Väyrynen devotes barely any space to thinking about the nature and character of thin terms and concepts, even though evaluation is clearly identified with them.

they think should not be viewed positively. Whatever the reasons for the rejection, critics will have to understand the point of the concept and how it is used in order to reject it.[24] In all of this, if they reject, then this rejection does not show that the evaluation is not an essential part of the concept. Indeed, the rejection may occur because of the evaluative point of the concept, not just how it happens to be being used on a particular occasion by some people.

We can repeat the point by making sense of Louie's situation. He has to understand what is going on when Huey and Dewey are talking. He has to appreciate that they are using an evaluative concept and what the dialogue is about; if he does not, then there is no meaningful rejection but just misfiring communication. Louie chooses not to use and apply 'lewd' and LEWD and refuses to enter into a detailed and sincere discussion in the same way as the two of them, because he rejects the evaluative point of the term and concept. (He may be rejecting the con evaluation specifically because he enjoys displays of a sexual nature. Or, alternatively, he may reject LEWD in a more holistic fashion: whether the pointed evaluation is pro, con, or neutral, he dislikes a concept that groups together certain sorts of sexual activity and then presents them positively or negatively.) He does so for reasons to do with how it picks out actions and gives them evaluative sheen. All of this does not cast doubt on the fact that LEWD is not an essentially evaluative concept. It shows only that Louie has made an evaluation of some (evaluative) concept, and has chosen to reject it. Similarly, we can presume that Huey and Dewey (if they are reflective) have evaluated the concept and decided to use it sincerely. The fact that Louie judges and rejects the concept after reflecting on its evaluative point and potential for use in a discussion seems to strengthen the claim that it is to be treated as an evaluative concept.

We can even go further than Roberts' line, if we need to. We could take any concept, it need not be evaluative. Perhaps for some reason I object to the idea of and application of BACHELOR or CHAIR or, for reasons of imaginative realism, some concept used by some group alien to me involving how one should count objects or classify actions. I might refuse to engage in meaningful, first-order discussion using the concept, just as Louie does in the case above. But would my rejection cast any serious doubt on any aspect of the concept being essential to the concept? I do not see that it would, at least without there being additional details provided for the rejection. In which case, it would then probably be those details that would be the deciding factor, not the overall nature of the concept itself.[25]

(ii) One can take three broad lines in response to Väyrynen's second argument. First, one can agree with Väyrynen: we have utterances such as (8) which do not

---

[24] If they reject it but do so based on inadequate understanding, then I could be accused of changing the rules of Väyrynen's set-up, since the scenario of an objector makes sense only if we assume that there is some meaningful dialogue between the parties and no talking past one another.

[25] There is one potential fly in the ointment of this entire counter. We assume that someone can understand a concept without thereby sharing it. Why this could be a problem and how nonseparationists can meet it is the topic of the next chapter.

admit of any semantic impropriety, think that the evaluations that are part of the concept cannot constrain one's literal use of the thick term or concept, and hence conclude that such evaluations therefore cannot be part of the semantic core of the term. Second, one can disagree with Väyrynen and argue that utterances such as (8) are semantically improper.[26] Third, one can question Väyrynen's set-up. Throughout his discussion of 'lewd' and other terms, he presumes a single specific evaluation, a pro or a con, and then the sort of tension in (8) arises because we seem to be negating it. What if we assume, instead, that a thick term and associated concept can embrace a range of different specific evaluations—pro, con, neither—in the way I have discussed earlier in this study under the heading of 'evaluative flexibility'? I take this third approach.

Väyrynen does consider this option, but what he says is not very convincing to my mind.[27] He notes that this position will make concepts and their mastery complex affairs. I agree. Unfortunately, he does not provide any discussion to show that this is implausible. (To my mind, it is a very plausible claim, given what we know about humans, their thought process, and their communication abilities.) However, he does say that even if concepts are complex, it is better to explain their evaluative complexity in other ways, "on the basis of various pieces of world knowledge, substantive evaluative beliefs and general-purpose abilities which aren't specifically conceptual".[28] I do not know what it would be to separate such matters from our use of evaluative concepts (or concepts that *prima facie* appear evaluative), especially 'substantive evaluative beliefs'. This may reflect and continue the difference between the two of us I expressed in §7.2 between essential and inherent evaluation.

The main point Väyrynen makes is to imagine that a proponent of the view will claim that "many words are correctly interpreted in different contexts". To illustrate the contention he considers the use of 'cut' and CUT via considerations from John Searle, who provides different examples of how 'cut' is used and what it implies: cutting a cake with a lawnmower and cutting the grass with a knife both seem wrong.[29] (We can add 'cut the cloth', 'cut to the chase', 'she cut me up' (re. driving), 'they cut in' (re. queuing), and 'he is all cut up' (re. being devastated); we can talk of the noun as well as the verb; we can distinguish piercing, slicing, separating, shaping; and so on.) Väyrynen simply casts doubt on whether there is a single concept CUT that the word refers to in all of its uses. But he does allow that there can be 'free enrichment' whereby an expression or word is given a pragmatically derived interpretation that is more specific than what the expression literally encodes. (So I take it that by this he imagines that the literally encoding may be very general, and is given different specific senses pragmatically.)

---

[26] Bedke (2014) claims this.
[27] Väyrynen (2013), pp. 226–9. As I do, Väyrynen refers to Dancy (1995) as the main source for this view.
[28] Väyrynen (2013), pp. 227–8.   [29] Searle (1980), pp. 222–3.

My response to this move is twofold. First, the conclusions Väyrynen draws might be true for 'cut' and the (clearly) different uses of the word in different contexts. The question that Väyrynen does not discuss head on is whether the same is true of concepts such as MACABRE, and even SIMILAR, which seem to have far fewer specific meanings and uses. The proposal is only that there will be a little variety of specific evaluation given, pro, con, or neither. Drawing doubt on the more varied 'cut' may do nothing to shift the nonseparationist proposal of evaluative flexibility that I favour.

Second, Väyrynen is happy to treat thin concepts as evaluative but not thick concepts. Yet the phenomena that I have discussed in this book put pressure on that clean division. DUTY for a start may convey different specific evaluations. In that case, Väyrynen may not treat it and concepts like it as inherently evaluative. Fine. So perhaps only those concepts that have a single specific evaluation whenever sincerely used (with no sarcasm, etc.) have a chance of being classed as inherently evaluative. But, even in that case, we saw that MORALLY GOOD, for example, may not fit the needed profile, for it could be objected to (it can be sincerely used by some to criticize others, and some nihilists may reject the concept altogether). In which case, it would be better to read the evaluation it conveyed as pragmatically given. But now we are getting fewer and fewer concepts counted as inherently evaluative. The whole picture building up is one where Väyrynen has very tightly conceived notions both of what evaluation is and of what inherently/essentially evaluative concepts are, and these may be applied to very few concepts.

This is reflected in the fact that he has quite a different view of concepts and conceptual understanding from that which I have offered. This takes me to my response to his third set of considerations.

(iii) The details of the considerations Väyrynen offers (shapelessness, etc.) need not hold us up. The key point to focus on is whether Grice's razor can be invoked and whether other things *are* equal. In his use of this philosophical principle, Väyrynen is raising the question of whether thick concepts are somehow special in how they relate to the evaluation that they carry and convey. He is, relatedly, questioning whether such concepts are any different from those obviously nonevaluative concepts such as CHAIR and OLD that can convey evaluation but which we would not want to classify as evaluative. He thinks that there is no difference in kind, at least in respect of the evaluation being inherent, and that any of the phenomena standardly invoked in the literature do not justify the classification of thick concepts as special. What difference or differences there are are differences of degree: certain concepts convey evaluative points more often than others (and far more often in some cases) and in certain ways that others do not, but the way in which they carry such points should be explained pragmatically, just as it is for OLD and CHAIR.[30]

---

[30] See, for example, Väyrynen (2013), p. 10.

There are three sorts of response to this challenge. The first is to show that Väyrynen is wrong in what he says about the various phenomena such as shapelessness. I do not take this route here, in part because I think that Väyrynen says some interesting and plausible things about the phenomena he discusses along the way. The second is to choose a different phenomenon that Väyrynen has not discussed in order to prove the special nature. I do not take this route because I think that sucks me into a position that I do not wish to defend, namely that the evaluative and the descriptive are starkly different. I prefer a third strategy, namely to question and undermine some of Väyrynen's assumptions; I have already begun to raise these at the end of the previous sub-section.[31]

He assumes that there has to be some division between evaluative and non-evaluative concepts or, better, some division between those concepts that are inherently evaluative and those that are not and which convey evaluation accidentally. As shown in the previous chapter, I think that the examples do not show this at all, even if we may wish to mark out some concepts as clearly and unquestionably evaluative, and mark others as nonevaluative even if they can be used to convey evaluative point every so often, such as CHAIR.

This links to how we regard differences among concepts. I think that there are differences, but I argue that we can determine what those differences are and where they lie through judgement, perhaps on a case-by-case basis, and indeed presumably we can spot trends. Inevitably there will be disagreements and, indeed, some grey area as to which concepts are evaluative and why. This, I very strongly suspect, will not satisfy Väyrynen (and others). He wants us to be able to say clearly, using a set of conditions (which may well be necessary and sufficient conditions in some form), what it is for a concept to be evaluative. Indeed, putting matters like this is one way of framing the narrative of his entire book. But imposing this sort of injunction on the phenomena creates problems, as we have seen in this chapter. He stresses at various points in his book that if we have a mass of concepts all treated as evaluative, then we will not be able to mark as we should important differences between concepts.[32] I agree that we should spot trends and differences. But I deny that all of these differences have to be so distinct as Väyrynen makes out, and one has to nail them with conditions that apparently have to be so clear-cut and final.

---

[31] Väyrynen does try to make sense of the type of position I mark out, namely that evaluation is not exhausted by PRO and CON; see Väyrynen (2013), pp. 208–13. Two points are worth making. First, by his own admission he struggles to make sense of this position, although to be fair there have been very few pieces of work to reference and work with, and no extended discussions at the time of his writing. Second, he latches onto the idea, from Roberts, that there could be marks of the evaluative, and then seeks to show that these marks do nothing to single out supposed evaluative concepts as special. I discussed this in Chapter Six, note 29.

[32] For example, see Väyrynen (2013), p. 37: "Moreover, even if paradigmatic thick terms and concepts turn out not to be inherently evaluative, a characterization that sorts *chocolate* and *athletic* into the same conceptual bin as *cruel, just, selfish* and *courageous* might still be thought to ignore important differences in evaluative depth and significance." I have not detailed it here, but he is interested in comparing and contrasting regular thick terms with pejoratives among other examples.

All of this reflects the different view of concepts we have, and a difference between us when it comes to semantics and pragmatics. I am not about to try to undermine this important linguistic distinction completely, but it is instructive to question the supposed clarity and strictness of it, and as Väyrynen's example of Lehrer shows, some linguists query how clear the divide is.[33]

Once we start to focus on terms exclusively, and assume that what goes for terms has implications for concepts, we can get sucked into the assumption that there is a clear difference between semantics and pragmatics: a clear difference between the literal meanings of terms and what they can be used to convey (and how they do so). We get sucked into thinking that, on the one hand, there are the terms in 'the page and the air', and what they standardly mean in the abstract, and, on the other, the meanings that are conveyed beyond this. Once this move is made and accepted, Väyrynen is able to identify his target. To say that a thick term (or concept) has inherent evaluation is to say that this is part of the meaning of the concept, which means that, because it is inherent, it is part of the literal meaning of the concept. But, as Väyrynen can show, when we think about how terms (and concepts) are used, we can see that the evaluations seemingly do not act as standard semantic entailments are supposed to act. So it is seemingly natural to infer that they are accidental to the thick terms (and concepts), and not inherent in them.

My counter-move from above, in (i), can be made to this. But we can also unpick the background assumptions. I prefer to focus on concepts rather than terms, even if I agree that we should pay attention to how terms are used. Terms and concepts are different, and not just because—*very* crudely—terms are 'speech-things' and concepts are 'idea-things'. It is not as if there is no link at all between the terms we use and the concepts that are employed, nor no link at all between the semantics of a term and the content of a concept. However, I am more liberal than Väyrynen.[34] The ways in which we use a concept build from a range of uses of a term in various contexts. To reuse previous thoughts, we understand what the concept THINKING means only by considering the various contexts in which it is used and how it is used. Aside from some simple and trivially correct synonym such as 'mental life', we develop and understand characterizations of 'thinking' (and 'mental life') only by appreciating various examples, their similarities and differences. And, yes, sometimes a term can be used in a wide variety of ways, and we may wish to resist the idea that all of those ways are part of the 'core' of the term or concept. 'Cut' and CUT show this phenomenon well. But just because some examples are like this, it does not mean that we then have to restrict the core meaning of every term and concept example in some very narrow fashion. I think that our use of concepts (and terms), and the variety of

---

[33] For more on this see Travis (1997). Despite his obvious commitment to a sharp division between the two, even Väyrynen acknowledges that the world of language is messy. See Väyrynen (2013), pp. 51ff.

[34] The relevance here of themes in the thought of the later Wittgenstein will be obvious to many readers.

uses that there may be, feeds into the meaning of the concept. It is clear that Väyrynen is far more resistant to this idea than I am.

That is why Väyrynen's citing of Lehrer's discussion of wine is interesting, and it also indicates the worry that he focuses too much on terms. Off the top of my head the term 'sweet' can be used to indicate at least three different concepts: the non-evaluative concept pertaining to a flavour, such as the flavour of normal cane-sugar; to indicate PRO, as in 'Look at my sweet set of wheels, man!'; and, third, the evaluative concept that typically indicates something pro, but which need not always.[35] Now, all three concepts may be at work in wine conversation, although the first is most likely to be used literally when thinking about something such as dessert wines. I presume that the concept Lehrer focuses on in wine conversation is something evaluative that can often be used to convey pro and con ideas. Is any evaluation of pro and con that comes forth in such wine conversations accidental to the concept as understood in this way? No. It is an important part of the concept that it has the potential to be used in these pointed ways, and the fact that it can be used in such ways, and that it is pregnant with these ideas itself all of the time, makes any use of it evaluative. We get specific ideas and it helps to build a certain context and picture of the wine. This leads into my final point in this sub-section.

All of this reflects the different views of how concepts can carry or convey evaluation that Väyrynen and I have. Evaluation is not a separate thing conveyed by concepts. I regard evaluation as something that is both conceptually basic and also a complex aspect of our lives that, in turn, is given life only by the concepts which are considered by mature users as evaluative. Although appealing, thinking of evaluation as something exhausted by PRO and CON and hived off from the concepts, even if such notions live in a few of them inherently, seems to me to be too narrow a view of evaluation and our evaluative lives. In this way Väyrynen shares a great deal with all separationists. And it is a view I have sought to challenge in this study.

7.5 Conclusion

In this chapter I have outlined some arguments against the idea that thick concepts are inherently or essentially evaluative. We have seen that these arguments can be questioned and found wanting. Their failure helps to cement my view. By saying that thick concepts are essentially evaluative we are indicating that certain concepts have certain roles and jobs to do, and we have a certain need for concepts that have as their prime and essential role the conveyance of evaluation. Even if we allow that such concepts can, even individually, carry a whole host of evaluations and be used in many ways, that does not detract from their essential role.

---

[35] Just to follow through on that, we might say that something is sweet (and I do not mean too sweet), where in fact we want something a bit edgy and dangerous, or something with a bit of bite. Sometimes we are in the mood for sweet pieces of music or dramas, and sometimes we are not.

8

Understanding Others and Having Confidence

8.1 Introduction

In Chapter Two, §2.6(d), I indicated two worries for nonseparationists, among four.[1] In this chapter I address them.

First, nonseparationists routinely say that in order to understand and fully master a concept one has to 'latch onto' the point of it and why people use it. It is a claim that has been prominent in the literature. But what does 'latch onto' mean? Does it mean sharing the evaluation involved in the concept and the entire point of it? If it does, that seems strange because it appears we can easily understand other people's evaluative concepts without sharing such concepts and sincerely agreeing with their point and use.[2] If such 'latching onto' is interpreted strongly and if it is further viewed as a necessary condition for understanding, then it would seem to make the understanding of others' concepts and points of view impossible.

Second, we saw that nonseparationists are accused of not having the resources to explain how normative criticism of others is possible. (Blackburn used the example of CUTE to make the point.) Apparently, if nonseparationism is correct, people can merely describe the fact that other people hold concepts different from theirs, and they must uncritically accept that there are just different ways of valuing the world, different 'organic whirls'.

---

[1] They were listed as the third and fourth concerns.

[2] For a detailed discussion of this and other issues, see Sreenivasan (2001). I do not have the space to discuss Sreenivasan's argument in detail, but it is worth sketching. His target is a combination of ideas, due to Hurley and Donald Davidson, such that if we assume an anthropologist has understood (supposedly) alien ethical evaluations and conceptual schemes then we must assume both that such evaluations and schemes are not so alien and, crucially, that our anthropologist must sincerely accept those evaluations. Sreenivasan argues that we can understand others (and treat them still as alien) without acceptance. I agree, although I believe he is too hard on the 'Hurley–Davidson' position and, unlike him, I do not believe at all that this position is committed to what he calls the 'descriptive equivalence thesis', which is the claim we met in Chapter Five: for every thick concept there is some nonevaluative equivalent concept that matches the thick concept extension perfectly.

For a standard-defining discussion about this issue from an anthropologist's point of view see Geertz (1973).

These are more or less the worries, but I articulate them further below. I begin with the first criticism, in §8.2, and explain why it is supposed to be a worry for nonseparationists. In §8.3 I show how we can solve it or, rather, show why it is not so much a problem at all. I do not have the space to pursue all of the details of a solution, but all that is needed here is an indication of how the problem is resolved. The real value, I think, is not in solving a potential problem, but in making explicit how understanding others' evaluations works from a nonseparationist point of view. Along the way I contrast nonseparationism with separationism again. This allows me to accommodate one of the desiderata mentioned in Chapter Two, namely an explanation of how disputes work. (The other desideratum mentioned was evaluative flexibility.) I also highlight a problem for separationism. I take this problem to be an echo of the problems discussed in Chapters Five and Six rather than a substantially new and different point. But it is worth highlighting all the same since it contributes to the narrative that separationism ends up looking odd.

In §8.4 I address the second concern. In §8.5 I move the discussion on a little, while staying within the general topic of encountering and trying to understand others. I discuss Williams' view of what is likely to happen when we meet other societies and consider how their members categorize matters evaluatively. I use this to provide perspective on the previous discussion. I do not have much to say about Williams' own account, aside from the fact that I believe he is slightly too pessimistic. At the end I introduce a criticism of separationism based on Williams' ideas due to A. W. Moore. This again echoes comments of mine from Chapter Six. In §8.6 I also offer a note on the thin in the light of Williams' views, as promised. In §8.7 I conclude.

8.2 The Problem of Understanding Others

Recall that Williams, in referencing the idea of a thick concept, cites Foot and Murdoch. His full words are:

The idea that it might be impossible to pick up an evaluative concept unless one shared its evaluative interest is basically a Wittgensteinian idea. I first heard it expressed by Philippa Foot and Iris Murdoch in a seminar in the 1950s.[3]

This is ambiguous as we will see. (We will also see that Williams clarifies what he means.) But one way of reading this—perhaps the natural way of reading this—is to think that if an anthropologist, say, is to understand the evaluative concepts of some group she is investigating, then we must assume that she holds and applies such concepts sincerely. That is, she is in agreement with the group's evaluations. If she is not in agreement, then she will fail to understand how their concepts should typically be withheld and applied.

---

[3] Williams (1985), note 7, pp. 217–18.

We normally think that anthropologists can easily understand other people and their concepts without sincerely holding the evaluations associated with such a concept. McDowell, in a throwaway line, assumes this is the case and the possible worry no worry at all.[4] Why, then, is this supposed to be a problem for nonseparationism? Recall that nonseparationists say that evaluative concepts are shapeless with respect to the descriptive because they are human tools and lying behind such things are highly complex human interests and motivations. The suspicion is that nonseparationists then have to say that unless you share the interests and motivations that shape, and are reflected by, an evaluative concept you will fail to judge what falls under it correctly. And if you fail to do that, then it (supposedly) shows you have not understood the concept. So it seems as if nonseparationists are committed to an implausible view of how people come to understand other people's evaluative concepts and outlooks.

Separationists are seemingly on firmer ground. (I mentioned this in Chapter Two §2.6(d) also.) If we assume that there is a division between descriptive and evaluative stuff, then we can easily conceptualize the success of anthropological investigation along separationist lines: an anthropologist follows and transcribes all of the situations to which a concept applies in descriptive terms, and then she can choose to apply or withhold some pro or con evaluation afterwards, in accordance with the group she is investigating or otherwise. Some separationist positions may complicate that story, but the core idea remains intact.

Furthermore, despite my use of anthropology and of 'seemingly alien groups', this is a worry for any sort of situation where we are called upon to try to understand those who evaluate differently from how we do. That includes understanding your neighbours and your close loved ones, as well as understanding societies that are quite different from you such as those on the other side of the world or on Mars.

8.3 Soothing the Worry

I introduce two examples so as to make some ideas clear. These pick up the final thought of the previous section. It may be that members of a group have a concept TABOO that is just like ours, and thus are somewhat close to us. However, they apply it to actions, people, and other things that an anthropologist would not normally think of as taboo. Second, and more radically, in a second case a group has a concept SCHMABOO. This is like TABOO but which incorporates interesting twists and grave departures; for example, 'it does not apply after dark', 'it applies only to the activities of physically disabled people', and 'is punishable by death'. They are a group that are, in conceptual terms, a lot further away from our anthropologist. Of course, an

---

[4] McDowell (1981), p. 144.

anthropologist and her team will need to exercise skill and judgement in working out the differences between these two cases.

How do we solve the problem or, better, soothe the worry and show that this is not such a problem after all? The key thing to note is that there is a shift across a vague and grey area. Nonseparationists are committed to thick evaluative concepts being evaluative, and therefore that in order to understand others' evaluative concepts you have to take that into account. Indeed, it is often said that non-users of the concept have to 'appreciate' its point. (I made much of this idea in Chapters Five and Six.) But to appreciate the point is one thing; to sincerely hold the evaluation expressed using the concept is another. It is this last possibility that creates the problem, and so nonseparationists need to make sure they can resist it and remain true to their position.

In order to show how they can easily do this, let us begin by returning to Williams. His wording of "shared its evaluative interest . . . " may suggest 'holding sincerely' the specific evaluation expressed by the concept, and even the reason or reasons behind it being used in the first place. Yet one can also read this remark as suggesting something else, namely that what must be held is some *more general* interest or set of interests that are given voice by the concept. (Indeed, in the main text, Williams voices this.[5]) Even if our anthropologist does not hold sincerely the specific evaluation expressed by SCHMABOO (that is, some con evaluation towards particular activities done by particular types of person on particular days), she has some general evaluative interests that the concept taps into, namely taking some negative evaluative stances to (non-specified) certain people in certain circumstances. After all, there will be concepts in her repertoire, such as TABOO as well as (perhaps) BLAME, APPROPRIATE, LIMIT, and REASONABLE (and LEWD, GRUESOME, and BARBARIC), that will have clear links and import. Indeed, TABOO is a thick concept. 'Taboo' means more than just 'impermissible'. It means that in certain, many, or all contexts a certain sort of behaviour is unacceptable because it contravenes serious rules and norms, with significant consequences to follow if certain actions are done. Taboo activities are 'beyond the pale'. With that in mind, our anthropologist will be able to make finer discriminations and interpretations of what the group does and how it categorizes. There is a keen interest among humans to conceptualize some matters in this fashion: to indicate things that are seriously wrong in a certain manner.

Indeed, this now shows us how the nonseparationist can resist the problem. When we compare the two concept examples I presume that attention focuses immediately on the radical SCHMABOO. But let us instead start with the case of TABOO. We imagine, indeed stipulate, that our anthropologist has TABOO. Part of her task is to work out whether the group has any concepts that map onto hers. After a while she is able to conclude that, although it maps onto different things—perhaps different foodstuffs, play activities, and sexual orientations—the concept is the same. She concludes there

---

[5] Williams (1985), pp. 141–2. See also Williams (1995), p. 206.

is just a difference in application. Part of the skill of being an anthropologist, at least through a philosopher's eyes, is being able to distinguish a situation where there is a difference in applications of the same concept and different conceptions of the same concept from a situation where there are just different concepts at issue. (And the criteria for this will be complicated and possibly difficult or impossible to articulate in a highly specific way.) The former sort of case places the anthropologist closer to the group, and we can use that to understand the latter sort of case.

In the former case she may employ the same concept, but she does not apply it to the same items. This may mean that there is a difference in conception of the concept.[6] Yet, despite this, it is easy to see how she could understand the different conception. Why? She holds the general evaluative interest of the concept—as we just saw when discussing the Williams' quotation—and, because of this, she is able to appreciate why the concept is applied to the items it is applied to, even if she is slightly surprised every so often with how the concept is used.

It is a short stretch from here to the more radical sort of case of SCHMABOO. For then she begins to note that not all is at it is in her social world. She finds that the word applies to types of thing she does not normally think it should apply to at all, and she finds that certain limits are put on the concept that, in her normative view, make little sense. This could be a long, frustrating process as she tries to make sense of what exactly is going on. Part of this process will be questioning whether she is dealing with TABOO or whether she is justified in describing the tribe as using a different, but related, concept altogether.

This is still all perfectly fine on the nonseparationist reading. As I have tried to draw out, understanding can occur while keeping fast to the chief nonseparationist idea, that evaluation is essentially what a thick concept is all about. So long as our anthropologist shows an appreciation of the evaluation involved in the concept, she

---

[6] I think that there can be a difference between these two cases: two people having the same concept and applying it differently, and two people having different conceptions of the same concept. But articulating clearly what that difference amounts to at a more specific level of detail than these two general descriptions will be hard if not impossible for many concepts. One may have to fall back to judging and commenting on any differences on a case-by-case basis. It will be hard because presumably any difference in conception will be shown mainly by the same term and concept being applied differently anyway. I do not attempt to say more about this topic here. However, I am merely indicating that in the scenario I envisage we should make space for there being these possible differences. As well as some radical tribe using SCHMABOO, our anthropologist may come across a people that she can justifiably say are using TABOO, but just with a different sharpening of that concept from her. This latter case is different again from a case where she disagrees with a colleague in her anthropology department who has similar cultural beliefs to hers. In that case the two of them differ merely on a few applications of TABOO, but where there are so few differences, or ones of such little significance, that it does not seem justifiable to label this difference between them as a difference in conception of the same concept. At this point it seems better to conceptualize this as a difference in application of the same concept. I say all of this while acknowledging that there may well be no difference in kind between these cases, certainly no stark ones, and much will depend on the narrative and reasons we can give for these summarizing labels in the cases we encounter.

will be able to understand it. We can see how she is able to do this by linking it to what she does know and how she does evaluate.

Two further points emerge. First, in this book I have often talked of the 'evaluative point' of the concept, or similar, something that we must appreciate. This is normally in the context of appreciation of the point of the concept, one's reason or reasons for holding it and applying it. Such a matter will be quite a complex affair, and mastery of a concept may sometimes not be easy. This connects with other times I have used the phrase 'evaluative point', to indicate some specific pro, con or neutral evaluation (of some strength) of some item. These two uses come together, of course: in appreciating what a concept is and how it should be used, one has to appreciate when and why one should take some pro or con stance towards something. What an anthropologist has to do is appreciate this range of specific evaluations, and understanding why it is that they apply and when.

This complicates our question, for we should strictly ask whether an anthropologist has to hold sincerely all of the specific evaluative points that a concept is used to convey across many contexts. But that is no real problem. And, all of this fits nicely with the above train of thought. For there is a general evaluative interest in using a concept and using it to express a range of ideas and seeing it function.

Second, I have set things up so that we have a difference between appreciation and sincere holding, and tried to articulate how 'appreciation' is consistent with non-separationism. As we see when we read anthropological accounts, and as we can easily suppose anyway, when understanding others and their concepts, certain states of mind, such as imagination, pretence and role-play will be used. We can understand other people's concepts only if we can draw on our own. Part of that process involves imagining what we would do in this situation and seeing how that possibility compares with what happens. Further, we might pretend to be the sort of person we are investigating: drawing on our concepts as a way to think our way into their mind. So in our imagined scenario, our anthropologist looks at the types of thing that the group is averse to, and plays around with her concepts that express types of impermissibility. She notes that *that* sort of impermissibility seems very similar to what she thinks of as being taboo, even if there are a few differences in some cases. All the time she has to have some general appreciation of the type of thing going on and what the concept is used for, and she can do that only if she has in mind her concepts.

This whole section is simply a sketch of what a nonseparationist can say. One question worth pursuing is how the different stances and states of mind, such as imagination and pretence, work in this context and how we can finely distinguish them. This would be interesting work in philosophy of mind, say. For reasons for space I do not do that work here.

So even if the details require more work, I think we can safely put the first worry of this chapter aside. Two last topics are required, however.

First, I have made out that we would expect that an anthropologist would draw on her concepts to understand others. But does she *have* to? Or, to ask this question in another way, where does separationism stand? Could an anthropologist understand others' concepts by thinking only in purely descriptive concepts?

What seemed to be a good position now looks odd, and its oddity underscores some of the points from Chapter Five. Is it really possible to note down all of the descriptive information in order to form the concept? We might be able to do that with a friendly insider's help, but after she leaves us would we be able to go on with confidence that we had mastered or captured the concept? It is only by appreciating the contours of our own concepts, and thinking about why they group certain events and situations together, that we can even hope to map the contours of other people's concepts and, at a second-order level, judge how alien or close to our own concepts they are. Separating the evaluative from the descriptive does not seem the best way to understand, simply because we are trying to understand other human's evaluations. Putting our evaluations aside and focusing just on the descriptive when understanding other evaluative concepts (or potentially evaluative concepts)—when put plainly like that—seems a recipe for disaster.

Furthermore, there is an oddity to be repeated from Chapter Six. There I cast strong doubt on there being a clear split between evaluative and descriptive concepts anyway. Trying to understand the contours of how a tribe uses a concept, which seems like a good candidate for our concept TABOO, and then deciding whether it is TABOO or perhaps even SCHMABOO, will require use of many concepts and ideas in the anthropologist's repertoire. What types of concept will be off-limits, according to separationists? Presumably INAPPROPRIATE, ILLICIT, and IMPERMISSIBLE. But what also of FORBIDDEN, PROHIBITION, VETO, and the like? The separationist response is obvious. With all of these we can supposedly offer some sort of separationist analysis: something descriptive combined with some negative element. The points I raise now are twofold. First, it is unclear to me whether these concepts are free from evaluation, or are simply nonevaluative, in the way separationists think. Second, even assuming that there exist some clear descriptive concepts (and I have allowed that), then this group may not be an adequate basis for an anthropologist to do her work effectively. CHAIR, TABLE, and their ilk will be in the group of kosher concepts, but they hardly make for a good basis for anthropological understanding. I have raised doubts about concepts such as JUSTIFIED, SIMILAR, and many more such concepts in Chapter Six. (This is just restating the first worry above, again.) I think it highly doubtful that unarguably nonevaluative concepts such as LEFT, RIGHT, TABLE, CHAIR, and their ilk, plus some separable and separated PRO and CON, will be enough basis on which to understand other societies, let alone allow one to achieve mastery of alien concepts.

A second topic needs to be cleared up. Recall that in Chapter Two I said that any account of thick concepts should explain how disputes work. I indicated that there was a tension between the two broad types of separationism. Simple separationists seemed better at accommodating (a type of) evaluative flexibility while complex separationists seemed better able to accommodate disputes and to ensure that people could understand one another and not talk past one another.

I have already shown how nonseparationism can accommodate evaluative flexibility. Everything is already in place to show how disputes work. The key, put simply, is that right at the heart of any nonseparationism is a focus on mastery of concepts and an appreciation of the point of their use, including the evaluative aspect. When one turns one's attention to others' concepts, one does so through the language of understanding their concepts. Right at the start the theorist states that one can understand others only by understanding their concepts. From here one can get easily to a point to explaining how disputes work, because unless one understands the concepts at issue, one will not be able to criticize.

So we have here a tightly drawn circle. But this is still an improvement on anything in separationism. In complex separationism, people were assumed to be speaking roughly about the same terms and using roughly the same concepts because there were general ideas that were *exactly* the same, with any differences (which are necessary for there to be a dispute) characterized with separable Xs, Ys, and Zs. The problems here are manifold, most of which I have just given above. Although this complex separationist analysis may seem neat and tidy on the page, it does not survive sustained thought. Communication, agreement, and disagreement are far more complex phenomena than such a separationist analysis can capture.

Here end my comments on this supposed problem of how we can understand others. In ending, we should notice one thing. When imagining our anthropologist encountering and interpreting groups and their concepts, we have not commented on any evaluative judgement she makes *about* them. Are they decent concepts? Illuminating? Awful? Evil? Silly? What do they tell her of her own concepts? These are questions that I now think about.

8.4 Criticism of Others

Recall that Blackburn thinks that nonseparationists cannot make room for normative criticism, and uses CUTE to support his claim. We can add to the examples. We are discussing disagreements and criticism that relate both to different and controversial applications of a shared concept (such as TABOO and CUTE) and the application and embracing of concepts that one would never use (such as SCHMABOO and also various common-or-garden racist and sexist epithets and slurs).

There are two parts to Blackburn's criticism. First, when explaining the situation of those that encounter others with whom they disagree, nonseparationists are supposedly committed to an overly conservative acceptance of anyone's use of thick concepts, such as CUTE. They cannot say more than the fact that people are so committed to seeing the world a certain way. Second, Blackburn thinks that separationists can explain how we can criticize normatively and, by implication, indicates that this is the best if not only way to criticize: namely to separate description of the world (a certain way of dressing, speaking, walking, and acting, for example) from one's evaluative stance towards it (seeing it as something to be encouraged in and emulated by women, for example).

I think that both of these claims are wrong.[7] I see no reason to think that separationism—and the sort of noncognitivistic, quasi-realism that Blackburn has long advocated—is better able to explain how we can criticize others. I have already worried about whether we can split evaluation from nonevaluative, descriptive content as cleanly as he may think. But we can put that aside and see that the criticism falls short anyway. First of all, it is not quite true that nonseparationists can literally say nothing. I see no reason to think that nonseparationists who encounter others (or who are explaining what people do when they encounter others) are stuck with merely describing the fact that others have different concepts. Nonseparationists can easily say that different way of viewing the world is an unjustified one, one that expresses unkindness, cruelty, or whatever else. Indeed, if we think through the more different types of concept, such as SCHMABOO and controversial slurs, when one is working out that they are different and how different they will be, one will realize that one would not adopt them oneself. It is but a short step from there to wish to criticize, if any step is required at all. The key question that Blackburn should raise, and which he may have in mind anyway, is whether one can criticize with any hope of one's judgement acquiring legitimacy. By this I mean that one hopes that one's judgement is more than just a disguised description of the fact that someone else's use of some concept is something that one would not adopt. One wishes to say that this other view is bad and hopes to at least have a chance of convincing others of this. One's view has to seem and be justifiable outside of one's own viewpoint and society. Again, I see no reason to think that nonseparationists cannot hope for this. They can point to how the use of the concept may create upset and hurt, may lead to certain lives going less well than they might, and so on. They reason and attempt to justify using their own concepts and, if they do seek to convince, attempt to find ideas and notions that provide bridges between their views and others'.

So I think that nonseparationists can explain how criticism of others is possible. It is just that they do it by using other thin and thick evaluative concepts. This takes me to the second part of Blackburn's worry. I do not see that assuming some sharp split between the evaluative and the descriptive helps in any way, even if we assume that this can be achieved. Imagine that *us* and *them* agree on a set of some evaluatively neutral descriptions of actions, styles of dress, and all the rest, and that while *we* take a negative view towards such actions, *they* take a positive view. *We* are then left with saying to them, and to any third parties who can hear us, that *they*

---

[7] I first considered this issue in Kirchin (2000).

should not take such a positive view. And why not? 'Because doing so is wrong', *we* will say. What is there left to defend such a position? Perhaps we can point to the upset, harm, and the like, all of the matters that nonseparationists will point to as well. There is as much chance of separationists convincing *them* and neutrals as there is of nonseparationists doing so.

As far as I can see, this supposed advantage of separationism over nonseparaton-ism is nothing of the sort, but is instead a red herring. The result applies not only to CUTE but, as I have indicated, it covers many concepts and their applications where we might not only differ but disagree. Nothing within nonseparationism says that we must accept what there is without challenge. Nonseparationists have as many, or as few, resources to criticize and do so legitimately. The difficulty lies not with the adoption of nonseparationism, or even separationism. The difficulty lies with trying to justify one's own view and being able to convince others to act differently. These are everyone's problems in philosophy, and are as old as the subject itself.[8]

8.5 Williams on Evaluative Knowledge

Some of Williams' most famous ideas in *Ethics and the Limits of Philosophy* concern the encounters we have with societies who categorize differently from how we do.[9] Some of it has a decidedly pessimistic flavour, although there are points of optimistic relief. I summarize what he says below, before linking it to what we have just discussed.

Williams imagines a 'hypertraditional' society, a society which is maximally homogenous and is given to minimal reflection about its practices. Williams asks whether such a society (or its members) can possess evaluative knowledge, specific-ally expressed using thick concepts. He uses this question to introduce a key distinction. If we think completely in terms of 'objective knowledge', that is (roughly) how the world is and exists outside of any human perspective, he thinks it is unlikely (to say the least) that the members of such a society possess evaluative knowledge. We can talk of scientific claims being claims of knowledge in this sense, but not evaluative ones. However, we can instead think in terms of 'nonobjective knowledge', and see evaluative claims as being both cultural artefacts and embodying ideas about how to live. In this sense members of the society could possess evaluative knowledge.

---

[8] An aside. Väyrynen mentions racist and sexist epithets and slurs more often than I do in Väyrynen (2013). But he does not discuss this worry of normative criticism, let alone argue that his pragmatic view has some advantage over a semantic view regarding it.

[9] This is drawn from across Williams (1985), although chapters 8 and 9 are particularly important. There are a number of good discussions about Williams' ideas. See in particular Altham (1995); Chappell (2010); Fricker (2001); Moore (2003); Thomas (2006), pp. 153–7; and Thomas (2007). Williams asks his question with regards to ethical knowledge alone because he thinks that the aesthetic, say, raises issues of its own (1985), p. 135. (Which is itself interesting in the light of my discussion in Chapter Six.) I run things in terms of evaluative knowledge since I see no reason why Williams' comments about ethics do not apply broadly to other forms of evaluation.

Yet, Williams then compares members of this hypertraditional society with members of a society that is not immune to reflection at some higher level, as the hypertraditional society is really introduced so we can think harder about ourselves. What happens at this level is that members of the group consider whether they really are categorizing as they should, whether the world is as they depict it with their thick concepts, and so on. In brief, Williams thinks that once we or any members of a group think at the reflective level we will see our thick concepts for what they are: local attempts to capture what we think the world is like. For Williams, reflection "characteristically disturbs, unseats or replaces…traditional concepts" and it leads him to say "if we agree that, at least as things are, the reflective level is not in a position to give us knowledge we did not have before—then we reach the decidedly un-Socratic conclusion that, in ethics, *reflection can destroy knowledge*".[10]

As A. W. Moore points out in a nice discussion, this sort of reflection is interesting because it undermines some of the concepts (perhaps all of the concepts) that are required to think in the relevant terms to justify our concepts. (This sort of role Moore labels 'constitutional'.) Some of the justification for ethical concepts may itself be ethical. Someone might ask, 'Should we really continue to justify our actions in this way?' The worry here is obvious. Moore continues from this point and says:

The people engaged in reflection can no longer make judgements of the relevant kind that constitute the knowledge, although they can still have enough grasp on concepts of that kind, from without, to *see* that they constitute knowledge. They may eventually recover the knowledge: various social forces may bring this about. But such forces may also prevent them from thinking, at the relevant level, about what they are up to. They will never recover the knowledge in the full light of reflection.[11]

We can pick up on the last comment. Once we are in the grip of reflective thinking it is very hard, if not impossible, for us to see our ethical justifications of our ethical concepts, say, in a genuine way: we will always be drawn to the thought that this is all local. In addition, we will no longer see such judgements as embodying any sort of knowledge.

Some claims may survive such reflection, however; Williams' example is 'one has to have a special reason to kill someone'. But he remarks that this and similar beliefs fall short of what will be required by an extensive and practical body of evaluative knowledge. Furthermore, as I have mentioned in other parts of this book, he has little time for thin concepts, given that they are, in effect, pale abstractions from the evaluative concepts that do some real justificatory and categorizing work. Assuming that we can have a system of evaluative knowledge based around some network of thin concepts is, for Williams, a rose-tinted view and shows the false ambitions of much of modern philosophy. Thin concepts are simply not world-guided in the right sort of way.

---

[10] Williams (1985), p. 158.   [11] Moore (2003), p. 344.

I have so far not pointed out something obvious, but very important. Clearly societies and their individual members will be shaken to think reflectively about how they justify and categorize if there is some encounter with a society that thinks in different ways. Not every society will matter. On reflection, we may think there are some societies that are so different from ours that any comparison with them—certainly an evaluative comparison—will make no sense. There is a certain 'relativism of distance', whereby it is only if a society is close to ours, if it thinks and justifies in ways we judge to be similar to our own, that we can talk of one or other of us being correct and incorrect. Williams uses these thoughts to distinguish between 'real' and 'notional' confrontations: those ways of thinking and living which could be possible for us and those which are not.

Within these thoughts he makes an optimistic claim.[12] He admits that some thick concepts can be seen to be the best and most appropriate ones to use. But this optimism is couched in a pessimistic general discussion that compares science with ethics. The former can aspire to objectivity, and even societies that are conceptually distant from our own can be correct or incorrect, for science aims to depict the world as it really is, free from human perspective. Ethics (and evaluative knowledge) can never aspire to this sort of objectivity, but it can try to ape some of it, simply by thinking through what sort of society is best. Williams entertains the idea that we could try to base the best sort of society on ideas of human nature.[13] Although he admits that this is a "comprehensible" project, he is pessimistic about it, for he thinks, chiefly, that any theory of human nature will radically underdetermine what ethical options there will be in particular situations and in societies as a whole.

So, in short, the particular ideas of Williams add up to a general idea: that when we come into contact with people from a society who think differently from how we think, be they fairly close or somewhat distant, we may well reflect on how we categorize and justify using our thick concepts. What we will see is that our way is one way among others, and that is likely to unseat our concepts and, probably, destroy our use of them. We could try to get back to a more innocent and pre-reflective time but, as Williams points out, we cannot do that consciously, and it may be hard to do that as a society.[14]

For those who find this discussion too pessimistic there are two bright spots. The first I find curious. Williams accords a special place to JUST or JUSTICE, particularly related to social organization.[15] He makes a case for thinking that we can usefully apply this notion to past societies, while acknowledging that it need not apply to every society. We can put the thought thus: the idea of justice may transcend the phenomenon of the relativism of distance more than other ethical notions. He speculates as to why this is. One reason is that many older societies had notions of justice. Another is that we find echoes of these notions in our notions, and hence they

---

[12] Williams (1985), p. 155.   [13] Williams (1985), pp. 153–4.
[14] Williams (1985), pp. 163–4.   [15] Williams (1985), pp. 164–7.

may not be as far away from us with regards to justice as they are when it comes to other evaluative ideas. Other considerations may apply, such as the fact that many medieval societies, for example, had knowledge of different social organizations and could not excuse their arrangements on the basis of ignorance.

Why do I find this curious? Quite simply because these considerations seem to apply to more than JUST or SOCIAL JUSTICE. They apply to KIND and BRAVE, I think. They may not apply to more specific and related concepts, such as COMPASSIONATE and VALOUR. But the change in these concepts is itself something that shows how we have different conceptions of KIND and BRAVE from many medieval Europeans, just as Williams claims about JUST. And, there may be rival conceptions of KIND and BRAVE in today's society (and philosophy), and these find echoes in conceptions from the past. Also, many of his other points repeat, as far as I can see. Furthermore, they seem to repeat for evaluative concepts other than ethical ones, such as BEAUTY and WISDOM. Perhaps there is something special about these thinnish sorts of thick concept. Although, to pick up on an example from earlier in this book, perhaps the same can be said for a specific concept such as VOCATION, and if we want to make out that JUST is special, I am pretty confident that DUTY will get in as well, and if it does it raises the question of what we say about thin concepts.

Of course, in one sense Williams keeps to his ideas regarding the relativism of distance. Recall that he thinks that JUST is special because more meaningful comparisons can be made, not that there is some sharp cut-off point indicating some difference in kind between it and other concepts. My comment is that he should be more optimistic—if that *is* the right word—here, and see that his thoughts apply to many evaluative concepts.[16]

For those who find Williams' ideas too pessimistic, the second bright spot opens up things quite generally. After articulating his worries about knowledge, Williams introduces the notion of confidence. In short, he thinks that when we lose knowledge we still go on living. We go on making ethical judgements and using ethical and evaluative concepts. We do not forget completely the fact that we no longer have knowledge. And, we may well not have conviction that we have the correct cognitive capacities and ideas. But there is *something* to support and underpin our use and this something is a confidence in how we think and act. Although he does not use the word, I suspect Williams is not talking about 'blithe' confidence: it is a certain doubting confidence, constantly on the watch for worries and challenges. (At one stage he contrasts this state of mind with optimism, citing Nietzsche's 'pessimism of strength', and also contrasts confidence with dogmatism.[17]) Williams thinks it is a social and psychological matter which concepts are retained and which we have confidence in, and this may be one of the ways in which his book's title is justified:

---

[16] For an excellent discussion and continuation of Williams' thoughts on justice, see the exchange between Brady (2010) and Fricker (2010).

[17] Williams (1985), p. 171.

philosophy's limits are shown because which concepts survive and thrive is not strictly or mainly a matter of philosophers arguing which concepts are better.

There ends my whistle-stop summary of Williams. I offer one point of criticism and draw out one idea about separationism. Both relate to our earlier discussion.[18]

First, as indicated, I find Williams slightly too pessimistic, as do some other commentators.[19] We need not doubt that when someone comes into contact with other societies who think differently from her, she will reflect on the fact that hers is not the only way to think. (Presumably this does not describe our anthropologist, for she would be poor at her subject if she had not realized this already!) But, having had this thought and lived with it for a while, why assume that the eventual outcome has to be something negative? There may be some unseating and unsettling, but only in the sense that further thought is required. If our imagined person is of a certain cast of mind she may realize that what she is making claims about are of a practical nature, in the way Williams discusses. And, from that, she may conclude that her way is at least as good as any other way, if not better. She may trace in a tight fashion which set of concepts is illuminating and allow for neat expressions, but she may also think more broadly and compare how much pain is generated in a society, whether certain groups are marginalized, what art and medicines have been produced, and which society has the better average life expectancy. In short, she may have the confidence both to justify her way of living and set of concepts as good ones, and also criticize others. There need be no reason to think that an initial unsettling will lead to a pessimistic conclusion.

I detect in Williams the idea that the pre-reflective state comprises much false knowledge, and people will be in an optimistic state of ignorance. After the Fall, as it were, we can get along, but we will be pessimistic at best. (This is *crude*, but not a hopelessly false reading.) Yet, why not assume a different mythology: the scales fall from our eyes, and in treating our evaluative concepts as they really are we can be more optimistic about us and how we judge, even if we constantly question whether we are judging correctly. When we look to other societies we can be confident about what we do as well as learn from them. Comparison can lead to a loss of knowledge, and a loss of confidence. But there is no reason to think it cannot lead to an increase as well.

This is just a claim about those cases where we feel confident in our judgements. But beyond that we have seen that Williams can be challenged about the number of times such comparisons can be made. This was the curiosity involved in his treatment of JUST. Williams makes an exception of it, but it is less exceptional than he thinks.

---

[18] There are many other things to comment on, but I restrict myself. One interesting idea is whether the existence in a society of claims that are treated as knowledge (such as the earlier example about killing) will itself effect how much confidence (rather than knowledge) we have in other claims. Categorizing them in this way seems to involve an explicit acknowledgement that they are of a lesser sort, and this in turn may lead us to have even less confidence in them. See Altham (1995), p. 157.

[19] For example, of those mentioned in an earlier footnote, Altham and Fricker stand out.

Second, despite what I have just said, I find much of Williams' discussion healthily refreshing. Evaluative concepts *do* fade away or are abruptly dropped, and often there is no way to think in those terms again. Such change is often caused by reflection. (So the best way to read my first criticism is that while Williams is correct in claiming that reflection can destroy knowledge, he may overstate the case.) This raises an issue for separationists. Here is Moore again. He imagines what separationists have to say about reflection destroying knowledge in the way Williams sketches:

> If [separationism] were right, and if what reflection did were simply to undermine the evaluative component in thick ethical concepts, then there would be a clear sense in which what had *strictly speaking* been known, in a way that had found expression through judgements involving the concepts, was still available to be known, in a way that could find expression through judgements involving purely factual counterparts of the concepts. The claim that reflection can destroy knowledge, in the sense intended by Williams, *would* then be a needlessly paradoxical way of putting something innocuous.[20]

Moore's point is that separationism does not seem to respect the phenomenon of reflection destroying knowledge in the right way. After a concept is dropped we should, if separationism is correct, be able simply to pick up similar, nonevaluative categorizations with the only difference being that now there is no attachment of some pro or con evaluation. Yet, for Moore, Williams' point is that this fails to capture the phenomenon adequately. For using such categorizations is also a matter of caring about our use of them. What seems pertinent is not that we would be unable to adopt a purely descriptive version of a concept (although that may the case), but the very fact that we do not adopt such a version and do not attempt to.[21]

The fading of the concept is primarily caused by us not wanting to evaluate this group of things in a certain way, and our evaluation of them is precisely what makes them a group. Or, to put it another way, we could continue to group these things using a different descriptive concept, but there would be no point because we have lost the evaluative reason for doing so. For Moore, Williams is not simply saying that after reflection we no longer want to group together, it is that we now judge the evaluative point of such a grouping as being silly, unjustified, hopelessly biased, or something else. And that is why such knowledge is destroyed. Why bother grouping these things after that revelation?

All of this second point echoes Foot's point outlined in Chapter Six. There is some internal relation between a thing as categorized and our attitude towards the thing. We cannot just attach and drop evaluations at will. There has to be some point and justification to our doing so, which will in some inevitable way call

---

[20]   Moore (2003), p. 345.
[21]   We very often speak of medieval Europeans' concept of VALOUR, but that is a different thing: that is a reference to some others' concept, not the sincere use of a different, wholly descriptive replacement concept.

forth more evaluative concepts, and thick ones at that. Importantly, we work within a tradition and social context, so any justifications have to make sense within certain confines.

8.6 A Note on the Thin

I think Williams is wrong about many things he says about thin concepts. He may be correct to think that philosophers, or at least some of them, concentrate too much on thin concepts and try to magic too much out of them. But he goes wrong in claiming that thin concepts are just pale abstractions of the thick and that they can do little justificatory work of importance.

Throughout this book I have indicated that thick concepts are best seen as doing certain sorts of job. We have a need for evaluative concepts and, at least for a society at a certain point in its history, we have a need for *these* concepts. The same is true, I think, of thin concepts. They may be less specific, but they can justify as much as thick ones. As I said in Chapter Four, sometimes we need a clear and direct 'right' or 'wrong' to tell us whether to do something. There is a clear need for them to fulfil and a role for them to play.

I certainly appreciate why Williams was led to say what he said. In some ways thick concepts are closer to everyday concerns. But I cannot see that thin ones have no purchase either. I have earlier captured Williams' thinking in this book with reference to the idea of an 'abstraction tree'. One may suggest the following: thin concepts *can be* seen as abstractions from thick concepts, so that *is* the best and only way of viewing them. But that latter claim does not follow. Just because thin concepts can be seen as linked in this way to thick concepts, this does not mean that they are lesser sorts of concept, just as one should not conclude that thick concepts are lesser than thin ones because they can seemingly be created from thin evaluation and something else.

There may be some genetic aspect to Williams' view. Perhaps humans use thick concepts and then thin ones come later only because we notice points of comparison among the thick and want to record such comparisons. This story can be told at the level of individual families of concepts, or it can be told as part of some evolutionary story about how humans and our concepts arose, or it can be told with reference to how societies meet and share points of comparison among how they compare. Even if—*if*—there is some truth in these just-so stories, why assume that these histories should determine our view of thin *or* thick concepts? What matters, I think, is that we can easily understand the idea of a thin evaluation, see how it justifies, and see how it can have and does have a life of its own apart from the thick. Surely it is this set of thoughts that is key. To put the point provocatively, one person's justification trading on the (true or mythical) genealogy of a concept or idea is another person's genetic fallacy.

8.7 Conclusion

In this chapter I have dismissed two problems for nonseparationsism. Nonseparationists can explain how it is that we can understand others' evaluative concepts without sharing them, and they can explain normative criticism as well as separationists. In contrast, we have found echoes of my previous criticisms of separationism when we dig deeper into these worries.

Chapter Eight has tied a few ends together. The final chapter, Chapter Nine seeks to face up to a challenge that has been lurking in the background throughout much of my discussion. If thick concepts are nonseparable concepts, what does this mean for how we conceive the world to be? Or, in other words, if we have thick concepts, do we also have thick properties? Despite my criticism of Williams in this chapter, his thoughts show us a plausible and mature response to this question.

9

Evaluative Cognitivism

9.1 Introduction

As advertised, this concluding chapter deals with an issue that has bubbled up every so often, namely what we are to say of the ontology that lies behind our conceptual categorizations? This is, to be frank, a topic worth a book or more itself.[1] My aim here is very modest, namely to sketch some recent philosophical currents and draw together some of my thoughts to show what we may begin to say on this issue in connection with points made in this book. Although this chapter uses 'cognitivism' in its title, 'realism' could have been used in its stead.

In §9.2 I set out a train of thought that leads us into territory that I regard as incorrect. In doing so I am offering a deliberately broad sweep of recent metaethical thought. In §9.3 I respond to that train of thought to show the possibility of a better position. In §9.4 I conclude, both this chapter and the overall book. However, I cannot resist a look beyond the confines of my main focus and so in §9.5 I permit myself one last thought.

9.2 A Train of Thought

The concepts that we use are typically couched in and expressed by various judge-ments we make.[2] It is natural to think that many of these judgements can be true or false, correct or incorrect, and we think it is important that such judgements are this way. The truth value of 'Jupiter is bigger than Saturn' really matters for many reasons, one of which is just that we think there is a fact of the matter about the comparative sizes of planets. Some judgements and issues are more important than others. It really matters how those bacteria behave and what we say about their nature, for people are getting very ill and the bacteria may be the cause. In contrast, it is typically not so important exactly how many worms are in my compost heap.

---

[1] As noted earlier in this book, I discuss ontology and metaethics generally in Kirchin (2012). In that book I also discuss all of the main metaethical positions, questions, arguments and ideas in far more detail than in this brief chapter.

[2] We might replace 'judgement' here with 'sentence', 'proposition', 'belief', etc. Because I focus on other things, I am being deliberately broad and unspecific here.

We often express thick concepts in ways that indicate we are trying to make judgements about the world. We are categorizing the world in certain ways, and want to present it correctly. And, when it comes to evaluations, we are often doing things of importance. It really matters whether the action was cruel or kind, and it really matters whether the dress is classy or vulgar. If so, and if they are important, we had better make sure that we can support the idea that evaluative judgements get to be true and false.

When it comes to many other sorts of judgement and concept, we typically assume that we should look to the world. Rightly or wrongly we might assume a sort of correspondence theory of truth: our linguistic expressions are attempts to map onto the world in some way, and when they do it successfully we call such expressions true, and when they fail we call them false. Now, there is much to be said about the correspondence theory of truth, and the problems it faces, but it has a strong grip on people, be they philosophers or not. If we go down this path, we confront the obvious question, 'What sort of thing is there which makes evaluative judgements true?' The obvious answer is to postulate the existence of a type of evaluative entity: a property, fact or similar thing. There is some evaluative stuff that is real and which is such that if judgements correspond with it (whatever 'correspond' may mean), such judgements are true. If we do not postulate the existence of such stuff, then it is unclear how such judgements could be true. When it comes to evaluations and evaluative concepts, in particular, people have different views and employ different concepts. There is no way that there can be truth unless there are things—evaluative things—that anchor all of those judgements.

Indeed, once we reflect on that last point we must realize that we have to conceive of the existence of these evaluative things in some way which is free of human influence. Built into the train of thought I am following is the idea that people have all sorts of views and employ all sorts of concepts. We can thus distinguish two ways of going wrong: applying a concept to the wrong thing (because we are foolish, or uninformed, or mad, say), and using a bogus concept in the first place (perhaps by using SCHMABOO instead of TABOO, perhaps by using racist slurs). If we base the existence of the evaluative things that make judgements true and false on anything to do with humans and our influence then we are basing them on biases, prejudices, and other undesirable things. We need to assume such things are created and maintained in some mind-independent fashion. Or in other words, while it is a human matter which judgements we make, if we want to ensure the legitimacy and authority of evaluative judgements, we should say that the things which the judgements are judgements of, are decidedly not human matters: humans do not determine or influence what evaluative things exist and their nature.

So, in short, when we say that some action is cruel, or some dress is vulgar, there really is a fact of the matter that determines whether we speak truly. Further, this fact of the matter is not itself based on anything human, be it whim or something more solid and measured. It is determined mind-independently. Indeed, once we think like that, it could be that the dress is neither vulgar nor elegant. That is, the concepts and terms we use are all hopeless; none of them capture or 'cut' the world correctly. Why think that our human-based concepts are correct, particularly as we have now invoked the notion of mind-independence? Perhaps there are better ways to categorize the world, such as those the Martians use. Perhaps the dress is schmelegant not elegant.

9.3 Thoughts about that Train of Thought

There is a lot that goes wrong in this train of thought. I will not worry too much about the end point. Mind-independent evaluative realism, particularly in ethics, will always have its supporters, both within philosophy and outside. It is easy to see why. It is fuelled by a fear of relativism and clamour for a certain sort of certainty. While some people (even philosophers) may be more inclined towards relativism of at least some variety when it comes to aesthetics, in ethics the stakes seem higher. Even if we care passionately about the transcendence of art, in ethics we are thinking about suffering and death, and prolonged happiness and freedom. We may feel happier to live and let live in art, but in ethics we cannot leave things there. (Or so many philosophers assume.) It seems to matter strongly whether we keep promises and whether a society is just. And these matters cannot be left to human judgement alone. We had better get these judgements right, and getting it right cannot simply be a matter of reflecting our own prejudices and biases, because for all we know we may be simply repeating what we are comfortable with, not getting at the truth.

I can understand why this view of ethical matters has it adherents, and why the quest for truth turns into a postulation of mind-independent ethical or evaluative entities. I believe, however, that this position is fundamentally misguided. But I am not going to argue against it here, and instead I turn to think about the various ways in which we can respond once we recognize it as an option.[3]

Many different sorts of theorist will reject this notion of an ethical or evaluative property. Some will think we can do away altogether with any notions of truth and will fall back on to a type of relativism or nihilism. Others will try to retain something of the idea of truth while rejecting the ontology. These are the more interesting positions in contemporary metaethics.

But of these more interesting positions some still go wrong, in my view. Let me sketch two. Error theorists, particularly those influenced directly by the arguments of John Mackie, think that the ethical properties—or 'objective prescriptions'—that everyday moral thought and language can be seen to rely on simply do not exist. Why not? Because, according to those that follow Mackie, the sort of conception of ethical properties to be found in everyday moral thought and language is that given above, and the idea of a mind-independent value property is an incoherent notion. So

---

[3] For arguments against, again see Kirchin (2012).

ethical thought as a whole is in systematic error, for we are making judgements using a bogus notion. There is a lot to say about Mackie's version of error theory, and error theory generally.[4] One main worry is that Mackie and others have misidentified their target. It is unclear how strong this conception of ethical properties is in everyday moral thought and language. If other options are on the table, ones that make the truth of true moral judgements more palatable, then we should not reject something as old and as useful as ethical thought at all. And, further, what are we to say about other sorts of prescription and evaluative property, particularly such as those found in epistemology where there seem to be requirements or reasons to believe such-and-such?[5]

A second position that goes wrong is noncognitivism/expressivism.[6] Things are tricky here. Noncognitivism is, strictly, a view about the mental states that typically accompany everyday ethical judgements (or should be viewed by philosophers to accompany them). Similarly, expressivism is strictly a view about how language works (or how it should be seen to work). It is not, strictly, a view about ontology. However, ontological and conceptual claims about ethics come in noncognitivism's (and expressivism's) wake. For if we can show that ethical language and thought work in a certain way, and work fairly well in a certain way, without the need for a postulation of ethical properties at all, then why bother postulating such things?

Why and how does noncognitivism go wrong? Again, there is much to comment on, and some of this has already occupied us in this study. As with error theory, I think its failure is due to a misunderstanding about what a sensible sort of realism could be: a realism that can respond to the challenge of relativism sensibly, yet which does not go as far as postulating mind-independent properties and which accommodates some of what is good in noncognitivism.

During the 1980s and beyond, analytic philosophy saw the rise of this sort of sensible position, labelled in various ways. For simplicity's sake, let me call it 'sensibility theory'. (The name relates to people's sensibility, not the fact that many regarded it as sensible.) It was associated most famously with the work of McDowell and Wiggins. In short, values were seen to be analogous to Locke's idea of secondary qualities.[7] There were not mind-independently existing things, but things whose reality could be said to depend, in some way, on human beings and how they perceive and experience the world. In forming his view, McDowell was, famously, explicitly arguing against error theorists and noncognitivists.

There are questionable aspects of this view. For example, we require details of how some natural stuff and some human stuff combine to create some value stuff that in turn can be seen, by philosophers, to constitute the stuff to which our judgements are

---

[4] See Kirchin (2010b) for commentary and discussion.
[5] See Cuneo (2007) for an extended discussion of this idea.
[6] Schroeder (2010) is a great survey and history of noncognitivism.
[7] McDowell (1985) is the *locus classicus*. See also some of the essays in Wiggins (1998), especially III and IV.

answerable. There *is* devilish detail here. Despite that detail, I believe this view broadly get things right, or at least it is better than error theory and noncognitivism.

And yet... the sort of realism that is developed is, perhaps, far too optimistic. (In fairness, as I read them Wiggins was more reluctant than McDowell in his use of 'realism' and 'features'.) There is a confidence that ethical judgements are true and false, and that we can determine which ones are which and why. There is a confidence that we can indicate the better sorts of judge—the virtuous and wise judges—who will act as our determiners (if not stipulators) of the moral compass.

Williams' views on these matters, which I summarized in the previous chapter, are more nuanced. They are also more realistic, realistic in that everyday sense of the word that sometimes goes unconsidered in philosophical debates. Forming moral judgements is a hard process, and not just because there may be many considerations to bring to bear. It is hard because there is no clear sense that we have a best judge who can determine what we should say; even a philosophical fiction of such a person designed to further certain intuitions may stand in the way. It is also hard because it is one thing to say that we want to be able to distinguish the better concepts from the worse concepts; far harder to arrive at neutral criteria that would enable such a comparison. Perhaps the confidence on show in sensibility theory is misplaced.

This is, as advertised, deliberately sketchy. Let me break out of this survey to make three points relevant to our concerns in this book. First, recall one of the notes from Chapter Five. It seems as if a commitment to the shapelessness of KIND involves a commitment to existence of something we can call kindness. The challenge is to reflect on the reality of kindness. I pointed out there that cognitivism and realism are distinct positions, just as noncognitivism and non-realism are distinct. However, this is not to say that the two cannot be embraced by one overall stance, nor that the insights of one position cannot be shared by the other. Williams and McDowell have their differences, a few of which I have touched upon in this book. The best hope I can see of forming a position concerning the reality of the thick, if we call it that, is one that, like Williams' position, does not give in to easy views about realism but which, unlike him, is optimistic about our confidence in forming views and using evaluative concepts. In the previous chapter I indicated the ways in which we should be more confident than Williams is. If, over time, we find that our use of concepts results in a better life—I leave this notion vague here—then why should we not be confident in how we live, categorize, and justify? Given that we categorize and justify by looking at how the world works, why not call this position a type of realism? Why not assume that we can, within our own justificatory system, have the resources to draw meaningful divisions between the better and worse and, therefore, between the true and the false? Why not think that such divisions and justifications that started from within a worldview could not gain legitimacy and authority that reached beyond these initial confines? This would take, of course, a focus on what sort of theory of truth we would wish to adopt.

We can also call this position 'cognitivism'. I am, as a second point, not too fussed about labels here. Despite my use of labels through this book, what really matters to me are the ideas that stand behind them. (And I hope my dissection of various labels shows how important that is to me.) Blackburn has often criticized McDowell, and other realists, for a seemingly simple postulation of something within one's philosophical view—reality, truth, knowledge—that really should be earned through honest toil, by which Blackburn means analysed, justified, and constructed in a plausible fashion. I am all for honest toil. Yet, in my view what we can earn has the right to be called a realist account, even if it falls short of the mind-independent realism I sketched earlier. Blackburn's position is labelled by him, accurately, as 'quasi-realism'. In my view there is no reason to think that we have to retain the 'quasi-' prefix, even if such a view postulates the existence of evaluative stuff that exists in a way different from the way in which, say, some scientific properties exist.

But this brings me to a third and most important point. Every so often I have mentioned the fact–value distinction, and I have discussed it earlier in this book. Thick concepts, it has been said, hold out the hope that this distinction is erroneous. A sensible challenge to those that advocate it does not claim that there are no value-free facts. Rather, it claims that there may be some things that appear to be factual but which, on closer inspection, are not as value-free as one thinks and, further, that the division between the two supposed groups is blurred. One reason noncognitivists, and possibly error theorists, go wrong is that they begin by thinking there is such a clear distinction, possibly influenced by the thought that if there are clear examples of both groups, then there must be a clear dividing line between the two groups (and, in effect, label them as two distinct groups). Ethical and other evaluative talk has to be part of one or other group, and therefore it is clearly not factual.

This is not, as I indicated in Chapter Five, to signal that ethical and other evaluative facts and properties are of the very same ontological cast as scientific properties and entities, and facts based on scientific ideas. To end on this point would be madness, I think. Yet, the importance of reflecting on thin and thick concepts is to show how far evaluative thought can go and how factual it can be. Understood in the right way, such thought can be the vehicle for claims that can be seen as true and as claims to knowledge. My discussion of Williams in the previous chapter began us on that road.

Williams was right, I think, to contrast the conceptual schemes of our making with the absolute conception of the world. Yet, the conceptual schemes that are imposed on such a world can be seen as better and worse than other schemes, and we can be confident, I think, in saying which ones are better.

9.4 Overall Conclusion

There were few details in the previous section. As I said, providing those details is a book in itself. The main point, instead, is that we should not think we have an impossible task here. We are not fated to embrace mind-independent evaluative realism, nor a type of relativism. And, within the middle ground, we are not forced to say that because the stuff of evaluative concerns is not science, it therefore cannot be factual or truth-apt. To echo a thought from Chapter Five, we can say that these issues call into question what might be meant by 'truth' and 'fact'. We should not cut off potential routes before we have begun: we need to think hard about truth and the factual, not assume we know about them already. Perhaps the correspondence theory of truth is not the right theory for evaluative concerns, for example.

That is one of the lessons of this study. In Chapter Seven I criticized Väyrynen. He argues that most standard thick concepts are not inherently or essentially evaluative because they do not conform to certain rules and norms about core semantic meaning. My criticism was partly based on the idea that we should think through how concepts are used and use this as a prompt to think about how the evaluative may be a broader category. In microcosm that is the overarching conclusion of this study. What I hope I have shown is that evaluation, and evaluative concepts, come in a variety of guises, but they are all no less the evaluative for that. Part of the point and joy of philosophy, particularly in its modern analytic variety, is an attempt to make clear various ideas. Yet it goes astray too often when it fails to realize that the phenomenon with which it is dealing is neither clear nor clean. It is pretty straight-forward to say that thick concepts are just specific types of evaluative concept, but beyond that there is not as much clarity as some suppose. Separationism imposes a clear division on matters where they may not be a division. Nonseparationism is to be preferred because it tries to understand thick concepts on their own terms. Thick concepts are simply evaluations of a sort different from thin ones.

9.5 One Last Thought

Having seemingly concluded, I break the rules and make one last point. In both Chapters Six and Eight I hid away in the main text and in footnotes a topic that could be one of the most important questions in this book. It is important to question how a concept can be held together as a single concept. We often find people agreeing about some idea, yet disagreeing because they have different conceptions that clash. The real-life debate between Rawls and Nozick over what it is for a distribution of resources to be just is one such example. Despite their differences—over particular points and over starting assumptions—no one could doubt that Rawls and Nozick were engaged in a dispute about the same concept, and had points of contact. But is it possible to pick out certain traits, or even necessary and sufficient conditions, that enable us to say when we have two ideas that are properly classed as conceptions of the same concept, and when those two ideas are just different concepts? If we can, what are they? And, further, do different sorts of concept (and conception) admit of different answers to these questions? Probing these ideas will give us a sense of some of the most everyday and fundamental of human social activities: communication with other people, understanding them, and agreement and disagreement with them. By getting a sound understanding of what it is for a concept to be evaluative, and what it is for it to be thick or thin, we can begin to make progress on these broader issues.

Bibliography

Altham, J. E. J. (1995) 'Reflection and Confidence', in J. E. J. Altham and Ross Harrison (eds) *World, Mind and Ethics* (Cambridge: Cambridge University Press), pp. 156–69.

Appiah, Kwame Anthony (2008) *Experiments in Ethics* (Cambridge, MA: Harvard University Press).

Aristotle (1994) *Metaphysics*, Books *Z* and *H* (Oxford: Oxford University Press), (ed.) with commentary by David Bostock.

Aristotle (2000) *Nicomachean Ethics* (Cambridge: Cambridge University Press), (ed.) with an introduction by Roger Crisp.

Armstrong, David (1978) *A Theory of Universals* (Cambridge: Cambridge University Press).

Bedke, Matt (2014) 'Review of *The Lewd, the Rude and the Nasty: A Study of Thick Concepts in Ethics* by Pekka Vayrynen', *Notre Dame Philosophical Reviews*, posted 30 April 2014: http://ndpr.nd.edu/news/47974-the-lewd-the-rude-and-the-nasty.

Blackburn, Simon (1981) 'Rule-Following and Moral Realism', in Stephen Holtzman and Christopher Leich (eds) *Wittgenstein: To Follow a Rule* (London: Routledge and Kegan Paul), pp. 163–87.

Blackburn, Simon (1984) *Spreading the Word* (Oxford: Oxford University Press).

Blackburn, Simon (1992) 'Morality and Thick Concepts: Through Thick and Thin', *Proceedings of the Aristotelian Society*, supp. vol. 66, pp. 285–99.

Blackburn, Simon (1998) *Ruling Passions* (Oxford: Oxford University Press).

Blackburn, Simon (2013) 'Disentangling Disentangling', in Simon Kirchin (ed.) *Thick Concepts* (Oxford: Oxford University Press), pp. 121–35.

Brady, Michael (2010) 'Disappointment', *Proceedings of the Aristotelian Society*, supp. vol. 84, pp. 179–98.

Brink, David (1989) *Moral Realism and the Foundations of Ethics* (Cambridge: Cambridge University Press).

Chalmers, David and Clark, Andy (1998) 'The Extended Mind', *Analysis*, vol. 58, pp. 7–19.

Chappell, Timothy (2010) 'Bernard Williams', in E. N. Zalta (ed.) *The Stanford Encyclopedia of Philosophy* (Fall 2010 edition): http://plato.stanford.edu/entries/williams-bernard.

Chappell, Timothy (2013) 'There Are No Thin Concepts', in Simon Kirchin (ed.) *Thick Concepts* (Oxford: Oxford University Press), pp. 182–96.

Crary, Alice (2007) *Beyond Moral Judgment* (Cambridge, MA: Harvard University Press).

Crisp, Roger (2000) 'Particularizing Particularism', in Brad Hooker and Margaret Little (eds) *Moral Particularism* (Oxford: Oxford University press), pp. 23–47.

Cuneo, Terence (2007) *The Normative Web* (Oxford: Oxford University Press).

Dancy, Jonathan (1993) *Moral Reasons* (Oxford: Blackwell).

Dancy, Jonathan (1995) 'In Defense of Thick Concepts', in Peter A. French, Theodore E. Uehling, and Howard K. Wettstein (eds) *Midwest Studies in Philosophy*, vol. XX, pp. 263–79.

Dancy, Jonathan (2004) *Ethics without Principles* (Oxford: Oxford University Press).

Dancy, Jonathan (2006) 'Nonnaturalism', in David Copp (ed.) *The Oxford Handbook of Ethical Theory* (New York: Oxford University Press), pp. 122–43.

Dworkin, Ronald (2011) *Justice for Hedgehogs* (Cambridge, MA: Harvard University Press).

Elstein, Daniel and Hurka, Thomas (2009) 'From Thin to Thick: Two Moral Reductionist Plans', *Canadian Journal of Philosophy*, vol. 39, pp. 515–35.

Enoch, David (2011) *Taking Morality Seriously* (New York: Oxford University Press).

Foot, Philippa (1958) 'Moral Arguments', *Mind*, vol. 67, pp. 502–13.

Foot, Philippa (1958-9) 'Moral Beliefs', *Proceedings of the Aristotelian Society*, vol. 59, pp. 83–104.

Fricker, Miranda (2001) 'Confidence and Irony', in Edward Harcourt (ed.) *Morality, Reflection and Ideology* (Oxford: Oxford University Press), pp. 87–112.

Fricker, Miranda (2010) 'The Relativism of Blame and Williams' Relativism of Distance', *Proceedings of the Aristotelian Society*, supp. vol. 84, pp. 151–77.

Geertz, Clifford (1973) 'Thick Description: Toward an Interpretive Theory of Culture', in his *The Interpretation of Cultures* (New York: Basic Books), pp. 3–30.

Gibbard, Allan (1990) *Wise Choices, Apt Feelings* (Oxford: Oxford University Press).

Gibbard, Allan (1992) 'Morality and Thick Concepts: Thick Concepts and Warrant for Feelings', *Proceedings of the Aristotelian Society*, supp. vol. 66, pp. 267–83.

Griffin, James (1996) *Value Judgement: Improving our Ethical Beliefs* (Oxford: Oxford University Press).

Harcourt, Edward and Thomas, Alan (2013) 'Thick Concepts, Analysis and Reductionism', in Simon Kirchin (ed.) *Thick Concepts* (Oxford: Oxford University Press), pp. 20–43.

Hare, R. M. (1952) *The Language of Morals* (Oxford: Oxford University Press).

Hare, R. M. (1963) *Freedom and Reason* (Oxford: Oxford University Press).

Heuer, Ulrike (2013) 'Thick Concepts and Internal Reasons', in Ulrike Heuer and Gerald Lang (eds) *Luck, Value and Commitment: Themes from the Ethics of Bernard Williams* (Oxford: Oxford University Press), pp. 219–46.

Hurley, Susan (1989) *Natural Reasons* (Oxford: Oxford University Press).

Johnson, W. E. (1921) *Logic*, Part I (Cambridge: Cambridge University Press).

Johnson, W. E. (1922) *Logic*, Part II (Cambridge: Cambridge University Press).

Johnson, W. E. (1924) *Logic*, Part III (Cambridge: Cambridge University Press).

Kirchin, Simon (2000) 'Quasi-Realism, Sensibility Theory and Ethical Relativism', *Inquiry*, vol. 43, pp. 413–28.

Kirchin, Simon (2003a) 'Ethical Phenomenology and Metaethics', *Ethical Theory and Moral Practice*, vol. 6, pp. 241–64.

Kirchin, Simon (2003b) 'Particularism, Generalism and the Counting Argument', *European Journal of Philosophy*, vol. 11, pp. 54–71.

Kirchin, Simon (2008) 'Review of *Beyond Moral Judgment* by Alice Crary', *Notre Dame Philosophical Reviews*, posted 10 January 2008: http://ndpr.nd.edu/news/beyond-moral-judgment.

Kirchin, Simon (2010a) 'The Shapelessness Hypothesis', *Philosophers' Imprint*, vol. 10, pp. 1–28.

Kirchin, Simon (2010b) 'A Tension in the Moral Error Theory', in Richard Joyce and Simon Kirchin (eds) *A World Without Values: Essays on John Mackie's Moral Error Theory* (Dordrecht: Springer), pp. 167–82.

Kirchin, Simon (2012) *Metaethics* (Basingstoke: Palgrave Macmillan).

Kirchin, Simon (2013) 'Thick Concepts and Thick Descriptions', in Simon Kirchin (ed.) *Thick Concepts* (Oxford: Oxford University Press), pp. 60–77.

Kirchin, Simon (ms) 'Concepts and Action-Guidance, and Motivation: Ethics, Aesthetics, Epistemology'.

Lang, Gerald (2001) 'The Rule-Following Considerations and Metaethics: Some False Moves', *European Journal of Philosophy*, vol. 9, pp. 190–209.

Lehrer, Adrienne (2009) *Wine and Conversation* (Oxford: Oxford University Press, 2nd edn).

Lovibond, Sabina (1983) *Realism and Imagination in Ethics* (Oxford: Blackwell).

Lovibond, Sabina (2003) 'Naturalism and Normativity: II', *Proceedings of the Aristotelian Society*, supp. vol. 77 (insert), pp. 1–12.

Margolis, Eric and Laurence, Stephen (2014) 'Concepts', in E. N. Zalta (ed.) *The Stanford Encyclopedia of Philosophy* (Spring 2014): http://plato.stanford.edu/cgi-bin/encyclopedia/archinfo.cgi?entry=concepts.

McDowell, John (1979) 'Virtue and Reason', *The Monist*, vol. 62, pp. 331–50.

McDowell, John (1981) 'Non-cognitivism and Rule-Following', in Stephen Holtzman and Christopher Leich (eds) *Wittgenstein: To Follow a Rule* (London: Routledge and Kegan Paul), pp. 141–62.

McDowell, John (1983) 'Aesthetic Value, Objectivity and the Fabric of the World', in Eva Schaper (ed.) *Pleasure, Preference, and Value* (Cambridge: Cambridge University Press), pp. 1–16.

McDowell, John (1985) 'Values and Secondary Qualities', in Ted Honderich (ed.) *Morality and Objectivity* (London: Routledge and Kegan Paul), pp. 110–29.

McDowell, John (1987) 'Projection and Truth in Ethics', Lindley Lecture, University of Kansas. Reprinted in his *Mind, Value, and Reality* (London: Harvard University Press, 1988), 151–66.

McKeever, Sean and Ridge, Michael (2006) *Principled Ethics* (Oxford: Oxford University Press).

McNaughton, David (1988) *Moral Vision* (Oxford: Blackwell).

McNaughton, David and Rawling, Piers (2000) 'Unprincipled Ethics', in Brad Hooker and Margaret Little (eds) *Moral Particularism* (Oxford: Oxford University Press), pp. 256–75.

McNaughton, David and Rawling, Piers (2003) 'Naturalism and Normativity: I', *Proceedings of the Aristotelian Society*, supp. vol. 77, pp. 23–45.

Miller, Alexander (2013) *An Introduction to Contemporary Metaethics* (Cambridge: Polity Press, 2nd edn).

Moore, A. W. (2003) 'Williams on Ethics, Knowledge, and Reflection', *Philosophy*, vol. 78, pp. 337–54.

Murdoch, Iris (1956) 'Vision and Choice in Morality', in *Proceedings of the Aristotelian Society*, supp. vol. 30, pp. 32–58. Reprinted in her *Existentialists and Mystics*. (ed.) Peter Conradi (London: Chatto and Windus, 1997), pp. 76–98.

Murdoch, Iris (1957) 'Metaphysics and Ethics', in D. F. Pears (ed.) *The Nature of Metaphysics* (London: Macmillan, 1957). Reprinted in her *Existentialists and Mystics*. (ed.) Peter Conradi (London: Chatto and Windus, 1997), pp. 59–75.

Murdoch, Iris (1962) 'The Idea of Perfection', based on the Ballard Matthews Lecture delivered at the University College, North Wales. Reprinted in her *Existentialists and Mystics*. (ed.) Peter Conradi (London: Chatto and Windus, 1997), pp. 299–336.

Nozick, Robert (1974) *Anarchy, State, and Utopia* (Oxford: Blackwell).

Oddie, Graham (2005) *Value, Reality, Desire* (Oxford: Oxford University Press).

Prior, A. N. (1949) 'Determinables, Determinates and Determinants', *Mind*, vol. 58, Part I, pp. 1–20, and Part II, pp. 178–94.

Putnam, Hilary (2002) *The Collapse of the Fact/Value Dichotomy and other Essays* (Cambridge, MA: Harvard University Press).

Railton, Peter (1993a) 'What the Non-cognitivist Helps Us to See the Naturalist Must Help Us to Explain', in John Haldane and Crispin Wright (eds) *Reality, Representation, and Projection* (Oxford: Oxford University Press), pp. 279–300.

Railton, Peter (1993b) 'Reply to David Wiggins', in John Haldane and Crispin Wright (eds) *Reality, Representation, and Projection* (Oxford: Oxford University Press), pp. 315–28.

Rawls, John (1971) *A Theory of Justice* (Oxford: Oxford University Press).

Roberts, Debbie (2011) 'Shapelessness and the Thick', *Ethics*, vol. 121, pp. 489–520.

Roberts, Debbie (2013) 'It's Evaluation, Only Thicker', in Simon Kirchin (ed.) *Thick Concepts* (Oxford: Oxford University Press), pp. 78–96.

Roberts, Debbie (2015) 'Review of *The Lewd, the Rude and the Nasty: A Study of Thick concepts in Ethics* by Pekka Vayrynen', *Ethics*, vol. 125, pp. 910–15.

Ryle, Gilbert (1966–7) 'Thinking and Reflecting', in 'The Human Agent', *Royal Institute of Philosophy Lectures*, vol. I (London: Macmillan). Reprinted in his *Collected Essays 1929–1968*, (ed.) Julia Tanney (London: Routledge), pp. 479–93.

Ryle, Gilbert (1968) 'The Thinking of Thoughts: What Is "Le Penseur" Doing?', University Lectures, 18, University of Saskatchewan. Reprinted in his *Collected Essays 1929–1968*, (ed.) Julia Tanney (London: Routledge, 2009), pp. 494–510.

Sanford, David (2006) 'Determinates v. Determinables', in E. N. Zalta (ed.) *The Stanford Encyclopedia of Philosophy* (Summer 2007 Edition): http://plato.stanford.edu/entries/determinate-determinables/#3.

Scheffler, Samuel (1987) 'Morality through Thick and Thin: A Critical Notice of *Ethics and the Limits of Philosophy*', *The Philosophical Review*, vol. 96, pp. 411–34.

Schroeder, Mark (2010) *Noncognitivism in Ethics* (London: Routledge).

Searle, John (1959) 'On Determinables and Resemblance II', *Proceedings of the Aristotelian Society*, supp. vol. 33, pp. 141–58.

Searle, John (1967) 'Determinables and Determinates', in Paul Edwards (ed.) *The Encyclopedia of Philosophy*, vol. II (New York: Macmillan), pp. 357–9.

Searle, John (1980) 'The Background of Meaning', in J. Searle, F. Kiefer, and M. Bierswich (eds) *Speech Act Theory and Pragmatics* (Dordrecht: Reidel), pp. 221–32.

Shafer-Landau, Russ (2003) *Moral Realism* (New York: Oxford University Press).

Skinner, Quentin (2002) *Visions of Politics* (Cambridge: Cambridge University Press).

Smith, Michael (2013) 'On the Nature and Significance of the Distinction between Thick and Thin Ethical Concepts', in Simon Kirchin (ed.) *Thick Concepts* (Oxford: Oxford University Press), pp. 97–120.

Sreenivasan, Gopal (2001) 'Understanding Alien Morals', *Philosophy and Phenomenological Research*, vol. 62, pp. 1–32.

Stevenson, C. L. (1944) *Ethics and Language* (New Haven: Yale University Press).

Tanney, Julia (2009) 'Foreword', in Gilbert Ryle *Collected Essays 1929–1968*, (ed.) Julia Tanney (London: Routledge), pp. vii–xix.

Tappolet, Christine (2004) 'Through Thick and Thin: *Good* and its Determinates', *dialectica*, vol. 58, pp. 207–21.

Thomas, Alan (2006) *Value and Context* (Oxford: Oxford University Press).

Thomas, Alan (2007) 'The Nonobjectivist Critique of Moral Knowledge', in Alan Thomas (ed.) *Bernard Williams* (Cambridge: Cambridge University Press), pp. 47–72.

Travis, Charles (1997) 'Pragmatics', in Bob Hale and Crispin Wright (eds) *A Companion to the Philosophy of Language* (Oxford: Blackwell), pp. 87–107.

Väyrynen, Pekka (2009) 'Objectionable Thick Concepts in Denials', *Philosophical Perspectives*, vol. 23, pp. 439–69.

Väyrynen, Pekka (2013) *The Lewd, the Rude and the Nasty: A Study of Thick Concepts* (New York: Oxford University Press).

Väyrynen, Pekka (2014) 'Essential Contestability and Evaluation', *Australasian Journal of Philosophy*, vol. 92, pp. 471–88.

Wiggins, David (1993a) 'Cognitivism, Naturalism and Normativity', in John Haldane and Crispin Wright (eds) *Reality, Representation, and Projection* (Oxford: Oxford University Press), pp. 301–14.

Wiggins, David (1993b) 'A Neglected Position?', in John Haldane and Crispin Wright (eds) *Reality, Representation, and Projection* (Oxford: Oxford University Press), pp. 329–38.

Wiggins, David (1998) *Needs, Values, Truth* (Oxford: Oxford University Press, 3rd edn).

Wiggins, David (2006) *Ethics: Twelve Lectures on the Philosophy of Morality* (London: Penguin).

Wiland, Eric (2013) 'Williams on Thick Ethical Concepts and Reasons for Action', in Simon Kirchin (ed.) *Thick Concepts* (Oxford: Oxford University Press), pp. 210–16.

Williams, Bernard (1978) *Descartes: The Project of Pure Enquiry* (Harmondsworth: Penguin).

Williams, Bernard (1981) 'Internal and External Reasons', in his *Moral Luck* (Cambridge: Cambridge University Press), pp. 101–13.

Williams, Bernard (1985) *Ethics and the Limits of Philosophy* (London: Fontana).

Williams, Bernard (1995) 'Replies', in J. E. J. Altham and Ross Harrison (eds) *World, Mind, and Ethics* (Cambridge: Cambridge University Press), pp. 185–224.

Williams, Bernard (1996) 'Truth in Ethics', in Brad Hooker (ed.) *Truth in Ethics* (Oxford: Blackwell), pp. 19–34.

Zangwill, Nick (2013) 'Moral Metaphor: what Moral Philosophy can Learn from Aesthetics', in Simon Kirchin (ed.) *Thick Concepts* (Oxford: Oxford University Press), pp. 197–209.

Index of Notable Examples

I have not included every thick concept discussed, such as ELEGANT and FAIR, nor have I included every instance of all the notable examples, such as every instance of CHAIR. However, I have listed some notable discussions and mentions of a number of concepts, and of other examples.

PRO and CON / pro and con is in the general index since the mention and use of these concepts *as* concepts bleeds into discussion of the topic of evaluations with clear positive and negative point.

General Index